Evangelicals and Abortion

OTHER BOOKS BY J. CAMERON FRASER

Thandabantu: The Man Who Loved the People

God Is Always Good: Cassidy's Story
(with Sonya M. Taekema)

A Personal Appreciation of D. A. Macfarlane

Developments in Biblical Counseling

*Learning From Lord Mackay:
Life and Work in Two Kingdoms*

*Missionary Baptism & Evangelical Unity:
An Historical, Theological, Pastoral Inquiry*

Evangelicals and Abortion

Historical, Theological, Practical Perspectives

J. Cameron Fraser

FOREWORD BY
Kristy L. Johnson

WIPF & STOCK · Eugene, Oregon

EVANGELICALS AND ABORTION
Historical, Theological, Practical Perspectives

Copyright © 2024 J. Cameron Fraser. All rights reserved. Except for brief quotations in critical publications or reviews, no part of this book may be reproduced in any manner without prior written permission from the publisher. Write: Permissions, Wipf and Stock Publishers, 199 W. 8th Ave., Suite 3, Eugene, OR 97401.

Wipf & Stock
An Imprint of Wipf and Stock Publishers
199 W. 8th Ave., Suite 3
Eugene, OR 97401

www.wipfandstock.com

PAPERBACK ISBN: 978-1-6667-8451-0
HARDCOVER ISBN: 978-1-6667-8452-7
EBOOK ISBN: 978-1-6667-8453-4

VERSION NUMBER 04/12/24

For Margaret

Contents

Permissions | ix
Acknowledgments | xi
Foreword by Kristy L. Johnson | xiii

Introduction: Why *Evangelicals and Abortion*? | 1

PART I—Historical: Understanding Evangelicals and Abortion

1. Abortion, Women's Rights, and Evangelical Religion | 9
2. Evangelicals and Abortion: Who Are Evangelicals? | 21
3. Lessons from the Early Church and Beyond | 46
4. Developing Evangelical Views in the Twentieth Century | 55

PART II—Theological: Why Evangelicals Should Be Pro-life

5. Changing Views: An Interpretive Review of Exodus 21: 22-25 | 73
6. Abortion and the Image of God | 80
7. Some Related Implications of Life in the Image of God | 95

PART III—**Practical: Mainstream Society and the Evangelical Pro Life Position**

8   "Adoption Not Abortion" | 113
9   Evangelicals and Abortion in a Post-*Roe* World | 120
10 Evangelicals, Abortion, and the Politics of the Cross | 159

Appendix: The Prolific Deceivers at the Heart of Roe v. Wade | 171
Bibliography | 179
Index | 197

Permissions

Scripture quotations are from THE HOLY BIBLE, NEW INTERNATIONAL VERSION®, NIV® Copyright © 1973, 1978, 1984, 2011 by Biblica, Inc.™ All rights reserved; The Holy Bible, English Standard Version® (ESV®) Copyright © 2001 by Crossway, a publishing ministry of Good News Publishers; The New American Bible Copyright © 1970 by United States Conference of Catholic Bishops. All rights reserved; and the King James Version.

Quotations from *Abortion and the Early Church* by Michael J. Gorman, Copyright © 1982. Wipf & Stock edition, 1988. Used by permission.

Quotations from John M. Frame, "Book Review: *Abortion: The Personal Dilemma*," Copyright © 1972 and Dr. Chris Richards, "When Does Life Begin?" Copyright © 2020 The Banner of Truth Trust, Edinburgh, UK, EH12 6EL, *https://banneroftruth.org.uk/*. Used by permission.

Quotations from "Abortion Perspective" by Klaas Runia, "When Does Life Begin?" by Nancy Hardesty, as well as "Fetal Life" and "ETERNITY's Analysis" by the editors in *ETERNITY* magazine, February 1971, and Matthew Miller, "How the Evangelical Church Awoke to the Abortion Issue." Copyright © 2013 Alliance of Confessing Evangelicals, Lancaster, PA, 17601, *www.alliancenet.org*. Used by permission.

Quotations from "A Protestant Affirmation on the Control of Human Reproduction" (November 8, 1968); Ericka Andersen, "When Pro-Life Isn't Enough: Abortion 'Abolitionists' Speak Out" (August 2022); Mark Galli, "'When Evangelicals Were Pro-Choice'—Another Fake History" (October 2012); Paul Miller, "What is Christian Nationalism?" (February 2021); Kathryn Watson, "They're Not Religious," (November 2022); John Stott, "Does Life Begin Before Birth?" (September 1980); Daniel K. Williams, "The Prolific Deceivers at the Heart of 'Roe v. Wade'" (December 2021), Copyright © *Christianity Today*, Carol Stream Ill, 60189. Used by permission. *www.christianity.com*.

Quotations from *Report of the Committee to Study the Matter of Abortion*. Copyright © The Orthodox Presbyterian Church, Philadelphia, PA. 19412, *www.philadelphia.opc.org*. Used by permission.

Quotations from *The Story of Abortion in America* by Marvin Olasky & Leah Savas, Copyright © 2023, pp. 1, 22, 35, 70-72, 142-43, 159, 326-28, 377-78, 439-43. Also, from David VanDrunen, *Bioethics and the Christian*, p. 168. Used by permission of Crossway, a publishing ministry of Good News Publishers, Wheaton, IL 60187, *www.crossway.org*.

Acknowledgments

THIS BOOK IS DEDICATED to my wife Margaret in appreciation of her past leadership in Christians for Life (see Introduction), for first urging me to get involved in this issue, and for her patience with me as I struggled with what to write on an emotionally difficult subject.

A number of friends and others read all of part of the manuscript over more than two years, and I thank them all for their helpful feedback, evaluations, criticisms, and encouragements: Tom Albaugh, Mark Archibald, Bill Davis, D. Clair Davis, Blane Després, Glenn Davies, Richard B. Gaffin, Adam Harris, Kristy Johnson, Duane Konynenbelt, Danielle Koop, Monica Loewen, Sam Logan, Frederica Matthewes-Green, Tom McCormack, Andrea Mrozek, Andrée Seu Peterson, Chris Richards, David Robertson, Ken Stewart, Troy Taylor, Karen Thompson, Daniel K. Williams, John Van Eyk, Mary Ziegler. In particular, Kristy Johnson and Tom McCormack provided invaluable editorial assistance. Besides, Kristy prepared the discussion questions and Tom helped edit them, having been the one to first suggest using them. Kristy also kindly provided the gracious foreword. Dan Williams pushed me to get the help that makes this a better structured and hopefully more readable book. All remaining infelicities are my responsibility. I thank Dan for also allowing me to use, as appendix, a book review he originally wrote for *Christianity Today*.

I am grateful to several staff at Wipf & Stock, especially Caleb Kormann, Savanah Landerholm, Caleb Schupe, and Calvin Jaffarian for their expert help and flexible cooperation throughout the publishing process.

I thank God for allowing me to complete this project in some difficult circumstances and pray that it may serve some useful purpose as a distinctively Christian and evangelical approach to the abortion issue.

Foreword

I HAVE KNOWN THE REV. DR. J. CAMERON FRASER since 1994, when he accepted the call to be the pastor at my rural, Southern Alberta (Canada) Christian Reformed Church. Even at eight years old, I felt a tremendous amount of respect for how passionately he preached and inspired his congregants' spiritual life. Over the years, I have been taught, challenged, and mentored by Cameron, and one thing has remained consistently true; he makes you think and think deeply. He asks the tough questions, he's intentional about his words, and he encourages those around him to be purposeful in their lives. All of which is housed in an unwavering commitment to follow Jesus. He speaks not only from an intellectually considered position, but also from a deeply spiritual one.

As a psychologist, I have worked with women experiencing all kinds of pregnancy-related grief, including grief before and after an abortion. Regardless of the nature of the grief, the emotion remains the same—loss, sadness, confusion, pain, and uncertainty. These women are, most often, acutely aware of the pro-life/pro-choice debate. At times in their lives, they had even held a pro-life position, but due to circumstances, fear, and pressure they then found themselves in a place of desperation that they never thought they would be in. The women who have identified themselves as pro-choice come with similar emotions much of the time. They hope for someone to acknowledge their suffering. So often, people mistake this kind of acknowledgement and understanding as acceptance of and agreement with their choices. This doesn't have to be true! People are best able to accept influence when they feel understood and known by the other. Cameron's book, informed by his myriad of experiences across borders, emphasizes the value of understanding this grief and the desperation felt by those faced with this decision.

This is an evangelical Christian's must-read. Cameron Fraser not only provides a thorough historical review of the pro-life movement; he, more importantly, challenges evangelical Christians to return to the gospel as a foundation for our engagement with this generally divisive issue. The book outlines a clear biblical approach to addressing the abortion issues in our world today, all the while emphasizing the need for Christ-like compassion and love as a primary catalyst for change.

To tackle the topic of abortion from a strong, unapologetically pro-life position, takes courage, faith, and conviction. This notoriously contentious topic can make even the most committed pro-life thinkers balk and water down their position to avoid the inevitable attack from the pro-choice side. Cameron writes from a strong and clear position of advocacy, love, and compassion.

Kristy L Johnson, PHD, R.PSYCH

Registered Psychologist and Owner of Ascend Psychology Ltd.

Introduction

Why *Evangelicals and Abortion?*

THE WRITING OF THIS BOOK arose out of a conversation with a middle-aged pastor who had expressed astonishment at learning that evangelical Christians had not always believed that human life begins at conception. Instead, they had understood this to be the Roman Catholic position. As someone who has been a strong advocate of the pro-life position for decades, I understood my friend's bewilderment and shared his concern. But as a lifelong Reformed evangelical, I also knew that the evangelical position on abortion that we might like to think is an obvious reading of Scripture is less than fifty years old as of this time of writing.

In another conversation of the relatively recent past, a highly respected evangelical friend assured me that the biblical view is that life begins at birth. It is rare to hear this viewpoint in evangelical circles today, but it is the position taken by R.F.R. Gardner in *Abortion: The Personal Dilemma*, a book published in 1972 that exerted considerable influence at the time. It was also the view of the influential Southern Baptist preacher, W. A. Criswell, although he later changed his mind. It was not until the late 1970s with the Schaeffer-Koop film series and book, *Whatever Happened to the Human Race?* that evangelicals in large numbers got on board with the pro-life movement and the view that life begins at conception. Following the 2022 *Dobbs* decision in the USA, overturning *Roe v. Wade* (which had found abortion to be a constitutional right), *First Things*, a journal founded by the late Lutheran pastor-turned-Catholic priest Richard John Neuhaus, published an article suggesting that without Schaeffer's work and influence "*Dobbs* may never have come to pass."[1]

Like many others, Margaret and I were influenced by the Schaeffer–Koop film series. We attended its world premiere in Philadelphia, where we lived at the time, in 1979. Shortly thereafter, we joined the local chapter of the Christian Action Council (CAC), an evangelical organization that had been formed in 1975 to press for legal changes to abortion. In 1981, we moved to Vancouver, Canada, and shortly thereafter Christians for Life (CFL) was formed as an affiliate of the CAC, with Margaret as founding president. She also served as CFL's representative on the provincial (British Columbia) pro-life board. The goal of CFL was to promote an explicitly Christian pro-life approach in educating local churches and seeking to motivate interest, support, and prayer.

The desire to begin a Crisis Pregnancy Centre (CPC) in Vancouver had preceded the formation of CFL and some initial research had been done, prompted by several developments, including the showing of *Whatever Happened to the Human Race?* in February of 1981, sponsored by a pastors' fellowship. Then, after the formation of CFL, two of its members recruited six others, mostly from CFL, to form a steering committee in 1983 that got in touch directly with the CAC which at that time was combining political advocacy with the establishment of CPCs in the USA. Following training by a CAC representative, the Vancouver CPC was established in 1985 with some twenty supporting churches.

The Vancouver CPC is now an outreach of the Christian Advocacy Society of Greater Vancouver, that also includes a CPC in Burnaby (a suburb of Vancouver), Burnaby Safe House, OnlineCare Canada, Post Abortion Community Services, and Rape Victims Support Network. Similar organizations exist across Canada, as well as the United States and other countries.

Meanwhile, the CAC in the USA has changed its name to Care Net, abandoned its direct political involvement, and now focuses on CPCs and related ministries as the most effective means of providing a biblically-based alternative to abortion. There are now more CPCs in the USA than there are abortion clinics.

CFL as such no longer exists, but during the eighties and into the nineties (latterly under different leadership), it continued to promote the more educational and political wings of the pro-life movement, including (but not limited to) organizing pro-life rallies, media outreach, public speaking, and picketing of hospitals where abortions were performed. We had friends who went to jail for taking part in abortion clinic sit-ins. I subsequently served on

---

1. Talbot, "Pro-life Legacy of Francis Schaeffer," §2.

local pro-life boards in two provinces (we moved to the neighboring province of Alberta in the mid-nineties) and, among other things, organized Life Chain events (where lines are formed in communities across North America and elsewhere to protest silently and prayerfully against abortion). In other words, in the past we have been fully engaged in most educational and political aspects of the pro-life movement. I do not discount the value of such efforts (think of the frequently made comparison with William Wilberforce and the abolition of slavery) but have become increasingly convinced that the mercy ministry approach of CPCs and related ministries is the most effective and most biblical response to the tragedy of abortion. This perspective was developed early on and was reinforced by having two single mothers (at different times) live with us, as the struggles they went through both before and after giving birth were very evident.

Partly because of these experiences, as well as due to reflections on the increasing drift in Western societal ethical values, this book presents an argument that, contrary to much pro-life rhetoric, abortion is fundamentally a religious issue that requires a religious (biblical or evangelical) solution. I am aware that those who support and promote abortion rights often characterize pro-lifers as religious zealots, and this may seem to be playing into their hands. But I want to admit that, up to a point, they are correct, and this is why educational and political efforts have had such a limited effect on society at large. The political backlash to the reversal of *Roe v. Wade* is a case in point. What is needed more than legislation and education is a societal change of heart, coupled with (dare I say?) perhaps greater humility, realism, and Christlikeness in pro-life advocacy.

All Christian pro-lifers seek, however imperfectly, to heed the biblical admonition to "act justly, and to love mercy, and to walk humbly with your God" (Mic 6:8b). However, some of those most involved in the mercy aspect of pro-life ministry avoid use of the label "pro-life" because of the negative connotation it has in the public mind which associates it with strident political advocacy that can sometimes come across as insensitive. One person interviewed for this book did not want her name mentioned in the acknowledgements because I address the political (justice) wing of pro-life advocacy. Another simply stopped corresponding with me. This separation between what I am calling the justice and mercy aspects of what it means to be pro-life, while understandable, can have the unfortunate effect of reinforcing the perception that pro-lifers are concerned only about the unborn (justice), and not about the women who have conceived them (mercy). Such a perception is patently false, as any careful research will demonstrate, but why is it that so many see a conflict between these two aspects of pro-life advocacy that should and do really belong together?

My aim is not to discourage those committed to political and legislative activism for the unborn, but to be realistic about the spiritual nature of the battle in which we are engaged (Eph 6:12), and the requisite spiritual fruit needed to engage in it (Gal 5: 22-26).

Accordingly, in chapter 1, I make the case that abortion, which is widely viewed as exclusively a women's rights issue, is in fact a religious one in that it reflects foundational beliefs about the value of human life. I return to this in chapters 9 and 10 with some examples of biblically based pro-life ministries, as well as examples of why a politically and legally based solution does not resonate with Western (specifically American) society in general. Before getting there, by way of background, chapter 2 provides a brief history and definition of evangelicalism in the context of public perceptions of what it means and how it relates to the abortion issue. Chapter 3 provides a short historical survey of biblical/evangelical approaches to abortion from the early church onwards. Then there is a discussion (in chapters 4 and 5) of more recent evangelical debates, leading to the majority (but not exclusive) position among evangelicals today.

In chapter 6, I offer a definition of the often asserted, but seldom defined, understanding of what it means to be created in the image of God as that concept relates to prenatal life. This includes a fairly detailed discussion, in the second part of the chapter (which some readers may prefer to skip), of when the soul enters the body. Chapter 7 discusses some implications of the image of God for the related issues of contraception, embryo research, and vaccinations, as well as the connection between a pro-life stance on abortion and support of capital punishment for murder, often cited as evidence of pro-life inconsistency.

Chapter 8 asks why the seemingly reasonable and compassionate alternative of adoption meets with so much hostility from abortion advocates. Chapters 9 and 10 are as described earlier.

The connection between these various chapters may not appear to all readers to be as obvious as they are in my mind! I hope it helps that the book is divided into three distinct if related parts: (I) Historical: Understanding Evangelicals and Abortion (1-4); (II) Theological: Why Evangelicals Should Be Pro-Life? (5-7); (III) Practical: Mainstream Society and the Evangelical Prolife Position (8-10). Each chapter is completed with discussion questions such as might be useful, for instance, in an adult Sunday School class.

In much (not all) of what follows, the focus is on the American abortion scene, including the post-*Roe v. Wade* era in which we now are. I am not a US citizen, nor do I live in the USA, although (as previously indicated) I once did with my American-born wife, and we closely follow developments there. My background is British, having grown up in Scotland. I have lived in

Canada for most of my adult life. I make passing references to the situation in these nations and a few others, but it is the USA that attracts most attention from north of the border as well as elsewhere in the world. Some may question my right to comment on the politics and pro-life activism there, but it is where abortion continues to be a highly divisive issue, whereas in most other liberal democracies there are active pro-life organizations, and they occasionally experience some minor gains as well as setbacks, but not nearly the same level of political and legal controversy. It is where, I believe, most lessons can be learned, and just possibly a sympathetic, if sometimes critical, outsider's observations may have some value.

Much of the book deals with historical and theological issues that do not change, but there are also references to contemporary political issues and leaders. I am aware that these may soon become dated. One of the challenges of addressing fast-moving contemporary issues is that, by the time of publication, the situation may have changed. In that case, what becomes obsolete is then part of the historical record. It seems that there are new developments in the USA on an almost daily basis affecting questions of access to abortion, but a writer who hopes to be published must stop reporting them at some point. It might have been wise to wait until after the 2024 presidential election and the resolution of some ongoing court cases, except that I am doubtful that these developments will signal any significant change to the overall abortion landscape.

Note: as per the publisher's guidelines, all footnotes are in abbreviated form, followed by an extensive bibliography.

PART I

Historical: Understanding Evangelicals and Abortion

1

Abortion, Women's Rights, and Evangelical Religion

I AM A MAN AND A MINISTER. In the eyes of some (perhaps many), these two factors automatically disqualify me from having anything relevant or helpful to say about abortion. I do agree that abortion is a woman's issue to the extent that it obviously affects women more directly than men, although in too many cases the absence of support from the men in their lives is a factor in their choice to abort. (On the other hand, there are situations in which men have mourned the loss of their unborn children due to their partners' decision to abort.)

It is also fair to say that men, along with women, have been in the leadership of the abortion rights movement. One thinks of Dr. Bernard Nathanson (1926–2011) in the United States, before his conversion to the pro-life side of the debate, Dr. Henry Morgentaler (1923–2013), the pioneer of abortion rights in Canada, or British MP David Steel (now Lord Steel of Aikwood) who introduced Britain's 1967 Abortion Act. Consider also the webpage of URGE (Unite For Reproductive and Gender Equality) which urges men to take the *Bro-Choice Pledge*, stating that "Living Bro-Choice means being a vocal advocate for reproductive justice, and an authentic ally to women."[1]

I find it demeaning to women when men (as well as women) speak of abortion as a woman's right to control her own body and claim that

---

1. "Bro-Choice Links," §1.

to be anti-abortion is to be anti-women, or even (as we are increasingly hearing) to hate women, as if there were no other considerations and as if there were not an equal number of women opposed to abortion's widespread availability, with many of them involved in leadership positions in the pro-life movement.

The organization Feminists for Life states on its website:

> Established in 1972, Feminists for Life of America is a nonsectarian, nonpartisan, grassroots organization that seeks real solutions to the challenges women face. Our efforts are shaped by the core feminist values of justice, nondiscrimination, and nonviolence. Feminists for Life of America continues the tradition of early American feminists such as Susan B. Anthony, who opposed abortion.[2]

Then there is Susan B. Anthony Pro-Life America, which also claims the suffragette mantle in its pro-life advocacy, supporting "the election of women and men who will fight for life."[3] Women are also involved in leadership of National Right to Life,[4] among other pro-life organizations.

Marvin Olasky in *The Story of Abortion in America* (co-authored with Leah Savas) documents how female doctors in the nineteenth century opposed abortion, not just, as is sometimes claimed, simply because it was then illegal and dangerous for women:

> The woman-to-woman educational efforts began in the 1850s when Dr. Elizabeth Blackwell, the first female to receive a medical degree in the U.S., included in her book, *The Laws of Life*, a plea to "look at the first faint gleam of life, the life of the embryo. . . . The cell rapidly enlarges . . . each organ is distinctly formed. . . . It would be impious folly to attempt to interfere directly with this act of creation."[5]

In the 1890s, Dr Prudence Saur "hit the lecture circuit with her new book, *Maternity: A Book for Every Wife and Mother*." She encouraged single women not to have sex (and thus possible pregnancy) outside of marriage. But once a woman was pregnant, Saur dissuaded her readers from abortion, reminding them that "'the embryo is alive and hence quick [alive] from the moment of conception, [as] modern science has abundantly proven. It

---

2. "Feminists for Life, About Us" §4.
3. "Susan B. Anthony Pro Life, About."
4. "National Right to Life," see: https://www.nrlc.org.
5. Olasky and Savas, *Story of Abortion in America*, 205. Cf. Blackwell, *Laws of Life*, 70–72.

follows, then, that this crime is equally great whether committed in the early weeks of pregnancy or at a more advanced period in the life of the foetus."[6] Olasky gives other historical examples of women taking a pro-life position, just as examples could be given of pro-life female physicians today or in the recent past, such as Dr. Mildred Jefferson (1927–2010), past president (1975–78) of the National Right Life Committee.[7]

It is one thing to say, as Bill Clinton once did, that abortion should be safe, legal, and rare, or that it is a tragic but sometimes necessary choice that should be kept safe and well regulated as much as possible, especially in the later stages,[8] but it is quite another to see it as one among many positive rights of women to be actively promoted. I am offended when men like the late Henry Morgentaler dismiss any suggestion that abortion can have negative effects on women as anti-abortion propaganda.[9]

It does seem to be true that for many women there appear to be mainly positive consequences (relief, career advancement, financial freedom etc.). A not untypical experience quoted approvingly by the Religious Coalition for Abortion Choice is of a then twenty-one-year-old woman who had an abortion at sixteen: "Even though I love children, I had no doubt that an abortion would be the right thing in this particular situation. That was five years ago, and every time I think about it I always have the same feeling—relief, almost a sense of deliverance. It would have been unbearable to have had to live with that mistake for a lifetime. My life was changed in this experience, transformed. I like to think I'm stronger now,

---

6. Olasky and Savas, *Story of Abortion in America*, 207. Cf. Saur, *Maternity*, 150.

7. March for Life, "Women of the Pro-Life Movement: Dr. Mildred Jefferson."

8. See e.g., Denes, *In Necessity and Sorrow: Life and Death in an Abortion Hospital* (1977).

9. I am basing this on personal experience of confronting Morgentaler on a radio call-in talk show back in the 1980s. In his book, *Abortion and Contraception*, Morgentaler is slightly more nuanced. He cites a 1972 research study conducted in Quebec which showed that "four out of five women who had a medical abortion in safe and sanitary conditions felt mainly relieved." The women "who felt intense regret or persistent remorse fall into two groups: the first felt that abortion was against their ethical or religious principles (in all these cases, Roman Catholicism); the second had strong pressure exerted on them to terminate their pregnancies by people close to them," but "a woman who is truly determined to terminate her pregnancy does not regret the act. . . . Fortunately, the women who experience intense feelings of guilt after an abortion are a minority." Morgentaler notes that the study on which he is basing his findings (Rinfret, Giroux, and Boucher) "dealt with French-Canadian women in Montreal. It is encouraging to see that these women were able to shake off rather easily the guilt imposed on them by the Catholic Church. This is a trend which is continuing to this day." Morgentaler, *Abortion and Contraception*, 103–4.

more able to be my own person. I can't help think that making that decision was probably the beginning of a new life for me."[10]

Leah Savas gives a similar example that led to the founding of the organization, Shout Your Abortion, that encourages women to be proud of their decision to abort.[11] But she also documents several cases of women who have been damaged emotionally, even physically and fatally, from RU-486 abortion pills, also known as mifepristone, the first pill in a two-drug regimen with misoprostol, publicly declared very safe by the US Food and Drug Administration (FDA). "By December 2021 the official toll of adult female deaths associated with mifepristone was twenty-six. The FDA had reports of 4,207 adverse events for mothers. It is estimated 4.9 million women had taken mifepristone since its approval in 2000."[12] However, "Some pro-lifers were skeptical about those numbers. Since 2018, U.S. women have been able to buy abortion pills online from the European website Aid Access. This group and other international sources are unlikely to report to a U.S. government agency the number of abortion pills sold. . . . Aid Access also gives customers advice that could be obscuring the number of adult victims" by telling women who end up in the ER that "'You do not have to tell the medical staff that you tried to induce an abortion; you can tell them that you had a spontaneous miscarriage.' . . . Other abortion websites give the same advice."[13]

Dr. Bernard Nathanson, writing in 1996, devotes the better part of a chapter of his memoir to gruesome accounts of botched abortions, including fatalities to clients, under legal abortion.[14] The 1987 book, *Aborted Women: Silent No More*, by David C. Reardon, tells the harrowing stories of women who felt coerced into abortions and deceived about their potential consequences.[15] Another book by a woman who was active in Lutherans for Life is *Helping Women Recover from Abortion: How to deal with the guilt, the emotional pain, and the emptiness*.[16] Then there is *Forbidden Grief* by Teresa Burke and David C. Reardon.[17] Burke, a psychotherapist, is founder of Rachel's Vineyard, described as "a safe place to renew, rebuild and redeem

---

10. *Prayerfully Pro-Choice*, 25. Quoted in Gorman and Brooks, *Holy Abortion?*, 18.
11. Olasky and Savas, *Story of Abortion in America*, 382.
12. Olasky and Savas, *Story of Abortion in America*, 377–78.
13. Olasky and Savas, *Story of Abortion in America*, 378.
14. Nathenson, *The Hand of God*, 114–27.
15. Reardon, *Aborted Women* (1987).
16. Michels, *Helping Women Recover* (1988).
17. Burke and Reardon, *Forbidden Grief* (2000).

hearts broken by abortion."[18] Even Morgentaler recognized that forcing a woman to undergo an abortion against her will "is likely to cause psychological damage and difficulty in her relationship with those who forced her to do it."[19] (As a Dachau concentration camp victim in his youth, Morgentaler said that he was motivated, not only by the rights of women, but by a concern to end child abuse with every child being a wanted child. It seems clear, however, that the widespread availability of abortion has done little to eradicate child abuse. Some would say it has made it worse, and that abortion itself is a form of child abuse.)[20] Regardless of one's position on the pro-choice/life debate, we can surely conclude that the emotional and physical consequences of abortion are, at the very least, varied.

Abortion is typically advocated as a matter between a woman, her doctor, and perhaps her spiritual adviser, implying that the decision to undergo an abortion is made with fully informed consent as to the potential negative side effects and outcomes of the procedure. However, the reality in 2014, according to the Guttmacher Institute, was that "95 percent of abortions occur in freestanding abortion centres, apart from any established doctor-patient relationship."[21] More recently, self-medicated abortifacients available from certain pharmacies, sometimes through the mail, have accounted for more than half of first-term abortions, according to the same Institute.[22] Therefore, it is at least possible that many women are not fully informed or aware of the possible harm this decision could cause them.

The National Women's Coalition for Life is an umbrella organization representing 1.3 million women in the United States. It sponsored Real Choices, a research project conducted by Frederica Mathewes-Green, exploring the reasons women choose abortion, and exploring alternatives that included reaching out to pro-choice advocates for cooperation through an organization called the Common Ground Network for Life and Choice.[23]

18. "Rachel's Vineyard," §1.

19. Morgentaler, *Abortion and Contraception*, 49.

20. In a 1979 (and thus somewhat dated) study by Philip Ney published in the *Canadian Journal of Psychiatry*, the author argued, "Although permissive abortion has been advocated on the grounds it will reduce the prevalence of child abuse and infanticide, there is no evidence to prove it has. There is a growing concern that it may have contributed to the problem. This article outlines eight possible methods whereby an increasing rate of abortion will lead to an increasing rate of abuse" (abstract). For a contrary point of view, see Bitler and Zavodny, "Child Abuse and Abortion Availability," 363–65.

21. Olasky, *Abortion at the Crossroads*, 116. The Guttmacher Institute is a research and policy organization associated with Planned Parenthood.

22. Guttmacher Institute, "Medication Abortion," February 24, 2022.

23. Among the several endorsements for Mathewes-Green's book, *Real Choices*,

As Mathewes-Green once wrote, "No one wants an abortion as she wants an ice-cream or a Porsche. She wants an abortion as an animal, caught in a trap, wants to gnaw off its own leg." This statement in a *Policy Review* magazine article was "not just picked up by sympathetic pro-lifers, but it was 'Quote of the Week' in Planned Parenthood's *Public Affairs Action Letter*, and 'Quote of the Month' in *The Pro-Choice Network Newsletter*. Despite the profound differences and suspicion between the two sides, apparently all agreed that abortion was a miserable choice."[24] (A poll conducted by the pro-life organization, Charlotte Lozier Institute, found that 61 percent of women interviewed who have had an abortion said they had felt external pressure to do so, influencing their decision.)[25]

In 1994, Mathewes-Green published her findings in book form, then again in 1997 and 2013. Alternate chapters are interviews with women who regret their abortions, many of whom feel guilty, and some of whom are now actively pro-life. Interestingly, most, if not all, of the women had Roman Catholic backgrounds, which may account for their lingering sense of guilt. The author also points out that "Among all women having abortions nationwide, one in six says she is an evangelical or born-again Christian."[26] (A 2015 LifeWay study sponsored by Care Net found that four in ten women were churchgoers at the time of their abortion.)[27]

All of this brings us to the interconnectedness of religion with the abortion issue. As the study referred to by Morgentaler indicates (see note 1), those with religious backgrounds are the most likely to experience regret and guilt after an abortion. Morgentaler devotes a chapter to "Abortion and Religion," where he surveys the positions of various religions, then advocates secular humanism, noting that "Humanists wish to see women attain equality with men and be given all the same opportunities to realize their full human potential. It is clear that this goal will never be reached unless women are allowed to control their reproduction, which means effective contraception and access to safe abortions when necessary."[28] This is not to say that all

---

2013, is one from noted feminist author and theorist Naomi Wolf, who writes: "As a pro-choice activist concerned with getting at the root of why so many women choose abortion, I could only wish that her approach would be the one adopted by the pro-life movement in general."

24. Mathewes-Green, *Real Choices*, 1.

25. Anderson, "Most Women Who Had Abortions," §1.

26. Mathewes-Green, *Real Choices*, 107. She also notes that the Alan Guttmacher Institute reports that "Catholic women are as likely to have abortions as all women nationally; evangelical women are half as likely" (118).

27. LifeWay Study, "Women Distrust Church on Abortion," §2, 4.

28. Morgentaler, *Abortion and Contraception*, 142.

women who claim to feel no guilt are self-consciously secular humanists, or that all who feel guilty are from a religious background or are practicing Christians, but it does indicate that religious beliefs play a role.

In 1984, Dr. Bernard Nathanson was still an atheist, on his way to conversion to Roman Catholicism, although this did not officially take place for another dozen years. In 1979 he had co-authored *Aborting America* with Richard Ostling, then the *Time* magazine religion editor.[29] It told of Nathanson's involvement as a co-founder (with, among others, another man, Larry Lader)[30] in 1969 of the National Association for the Repeal of Abortion Laws, later renamed National Abortion Rights Action League (NARAL), and now the National Abortion and Reproductive Rights Action League. Nathanson claims, among other things, to have falsified the number of women who had died from illegal abortions. ("There were perhaps three hundred or so deaths from criminal abortions annually in the United States in the sixties, but NARAL in its press releases claimed to have data that supported a figure of five thousand.")[31] NARAL adopted a policy of targeting the Catholic Church as the main opponent of abortion in order to win over mainline Protestants to their cause. The Rev. Howard Moody, then pastor of the Judson Memorial Church in Manhattan's Greenwich Village was instrumental in forming the Clergy Consultation Referral Service, "a sizeable group of Protestant ministers and Jewish rabbis joined at the hip by a common disdain for restrictive abortion laws."[32] This evolved in 1973 into the Religious Coalition for Abortion Rights.

With the advent of ultrasound in the 1970s, Nathanson was able to witness a real time abortion taking place. This led him to begin rethinking his commitment to the movement he had helped found. Finally, in 1984, he produced and narrated *The Silent Scream*, showing a twelve-week-old fetus "being torn to pieces in utero by the combination of suction and crushing instrumentation by the abortionist." The abortionist in question, after viewing the film, "was so affected that he never did another abortion."[33] This film was followed up by another, *Eclipse of Reason*, dealing with late term abortions.[34]

29. Nathanson, MD, with Ostling, *Aborting America*, (1979).

30. Marvin Olasky, in *Story of Abortion in America,* devotes a chapter (289–95) to Lader as "The Father of Abortion Rights," noting *inter alia* his admiration of and association with Margaret Sanger, the founder of Planned Parenthood, and later with feminist icon Betty Friedan, also a co-founder of NARAL.

31. Nathanson, *Hand of God*, 91–92.

32. Nathanson, *Hand of God*, 105.

33. Nathanson, *Hand of God*, 148.

34. Nathanson, *Hand of God*, 184.

Copies of *The Silent Scream* were mailed to members of Congress. Ronald Reagan (1911–2004), who was US president at the time, said that if everyone in Congress could view it, abortion would be outlawed in America.[35] Not only did this not happen, but there was a flood of negative reaction from abortion rights advocates, claiming the film was manipulated and inaccurate. Nathanson sent it to Dr. Ian Donald in Scotland, the founder of ultrasound, informing him that "the New York Times had run several editorials saying that it was a fake. Donald looked at the tape and said that it was absolutely genuine" and swore an affidavit to that effect.[36]

More recently, Abby Johnson, a former prize-winning director of a Planned Parenthood facility, published *Unplanned*,[37] which became the basis for a controversial film of that name. Despite being director of the clinic, Johnson had not actually witnessed an abortion taking place until she was called to assist with one at thirteen week's gestation when no one else was available. She was horrified by what she saw on the screen and soon resigned her position. She subsequently formed And Then There Were None, to encourage abortion workers to leave the "industry," providing financial and other support to those who do. Not insignificantly, Johnson, now a Roman Catholic, grew up in an evangelical home. Both her parents and her husband questioned the work she was doing with Planned Parenthood.

Once again, extravagant claims were made about the effectiveness of Johnson's revelations, but equally they were met with a flood of denials from Planned Parenthood and others, even questioning whether the abortion in question had taken place.[38] When the dramatized film version of Johnson's story was produced and shown in movie theaters, it provoked demonstrations, denials of its scientific accuracy, and threats such that some movie theaters, including the one Margaret and I attended, had to hire additional security.

Why the backlash? Why was not everyone convinced of the evils of abortion, as Reagan had predicted they would be back in 1984? Why, as

---

35. I am unable to provide documentation of this but have a clear recollection of Reagan saying it. His pro-life position (which he apparently came to as president after having signed what was then the nation's most liberal abortion bill as Governor of California and saying at the time that he hadn't thought much about the issue) is evident in his book, *Abortion and the Conscience of the Nation* (1984), with afterwords by C. Everett Koop and Malcolm Muggeridge. The book is unusual in at least a couple of respects: that a sitting president should publish an essay on any issue, and that it should be on the most divisive political issue of the day. The book is based on an essay originally written for *The Human Life Review* (Spring, 1983).

36. Nathanson, *Hand of God*, 149.

37. Johnson, *Unplanned* (2010, 2014).

38. Blakeslee, "Sorting Fact from Fiction," §3.

the scientific evidence of fetal life has become more widely available, has societal acceptance of abortion increased rather than disappeared, with an increasing number of polls indicating that most respondents identify as pro-choice?[39] Perhaps this is because most people are considering the issue in shades of grey rather than as a for-or-against opinion. Polls commissioned by pro-life organizations, more so than others, report high percentages of respondents supporting some restrictions, but the majority of those respondents still tend to identify as pro-choice.[40] A February 13, 2023 article in *LifeNews.com* claimed that twenty-five recent polls had found that "a majority of Americans have taken a pro-life position wanting all or most abortions made illegal."[41] However, it seems that poll results depend somewhat on who is doing the polling and which exact questions are asked. Most supposedly pro-life Americans still want there to be exceptions, in some cases for rape, incest and the life of the mother, which constitute less than two percent of all abortions, but others seem more content with a gestational limit that would not exclude most abortions, the majority of which are performed by the thirteenth week.[42] (According to the Guttmacher Institute, incidents of rape account for 1 percent of all abortions, and incest accounts for less than 0.5 percent.[43] Incidents where the mother's physical life is at risk are likewise relatively rare, but the phrase "life of the mother" is open to a much broader interpretation, consistent with the World Health Organization's definition of health, to be discussed later.)

It follows, therefore, that the labels "pro-life" and "pro-choice" are, in reality, misnomers. Nathanson documents how the abortion rights lobby "sold" abortion to the general public by making it a matter of choice. Polls regularly show a small percentage of Americans (and other nationals),

39. According to a July 6, 2022 Pew Research Center poll, 62 percent of Americans say abortion should be legal in all or most cases. Almost a year later, a Gallup poll found that "close to half of Americans, 47%, now say abortion should be legal in all (34%) or most (13%) circumstances, while a similar proportion, 49%, want it legal in only a few (36%) or illegal in all (13%) circumstances." This represents a significant decrease from the 2022 Pew Research Poll's numbers of those supporting abortion in all or most cases. According to the Gallup poll, those wishing abortion to be legal in only a few cases or illegal in all now exceeds those with the opposing point of view, but it would be misleading (as some have) to represent this as endorsing a consistently pro-life position. See e.g., Ertelt, "Polls Show Majority of Americans Support Dobbs."

40. Gryboski, "Nearly half of Democrats support abortion restrictions," §9.

41. Ertelt, "25 Recent Polls Show Americans Are Pro-life on Abortion," §3.

42. See CDCs Abortion Surveillance System FAQs §3, "Nearly all abortions in 2020 took place early in gestation: 93.1% of abortions were performed at ≤13 weeks' gestation; a smaller number of abortions (5.8%) were performed at 14–20 weeks' gestation, and even fewer (0.9%) were performed at ≥21 weeks' gestation."

43. Finer et al., "Reasons U.S. Women Have Abortions."

being in favor of abortion at any stage of development, a smaller percentage opposing abortion except to save the mother's life, whereas most are somewhere in the middle, believing there should be some restrictions, but unwilling to impose a blanket restriction. The net effect, by making it a matter of choice, is that a woman's choice is paramount, even in some circumstances up to the admittedly minority of cases that involve viable fetuses. Pro-choice advocates will claim that they are not "pro-abortion," although their rhetoric often suggests otherwise.[44] Planned Parenthood prefers the euphemism, "pro-reproductive rights" for its position and "anti-abortion" for the opposing one. In its literature, this organization also perpetuates the notions that anti-abortionists care more for a fertilized egg than for pregnant women, and that they also oppose contraception (which some, but not all, do).[45]

On the other hand, the "pro-life" label reinforces the perception that abortion is the only issue pro-lifers are concerned about. Journalists are encouraged to use "abortion rights" and "anti-abortion."[46] "Pro-abortion" in the sense of wanting the procedure to be generally available, and "anti-abortion" would be more accurate, but we are more or less stuck with the monikers chosen by each side, although secular media often unfairly uses "pro-choice" versus "anti-abortion." It has become a slogan to say that "pro-choice" does not mean "pro-abortion," meaning that one might not choose abortion for oneself or one's partner, but this does not give anyone the right to make that decision for someone else. This makes it that much more important for there to be clear definitions and descriptions of the positions, perspectives, and values of each side of the issue.

Back to the question of why increasing scientific evidence has not turned the tide against "abortion on demand," but rather the reverse; the answer is that the abortion debate is not about biological science. From a strictly biological point of view, the life in a woman's womb is human life. It is not some other form of life. The question has shifted to whether that human life is potential or actual, or whether or not it is of a real person before birth.[47] If it is not, what is to prevent abortion at any stage of development? If on the other hand, the life in the womb is of a tiny human person, is abortion ever justified? Should the lives of living, breathing, grown women

44. See e.g., Pew Research Center, "Pro-Choice Does not Mean Pro-Abortion."

45. Planned Parenthood, "Can you explain what pro-choice means?"

46. *The Associated Press Stylebook*, 39th edition. Referenced in Williams, *Defenders of the Unborn*, xi.

47. Hillary Clinton came under criticism for stating in an NBC "Meet the Press" interview that an "unborn person doesn't have constitutional rights" ("Meet the Press," Apr 3, 2016.) The criticism was for referring to the unborn as a *person*.

have more value than those of unborn fetuses? These I submit and hope to demonstrate, are deeply religious questions. This, I realize, goes against the grain of conventional pro-life wisdom that abortion is a moral, human rights issue (which it is), but not a religious one. Granted not all pro-lifers claim a religious affiliation, but most do, and in any case, morality is based in religion. Religion allows us to define morality within the structure and parameters of culture, values, and belief. By thinking of these questions as religious considerations, we have a structure and a lens through which to evaluate and understand them on a deeper level than merely personal or emotional experience.

An article in the December 2022 issue of *Christianity Today* offers evidence opposed to the above position. It claims that "a growing number of non-religious people [are] joining the pro-life cause." It cites a 2022 Gallup poll which found that 21 percent of those who claim no religious affiliation say abortion is morally wrong. Monica Snyder, the executive director of Secular Pro-Life is quoted as saying that, contrary to pro-choice rhetoric, "abortion is not amoral." A Catholic priest is referenced as saying that "the pro-life movement has always involved nonreligious groups, but their visibility seems to be increasing." He also says that "the existence of these groups indicates that we can come to these pro-life positions with human reason alone."[48] I would question this assumption and argue that non-religious pro-lifers are being inconsistent with their fundamental (secular) presuppositions and worldview. Besides, oftentimes (as with Monica Snyder who grew up with a Roman Catholic background which she has rejected, but has been unable to throw off the pro-life convictions she inherited from her parents),[49] even if one rejects belief in God and with it awareness of having been created in his image, that awareness still exists "deep down" (see Rom 1: 18–19) influencing one's values and actions in life.

This is not to say that being openly and self-consciously religious, or even a professing Christian, makes one automatically pro-life. As noted, several mainline Protestant churches belong to the Religious Coalition for Abortion Rights, and they speak of being "prayerfully pro-choice" (see note 2). However, underlying this difference with pro-life evangelicals is a fundamentally different attitude to the authority of Scripture and other central doctrines to be alluded to in the next chapter. Also, despite the Roman Catholic Church's unequivocal stand on abortion, there is a dissenting group based in Washington, DC, called Catholics for Choice (originally formed in 1973 as Catholics for a Free Choice). Again, there are

48. Watson, "They're Not Religious."
49. Watson, "They're Not Religious."

underlying theological differences found within these groups regarding the interpretation and understanding of Scripture on this issue. According to the Pew Research Center, Islam, Buddhism and Orthodox Judaism (along with the Baptist National Convention) have no clear position on abortion.[50] However, I am not speaking of religion in a generic sense, but as it has been historically understood by those who call themselves *evangelical*, hence the title of this book.

Given the variable opinions on abortion found even within the church, it becomes necessary to define what group of Christians (evangelicals) I am referring to and how they are connected to this topic. The next chapter will offer a survey of evangelicalism and its connection with the abortion issue, beginning with the public perception of what it means to be evangelical, then briefly tracing its historical meaning, and ending with the example of the late C. Everett Koop, evangelical leader and one time Surgeon General of the United States.

Discussion Questions

1. From your perspective, what influence should fetal development have in the current discussion around pro-life/pro-choice debates?
2. Considering informed consent, what are the benefits and risks of fully informing women and men of both the supposedly positive and potentially negative consequences of abortion?
3. If, as the author suggests, the abortion debate isn't about biological science, what is it about? Do you agree with the author? Why or why not?
4. What are some of the main differences between the justice and mercy aspects of the pro-life movement?

---

50. Masci, "Where Major Religious Groups Stand on Abortion."

2

Evangelicals and Abortion
Who Are Evangelicals?

LATE IN 2019, THE RETIRING EDITOR of *Christianity Today (CT)*, Mark Galli, penned an editorial to the effect that then President Donald Trump should be removed from office on moral grounds. (Galli has since converted to Roman Catholicism, but this has no bearing on what he wrote as editor of *CT*.) The editorial sent temporary shockwaves throughout the secular media, not accustomed to criticisms of Trump by those they understood to be representative of mainstream evangelicalism, namely religiously motivated right-wing Republicans. Some opined that the *CT* editorial represented a shift in evangelicals' support for Trump, 81 percent of whom (mostly white) had voted for him in the 2016 election,[1] many of them because of his commitment to nominate pro-life judges, a priority that enabled them to turn a blind eye to Trump's many and obvious moral failings. (A similar number of evangelicals voted for Trump in 2020.)

Others downplayed the significance of *CT* as compared to the "millions" who are represented by TV evangelists and the like. *The New York Times* offered the opinion, which proved to be largely correct, that nothing would change as a result of the editorial.[2]

The current editor-in-chief of *CT*, Russell Moore's latest book is *Losing Our Religion: An Altar Call for Evangelical America*. Moore is an outspoken critic of what has come to be known as Trumpism and in this book he

---

1. Martinez, and Smith, "How the Faithful Voted."
2. Posner, "That Christianity Today Editorial."

pleads for conversion from Trumpism, as well as related issues like "Christian nationalism, white-identity backlash, the dismissing of issues like abuse as 'social justice secularism,'" and several others of which he says, some or all of them are "dividing almost every church, almost every family, almost every friendship I know."[3]

Another writer, Randall Balmer, announced that "After a long and lingering illness, evangelicalism died on November 8, 2016. On that day, 81 percent of white American evangelicals who for decades claimed to be concerned about 'family values' registered their votes for a twice-divorced, thrice-married, self-confessed sexual predator whose understanding of the faith is so truncated that he can't even fake religious literacy."[4]

The above quote is taken from a series of essays in *The Spiritual Danger of Donald Trump*, edited by Ronald J. Sider (1939–2022) and published in the 2020 election year. (Apparently Sider was recruited as editor by two others, Bandy X. Lee of Yale School of Medicine and Chris Thurman, a psychologist and author, both evangelical academics who did not think they had enough clout in the evangelical world to list their names as editors.) As with all such collections, some essays are better than others and there is some unnecessary repetition that comes across as overkill. One possibly valid argument is that, whereas Trump was good for pro-life and religious values in the short-term, he may have hurt them in the longer term by providing ammunition for the "liberal establishment" to "hate" evangelicals even more.[5]

Then there are other voices, among them prominent conservative American journalists like the late Michael Gerson (1964–2022), David French (a columnist for *The New York Times*) and Gary Abernathy (as Gerson was, a former columnist for *The Washington Post*) who continue(d) to self-identify as evangelical and are (or were) critical of excesses among fellow-evangelicals on the political right. It thus becomes apparent that not all evangelicals fit the popular perception, which begs the questions: who or what is an evangelical and who speaks for evangelicalism? There are a number of published works on this subject, one of which, *Who Is an Evangelical?* by Thomas S. Kidd has as its sub-title, *The History of a Movement in Crisis*, indicating at the very least the need for clarification.[6]

---

3. Moore, *Losing Our Religion*, 11.
4. Balmer, "Donald Trump," in Sider, ed., *Spiritual Danger*, 78.
5. Yancey, "Trump the Last Temptation," in Sider, ed., *Spiritual Danger*, 124–26.
6. Kidd, *Who is an Evangelical?* (2019).

WHO ARE EVANGELICALS?

Kidd and others focus largely on the history of evangelicalism in America, but the movement is broader and longer than that. The most commonly accepted definition is one offered by David Bebbington, emeritus professor of history at Stirling University in Scotland. Bebbington's terminology is somewhat technical, but what it boils down to is that evangelicals believe in the divine inspiration and authority of the Bible, in the need for personal conversion (Bebbington actually places this first), the centrality of the cross of Christ for our salvation, and in "activism," which includes world missions as well as social action. These four characteristics have come to be known as Bebbington's quadrilateral.

In his landmark work, *Evangelicalism in Modern Britain: A History from the 1730s to the 1980s*, Bebbington traces the roots of evangelicalism to the Evangelical Revival in England that crossed the Atlantic as the Great Awakening in the eighteenth century. At the same time, he also recognizes that:

> Historians regularly apply the term 'evangelical' to the churches arising from the Reformation in the sixteenth and seventeenth centuries. The usage of the period justifies them. Sir Thomas More in 1531 referred to advocates of the Reformation as 'Evaungelicalles.' Yet the normal use of the word, as late as the eighteenth century, was 'of the gospel' in a non-partisan sense.[7]

This is not surprising given that "evangelical" is derived from the Greek word *euangelio*, meaning "good news" or "gospel."

In 2008 Michael A. G. Haykin and Kenneth J. Stewart edited *The Emergence of Evangelicalism*, a collection of essays addressing various aspects of Bebbington's thesis, with a response from Bebbington.[8] In a separate article in the *Evangelical Quarterly*, a scholarly British publication, Stewart posits that there have been evangelical movements throughout church history. In "Did evangelicalism predate the eighteenth century?" Stewart begins: "If you or I had asked this question in evangelical company prior to 1989, we would certainly have drawn very blank looks. For until that year [the year Bebbington's book was published], it was taken as an elementary truth" that evangelicalism as we know it "stood in an unbroken

---

7. Bebbington, *Evangelicalism in Modern Britain*, 1.

8. Haykin and Stewart, *Emergence of Evangelicalism*. An American edition titled *The Advent of Evangelicalism* was published in the same year by Broadman and Holman.

succession of vital Christianity extending backwards to at least the Reformation of the sixteenth century and perhaps beyond."[9]

Besides his own historical research, Stewart quotes the late James Packer (1926–2020), one of the most recognized and respected evangelical theologians of his day. Writing in 1978 of the Christianity "which we inherit from the New Testament via the Reformers, the Puritans, and the revival and missionary leaders of the eighteenth and nineteenth centuries," Packer adds, "The reason why I call myself an evangelical and mean to go on doing so is my belief that as this historic evangelicalism has never sought to be anything other than New Testament Christianity, so in essentials it has succeeded in its aim."[10] Stewart references another "senior evangelical theologian," John Stott (1921–2011) to much the same effect.[11] (*New York Times* columnist David Brooks once quoted Michael Cromartie [1950–2017] of the Ethics and Public Policy Center as saying "if evangelicals could elect a pope, Stott is the person they would likely choose.")[12]

Diarmaid MacCulloch, in his massively researched biography of Thomas Cromwell (circa 1485–1540) notes that "evangelical" is a better term than "Protestant" in the early stage of the Reformation in England, "for in Cromwell's lifetime 'Protestant' was not a term used to describe English adherents of the Reformation and is best reserved for its place of origin in Germany. By contrast, the terms 'evangelic' or 'evangelical' were used in England at the time. . . ."[13] Iain Murray in *Evangelicalism Divided* observes that in William Tyndale's time (circa 1494–1536), he and his sympathisers were described as "'gospellers' or less commonly as evangelicals." It was over two hundred years later that:

> The latter term was to pass into more permanent usage at the time of the 'Evangelical Revival.' That it did not do so earlier is largely due to the fact that all the churches were 'of the gospel' in their creeds and confessions. By the eighteenth century, however, while the profession of the national churches in England

---

9. Stewart, "Did evangelicalism predate the eighteenth century?"13. An entirely different perspective in the *Evangelical Quarterly* by Robert Letham, (with a response by Donald Macleod), asks provocatively "Is Evangelicalism Christian? 3–33, precisely because of evangelicalism's supposedly recent emergence, thereby cutting itself off from the history of the Christian church in its entirety.

10. Stewart, "Did evangelicalism predate the eighteenth century?" 135. Cf. James Packer, "Uniqueness of Jesus Christ," 102.

11. Stewart, "Did evangelicalism predate the eighteenth century?" 136. Cf. John Stott, "Plea for Evangelical Christianity," 27–46.

12. Brooks, "Who is John Stott?"

13. MacCulloch, *Thomas Cromwell*, 18.

and Scotland remained orthodox there were many pulpits from which no gospel was heard and when the evangel was recovered a term was necessary to distinguish its preachers from others: they were 'evangelicals.'[14]

More recently, John G. Stackhouse Jr in *Evangelicalism: A Very Short Introduction* (2023) summarizes helpfully:

> Evangelicalism traces its roots back to the Bible itself—which is fitting enough since evangelicals describe themselves as Bible people. But evangelicalism as a definite something arises out of the Protestant Reformation of the sixteenth century and then taking shape via the English movement of Puritanism and the middle European movement of Pietism in the 17th century it blossoms into the transatlantic revivals of the eighteenth century. . . .[15]

Stackhouse expands on Bebbington's definition (without mentioning it): "Here then is a list of adjectives to define Evangelicalism: Trinitarian, biblicist, conversionist, missional, populist and pragmatic."[16] The first four correspond well to Bebbington's quadrilateral; the other two have more to do with the manner in which evangelicals typically operate.

All of which is to say that "evangelical" is a perfectly honorable term which has long been used to define adherence to the biblical gospel. As Olson and Winn write in *Reclaiming Pietism*, "If evangelical Christianity is anything, it is orthodoxy on fire, 'head belief' and 'heart experience' brought together. Evangelicals believe these two dimensions—doctrine and devotion—belong together for holistic, authentic Christian life."[17]

In 2019, Bebbington joined with noted American evangelical historians Mark Noll and George Marsden in producing *Evangelicals: Who They Have Been, Are Now, And Could Be*, a collection of essays by various scholars, some of which are reprinted from original sources. Part of the book involves interaction with Bebbington's quadrilateral of evangelical markers (see above). There are also essays with such titles as "Is the Term 'Evangelical' Redeemable?" (Thomas S. Kidd thinks maybe not) and "Can Evangelicalism Survive Donald Trump?" (Timothy Keller thinks maybe so).

---

14. Murray, *Evangelicalism Divided*, 1.

15. Stackhouse, *Evangelicalism*, 3. Since this was written, Stackhouse's employment at Crandall University in Newfoundland and Labrador, Canada was terminated for alleged sexual harassment. He subsequently sued the university for wrongful dismissal. This sad development does not affect the accuracy of what he is quoted as writing here.

16. Stackhouse, *Evangelicalism*, 24.

17. Olson and Winn, *Reclaiming Pietism*, 182.

Canadian contributor Brian C. Stiller in "To Be or Not to Be an Evangelical," makes the point that:

> While the recent sharp reaction to the use of the label has come about in the U.S. . . . a decision on what name suits us best globally is not a choice we can leave with Americans to decide. The U.S. does not set the agenda for the world, and we should not assume that what matters to them will define what matters globally. As influential as they are, and recognizing that American concerns do affect the world, the real place of evangelical growth is in the global south (Asia, Africa, and Latin America).[18]

A similar point is made about the definition of "evangelical" outside of the US, in Tim Alberta's recently published *The Kingdom, the Power, and the Glory*, by Australian professor John Dickson, currently teaching at Wheaton College, Illinois.[19]

EVANGELICALISM IN AMERICA

That said, there is no question that the American church has had its own unique evangelical history, beginning with the fundamentalist movement of the early twentieth century that sought to preserve biblical Christianity at a time when mainline denominations and seminaries were being overtaken by theological liberalism. This concern led to the publication of *The Fundamentals: A Testimony to the Truth*, a set of ninety essays, originally published quarterly in twelve volumes between 1910 and 1915. The authors consisted of a number of international scholars from different denominations, but the project was conceived of by a California businessman, Lyman Stewart, and the various volumes were published by the Testimony Publishing Company of Chicago, then republished in 1917 by the Bible Institute of Los Angeles (Now Biola University) as a four volume set.[20] Next, Princeton theologian (later founder of Westminster Seminary) J. Gresham Machen's book *Christianity and Liberalism*, first published in 1923, made the case that theological liberalism, with its denial of historic Christian doctrines, was another religion altogether. Machen and some others, including certain contributors to *The Fundamentals*, such as Machen's Princeton colleague B.B. Warfield, did not, however, self-identify as fundamentalists, as that label, over time, came to be associated with a narrower vision of the

---

18. Stiller, "To Be or Not to Be Evangelical," 274.
19. Alberta, *The Kingdom, the Power, and the Glory*, 137.
20. Marsden, *Fundamentalism and American Culture*, 118–19.

gospel focusing on end time prophesy, withdrawal from anything considered worldly (including politics) and a legalistic lifestyle.

Then in 1947, Carl Henry (1913–2003) wrote *The Uneasy Conscience of Modern Fundamentalism*, and a new movement, neo-evangelicalism was born, with Fuller Theological Seminary in California as its flagship academic institution and *Christianity Today*, founded by Billy Graham (1918–2018) with Carl Henry as its first editor, as its flagship publication. The National Association of Evangelicals had already been founded in 1942.

What came to be known as "neo-evangelicalism" sought to represent a more intellectually respectable, open-minded form of evangelicalism. Billy Graham's "cooperative evangelism" was typical. A greater concern for social issues, once identified with the "social gospel" of liberalism was another development. In time, this movement split into more "conservative" and "liberal" or "progressive" wings, in part over the nature and extent of biblical authority. Progressives have also highlighted social issues like the causes of poverty, and race relations that have come to be associated with left-wing politics. Evangelicals for Social Action and the Sojourners Community in Washington, DC are examples. In 2020, Evangelicals for Social Action became Christians for Social Action, largely in response to the identification of "evangelical" in the public mind with conservative evangelicals who have focused more narrowly on issues like abortion and same-sex marriage. These issues are not mutually exclusive from a biblical point of view, or even within modern evangelicalism. It is more a matter of emphasis and perception. (Some African-American church leaders with evangelical-compatible beliefs avoid using the term because of its past partial association with racism, even slavery.)

In 1975, Charles Colson (1931–2012) published *Born Again*, the story of his conversion from Richard Nixon's "hatchet man" to evangelical Christian and founder of Prison Fellowship. Meanwhile, Jimmy Carter was running for President of the United States. Carter made no secret of his Christian faith and so a reporter asked him if he were born again. Carter replied that he was, and the term "born again," along with the moniker "evangelical," entered the vocabulary of everyday English. *Time* magazine proclaimed 1976 the "Year of the Evangelical."

Carter may have been a born again evangelical, but his policies proved to be too liberal for some of his fellow evangelicals, leading to the emergence of the Moral Majority (see below) which claimed credit for the 1980 election of Republican president Ronald Reagan. Since then, the term "evangelical" has come to be associated with the Republican party and its "religious right."[21] Traditional family values and (over time) opposition to same-sex marriage and transgender issues came to be hallmarks of evangelicalism in the public mind, but the dominant issue throughout has been abortion.

It was in 1979 that fundamentalists like the late Jerry Falwell Sr. (1933–2007), abandoned their avoidance of politics and formed the Moral Majority, out of concern for the moral drift since the Supreme Court decisions outlawing school prayer (1963) and legalizing abortion (1973), although critics would say that this movement's first foray into politics was to support school segregation and that it tended to promote "laws, practices and ideas that limited or even sought to reverse the gains of the civil rights movement."[22] In 1989, the Moral Majority, having been absorbed into the newly founded Liberty Foundation in 1986, was disbanded, with Falwell declaring, "Our goal has been achieved.... The religious right is solidly in place and ... religious conservatives in America are now in for the duration."[23]

A decade later, two disillusioned former leaders published *Blinded by Might: Can the Religious Right Save America?* warning from experience of the danger of placing one's hope for moral change in political activism.[24] Their warning seems to have gone largely unheeded, with the religious right firmly in place, claiming "unprecedented" access to the White House during the Trump presidency. Falwell's son and namesake (prior to his fall from grace) was among them, as was Billy Graham's son Franklin. Others were more associated with the "prosperity gospel" and its message of health and wealth.

Another major figure in the linking of evangelical faith with conservative political (including pro-life) activism was Pat Robertson (1930–2023), founder of (*inter alia*) the Christian Broadcasting Network, Regent University, and the Christian Coalition. Robertson made an unsuccessful run for the Republican Presidential nomination in 1987 and subsequently formed the Christian Coalition to promote religiously and politically conservative values and candidates. According to Ralph Reed, that movement's first

---

21. This became increasingly true during the Trump presidency. As Ryan Burge points out in "Why 'Evangelical' is Becoming Another Word for 'Republican,'" rather than evangelicalism growing through spreading the gospel and bringing more people into the church, "What is drawing more people to embrace the evangelical label on surveys is more likely that Evangelicalism has been bound to the Republican Party. Instead of theological affinity for Jesus Christ, millions of Americans are being drawn to the evangelical label because of its association with the G.O.P." These include non-church-goers and even members of non-Christian religions like Hinduism and Islam, as well as Catholic and Orthodox Christians, and Mormons (§5, 8–9).

22. Tisby, *Color of Compromise*, 166.

23. Allit, *Religion in America Since 1945*, 198.

24. Thomas and Dobson, *Blinded by Might* (1999).

executive director, it "helped to turn the Republican Party irreversibly into a socially conservative, pro-life party that was populated increasingly by evangelical Christians."[25] Robertson later came to the conviction that "God is not a Republican," but on his death in 2023 it was his influence of the Republican Party that was remembered by the mainstream media.

CHRISTIAN NATIONALISM

Ever since the infamous storming of the US Capitol by Trump supporters on January 6, 2021, some carrying wooden crosses and other symbols of Christianity, the term "Christian Nationalism" has entered the conversation of what evangelicalism is. Some evangelicals embrace the moniker (see, e.g., *The Case for Christian Nationalism* by Stephen Wolfe),[26] others see it as the greatest threat facing American democracy.[27] More nuanced critiques are offered in a number of books and articles on the subject, among them, *The Religion of American Greatness: What's Wrong with Christian Nationalism*, by Paul Miller,[28] a former White House staffer under both George W. Bush and Barak Obama, now a professor at Georgetown University. Miller helpfully summarizes his views in a *Christianity Today* article, "What is Christian Nationalism?"[29] He distinguishes between patriotism as in "love for country," and Christian nationalism defined as "the belief that the American nation is defined by Christianity, and that the government should take active steps to keep it that way." Some would understand this as preserving America's "Anglo-Protestant heritage." Miller points out that "Christian nationalists do not reject the First Amendment and do not advocate for theocracy," but "they do believe that Christianity should enjoy a privileged position in the public square." Christian nationalism, according to Miller, "takes the name of Christ for a worldly political agenda, proclaiming that its program is *the* political program for every true believer. That is wrong in principle, no matter what the agenda is, because only the church is authorized to proclaim the name of Jesus and carry his standard into the world."

In answer to the question, "Can Christians be politically engaged without being Christian nationalists?" Miller answers:

---

25. McCammon, "Controversial televangelist Pat Robertson," §10.
26. Wolfe, *Case for Christian Nationalism* (2022).
27. Reynolds, "Powerful Minority."
28. Miller, *Religion of American Greatness* (2022).
29. Miller, "What Is Christian Nationalism?"

Yes. American Christians in the past were exemplary in helping establish the American experiment, and many American Christians worked to end slavery and segregation and other evils. They did so because they believed Christianity required them to work for justice. But they worked to advance Christian principles, not Christian power or Christian culture, which is the key distinction between normal Christian political engagement and Christian nationalism. Normal Christian political engagement is humble, loving, and sacrificial; it rejects the idea that Christians are entitled to primacy of place in the public square or that Christians have a presumptive right to continue their historical predominance in American culture. Today, Christians should seek to love their neighbors by pursuing justice in the public square, including by working against abortion, promoting religious liberty, fostering racial justice, protecting the rule of law, and honoring constitutional processes. That agenda is different from promoting Christian culture, Western heritage, or Anglo-Protestant values.[30]

Russell Moore defines Christian nationalism as "the use of Christian words, symbols, or rituals as a means to shoring up an ethnic or national identity," and accuses it of trading "the blood of Christ" (in the sense of his atoning sacrifice for sinners) "for blood-and-soil," adding "that is not an even trade."[31] Undoubtedly this is true for some, perhaps most, who self-identify with the label, but may be too broad a brush for others who are more theologically informed and understand Christian nationalism as simply an expression for Christ's lordship over the nations (see Matt 28:18–20; Eph 1:20–23, etc.) Besides, it is not only conservative Christians who have tried to influence the political discourse. Ever since the rise of the social gospel in the early twentieth century, and especially since mainstream churches got behind the civil rights movement in the 1960s, followed by support for feminism, gay rights and so on, liberal Christianity has reflected the values of the political left. As Paul Ramsay observed in *Who Speaks for the Church?* conservative and liberal wings of the church have come to look remarkably like "the secular variety of the same opinions."[32]

Advocates of Christian nationalism can point to Justice David Brewer of the US Supreme Court's judgment in 1882 that America was a Christian nation, an assertion he continued to make when in 1905 he published a series of lectures under the title *The United States: A Christian Nation*.

---

30. Miller, "What Is Christian Nationalism?" §15.
31. Moore, *Losing Our Religion*, 113–16.
32. Ramsay, *Who Speaks for the Church?*, 21.

According to *The First Amendment Encyclopedia*, "Brewer was not the first to make that assertion. Some state courts in the nineteenth century had also referred to the United States as a Christian nation or suggested that Christianity should receive special favor." Justice Brewer "did not make clear whether by 'Christian nation' he meant 'government' in a legal sense or whether he was observing that most Americans claimed to practice Christian morality or listed Christianity as their religion."[33] If only the latter, it still pointed to the existence of a generic Christian consensus that existed well into the twentieth century. Indeed, it might justifiably be termed a Protestant consensus, as was evidenced by the concern surrounding John F. Kennedy's election as president in 1960 that he might be influenced by directives from the Vatican. It was an admittedly imperfect consensus that tolerated slavery in the nineteenth century and racial segregation, among other forms of discrimination, in the first half of the twentieth. In any case, that consensus no longer exists, but this has not prevented the term "Christian Nationalism" from being associated with contemporary evangelicalism.

FROM CATHOLIC TO EVANGELICAL

Having established this background of evangelicalism in general, we return to the pre-eminence of abortion as the defining issue of modern evangelicalism. This was not always the case. The anti-abortion (pro-life) movement used to be associated with the Roman Catholic Church. Daniel K. Williams in *Defenders of the Unborn: The Pro-Life Movement Before Roe v. Wade* documents how, prior to the 1973 Supreme Court decision legalizing abortion in all fifty of the United States, anti-abortion activity had been driven mostly by Catholic doctors, lawyers, clergy and laypeople.

> The Catholics who launched the pro-life movement grounded their campaign not only in their Church's natural law theology, but also in the twentieth-century American liberal values of individual rights, legal protection for minorities, and societal recognition of human dignity. Many of the people who first began speaking against abortion in the 1930s, as well as those who created the first right-to-life organizations in the mid-1960s, were Catholic Democrats who were committed to New Deal liberalism.[34]

---

33. Rainey, "Church of the Holy Trinity v. United States (1892)." §6.
34. Williams, *Defenders of the Unborn*, 4.

So, what happened? "Only after *Roe v. Wade*, when the pro-life movement's interpretation of liberalism came into contact with another rights-based movement—feminism—and it became clear that pro-lifers would not be able to win the support of the Democratic Party, did the movement take a conservative turn. Yet because of the movement's liberal origins, its position in the Republican Party remains an uneasy one even today."[35] The American media now regularly associates opposition to abortion with evangelicals more so than Roman Catholics. While the Roman Catholic Church still officially opposes abortion, and many of its members are involved in the pro-life movement, several high-profile Catholics, such as current US president Joe Biden and former speaker of the House of Representatives Nancy Pelosi openly support abortion rights. The same is true of Canadian Prime Minister Justin Trudeau.

In *The Right Turn in Conservative Christian Politics: How Abortion Transformed the Culture Wars*, Andrew R. Lewis, building on Williams's work, notes that whereas rights-based advocacy has been identified with Catholic social justice and the political left, evangelicals have historically been committed to maintaining public morality and it was this emphasis, rather than fetal rights, that informed their opposition to abortion in the mid-to-late 1970s. Lewis rightly credits Francis Schaeffer with mobilizing evangelicals against abortion. In doing so, he "brought much of the Catholic human rights approach to abortion into Evangelicalism, yet simultaneously many of his appeals focused on lax morals, not human rights."[36]

As Williams makes clear, Catholic social justice theory has always had an affinity with issues usually associated with the political left: social programs for the alleviation of poverty, opposition to the death penalty etc. Evangelicals, on the other hand, have a different history that includes, *for some*, approval of slavery in the American South (along with condemnation of the barbarous slave trade that brought slaves to the colonies in the first place) and opposition to the civil rights movement of the 1960s under Martin Luther King Jr.[37] Thus, recent attempts to link the pro-life

---

35. Williams, *Defenders of the Unborn*, 4.
36. Lewis, *Right Turn*, 24.
37. Timothy (Tim) Keller, reflecting on his student days says this: "It marked the first time I realized that most older white adults in my life were telling me things that were dead wrong. The problem was not just a few troublemakers. Black people *did* have a right to demand the redress and rectifying of their many wrongs . . . Although I had grown up going to church, Christianity began to lose its appeal to me when I was in college. One reason for my difficulty was a disconnect between my secular friends who supported the civil rights movement and the orthodox Christian believers who thought the Martin Luther King Jr. was a threat to society. Why I wondered did the nonreligious believe passionately in equal rights and justice while the religious people could not have

movement with the abolition of the slave trade in the eighteenth century or the more recent civil rights movement can come across as a little disingenuous, even though it was evangelicals like William Wilberforce and his colleagues in the so-called Clapham Sect (or Saints) who were at the forefront of the movement to abolish the slave trade.

Wilberforce headed the parliamentary campaign against the British slave trade for twenty years until the passage of the Slave Trade Act of 1807 and, later, the 1833 Slavery Abolition Act which abolished slavery in most of the British empire. This act was passed three days before Wilberforce's death. He was a committed evangelical Christian who counted among his friends and supporters John Newton (1725–1807), the former slave trader turned Anglican clergyman and author of "Amazing Grace," and the evangelist John Wesley (1703–91). He and his Clapham colleagues advocated not only for the abolition of slavery but for a number of other causes, including penal reform, improved working conditions for laborers, the suppression of vice in society and animal welfare, the last of which led to the formation, in 1824, of the Royal Society for the Prevention of Cruelty to Animals.

Despite its overt religiosity at a time when it was still fashionable to attend church and it was mandatory in the Church of England at least twice a year, life in eighteenth century Britain was "brutal, decadent, violent, and vulgar. Slavery was only the worst of a host of societal evils that included endemic alcoholism, child prostitution, child labor, frequent public executions for petty crimes, public dissections and burnings of executed criminals, and unspeakable public cruelty to animals."[38] One of the problems faced by opponents of the slave trade was that "most Britons went about their lives with no idea of the universal horrors that existed under the British flag or the nightmarish way of life of the slaves, whose existence was nonetheless intimately intertwined with their own way of life thousands of miles away."[39]

Thus, one of the challenges faced by abolitionists was how to bring home to the British public what the African slave trade was actually like. In the same way, contemporary pro-lifers try various means to force upon the public the reality of what abortion looks like. These methods can include large-scale depictions of the grizzly reality of aborted babies, as well as pictures of the unborn at various stages of fetal development, sometimes juxtaposed with images of American slavery and the Nazi holocaust.[40] Such

---

cared less" (Keller, *Generous Justice*, xv–xvii).

38. Metaxas, *Amazing Grace*, 69.
39. Metaxas, *Amazing Grace*, 70.
40. The Genocide Awareness Project.

methods have proved controversial and have been banned on some university campuses, but it appears that they have had a positive influenced on at least some people who were previously uninformed and indifferent.[41] However, they have also provoked outrage among those who take offense at the comparisons made with slavery and the slave trade.[42]

41. The Genocide Awareness Project.

42. For evidence of evangelical complicity in Southern slavery (but not the slave trade), as well as in opposition to the civil rights movement, see Tisby, *Color of Compromise* (2019). *Reformed and Evangelical across Four Centuries: The Presbyterian Story in America* (edited by S. Donald Forston III and Kenneth J. Stewart, 2022,) includes a chapter on nineteenth century slavery debates. Broadly speaking, with exceptions, southern Presbyterian leaders like R.L. Dabney and J. H. Thornwell claimed that the institution of slavery (but not the slave trade) had biblical support, whereas northern churchmen, following the lead of Charles Hodge of Princeton Seminary (founded in 1812) advocated "a peaceful, gradual emancipation as the way forward for the United States" (177). It fell to smaller denominations like the Reformed Presbyterian Church (Covenanters) and the short-lived Free Presbyterian Church Synod of the United States to unequivocally advocate abolition and declare (as the Covenanters did in 1800) that "no slave-holder should be allowed the communion of the Church" (169).

Controversial evangelical and Reformed author Douglas Wilson in *Black and Tan* (2018), argues that the Civil War (which he prefers to call the War Between the States) resulting in the killing of over six hundred thousand men, could have been avoided if a more incremental approach had been taken to the abolition of slavery in the United States; that is if the New Testament model of regulating slavery leading to its ultimate demise had been followed, a demise of which Wilson positively approves. Instead, what resulted from the Civil War was an enlarged role for federalism that led ultimately to the imposition of legal abortion and other moral evils nationwide. Wilson claims that pro-lifers are open to the charge of special pleading when they oppose abortion on biblical grounds but refuse to admit that the Bible also condones and regulates slavery, thus "picking and choosing" which biblical teachings to defend. His concern, he says, is not to defend slavery, but to oppose the manner in which it was outlawed, and the implications of this for other issues such as abortion. Although controversial within evangelicalism, Wilson's argument that the practice of slavery can be justified on biblical grounds is not unique (though other details of his overall view may be), which makes it difficult to claim that all contemporary pro-lifers are heirs of the anti-slavery movement.

Besides, it is not only pro-lifers who claim an analogy with slavery. A federal judge has suggested that a constitutional right to abortion may be found in the thirteenth amendment to the U.S. Constitution that outlawed slavery. Bizarre as this may seem, it is not a new argument. See Jonathan Turley, "Federal Judge Suggests Abortion May be Protected," February 7, 2023. Also, see a 1994 law journal article on "Slavery Rhetoric and the Abortion Debate," by Debora Threedy, a self-described pro-choice feminist, who questions the validity of the comparison on both sides of the abortion debate. Regarding the pro-choice side, she notes: "both pregnant women and slaves, so the argument on this side runs, endure a condition of 'forced labor' that violates the Thirteenth Amendment of the U.S. Constitution which prohibits "the 'forced labor' of the slave." The fallacy of this argument, Threedy points out, is that the metaphor "masks the distinction that the slave had no choice in the condition of slavery, while in most cases the woman has some choice in the pregnancy" (Threedy, "Slavery Rhetoric and the Abortion Debate," 7–14).

PRO-LIFE EVANGELICAL FOR BIDEN

A recent evangelical who sought to promote a consistently pro-life position was the late Ron Sider, former executive director of Evangelicals (now Christians) for Social Action who in 1987 published *Completely Pro-Life: Building a Consistent Stance on Abortion, the Family, Nuclear Weapons, the Poor*. Sider was from a Mennonite background with a pacifist tradition and not all evangelicals will agree with his stance on nuclear weapons, or even all his prescriptions for relief of poverty, but he is at least to be commended for seeking to promote a broader vision of what it means to be pro-life, while pointing out some of the inconsistencies that exist among professing Christians on both the political right and left.[43]

In the context of the 2020 US presidential race, Sider, along with Fuller Seminary President Emeritus Richard Mouw, launched Pro-Life Evangelicals for Biden and issued the following statement:

> As pro-life evangelicals, we disagree with Vice President Biden and the Democratic platform on the issue of abortion. But we believe a biblically shaped commitment to the sanctity of human life compels us to a consistent ethic of life that affirms the sanctity of human life from beginning to end.
>
> Many things that good political decisions could change destroy persons created in the image of God and violate the sanctity of human life. Poverty kills millions every year. So does lack of healthcare and smoking. Racism kills. Unless we quickly make major changes, devastating climate change will kill tens of millions. Poverty, lack of accessible health care services, smoking, racism and climate change are all pro-life issues. . . . Therefore we oppose "one issue" political thinking because it lacks biblical balance.
>
> Knowing that the most common reason women give for abortion is the financial difficulty of another child, we appreciate a number of Democratic proposals that would significantly alleviate that financial burden: accessible health services for all citizens, affordable childcare, a minimum wage that lifts workers out of poverty. . .[44]

---

43. Sider's best-known book is *Rich Christians in an Age of Hunger*, originally published in 1978 by InterVarsity Press. Some of his economic prescriptions for ending world hunger were criticized and he later published a revised edition in 1984 that took some of these criticisms into account. Further editions have followed, most recently by Thomas Nelson in 2015.

44. Sider, "Pro-Life Evangelicals for Biden."

The reason for quoting this here is not to signal agreement with voting for Joe Biden or the Democratic Party, which includes access to "safe and legal abortion" among the rights of women for which it will fight.[45] It is, rather, to indicate that there are prominent evangelicals who take a center-left position politically and do not fit the caricature of extreme right-wing single-issue conservatives.[46] Not that all signers of the above statement were necessarily centre-left politically. They included, for instance, Joel Hunter, a long-time political conservative, and former mega-church pastor who in 2006 was elected president of the Christian Coalition identified with the religious right. Two years later, he wrote *A New Kind of Conservative*,[47] advocating a broader pro-life approach to politics, became a friend and pastoral adviser to Barak Obama, but then voted for Trump in 2016. He and the other signers of this document experienced considerable push-back from fellow-pro lifers who, among other things, questioned the use of the label "pro-life" for issues other than abortion.[48]

Following the election, Sider blogged that, among other things, he would work hard with Pro-Life Evangelicals for Biden "to urge the Democrats to say that as they continue to believe that abortion should be legal and safe, they will also want abortion to be rare and will embrace policies that promote that."[49] Commendable as this was, it proved to be a forlorn hope and an overestimation of the influence Pro-Life Evangelicals for Biden could have on the administration. Biden, a practicing Catholic and widely acclaimed to be a decent man with a history of working across the aisle, once supported the Hyde amendment (originating in 1976) that for decades prohibited federal funds being used to promote abortion, except in the cases of rape and incest (since 1993), and risk to the mother's life. More recently,

---

45. It states, "We oppose and will fight to overturn federal and state laws that create barriers to women's reproductive health and rights, including by repealing the Hyde Amendment and protecting and codifying the right to reproductive freedom." "2020 Democratic Platform," 42.

46. It seems fair to say that those evangelicals who fall into the center-left category are mostly intellectuals, a number of whom signed the above statement, but who unfortunately do not get the public media exposure given to more populist evangelicals (although *The Washington Times* and a few other media outlets did take notice of the formation of Pro-Life Evangelicals for Biden). For the most part, secular media outlets reference evangelicals as the core group of Republican supporters.

47. Hunter, *New Kind of Conservative* (2008).

48. See, for instance, Peter Jones, "A Plea." Jones responded to specific claims that various issues, like universal health care, were pro-life issues. See also Taylor, "Case Against Pro-Life Voting for Joe Biden." These were among the more respectful responses.

49. Sider, "Biden Won. Now What?"

likely under pressure from the more radical left of the Democratic Party, he has reversed that position and stated publicly and frequently in the wake of the US Supreme Court's decision to reverse *Roe v Wade* that given a sufficient Democratic majority in Congress, he would sign legislation to make *Roe v. Wade* the law of the land.[50] In his 2023 State of the Union address, Biden doubled down on his commitment, stating that "Congress must restore the right the Supreme Court took away last year and codify Roe v. Wade to protect every woman's constitutional right to choose." If, on the other hand, Congress passed any pro-life legislation, he promised to veto it.[51]

As a result of the 2022 midterm elections, Republicans narrowly gained control of the House of Representatives, thus defeating (or at least postponing) Biden's goal, but Democrats did not lose as badly as was predicted, and kept control of the Senate, in part because of their success in making abortion rights an election issue. Besides Democrats keeping things close in Congress despite the president's low approval ratings and concerns about inflation, three states entrenched abortion rights in their constitution, one defeated a referendum to deny abortion rights, and another had done the same previously.[52] In another rather shocking result, the state of Montana defeated a measure that would have designated babies who survive abortions as persons.[53] More than a dozen states have passed laws guaranteeing a right to abortion.[54]

Vice-President Kamala Harris, a professing Baptist, has stated frequently that she would fight to protect a woman's right to control her own body. She even urged pastors at a National Baptist Convention to take a stand on abortion rights.[55] Harris also used the fiftieth anniversary of *Roe v Wade* (January 22, 2023) to claim that the Declaration of Independence's guarantee of freedom and the pursuit of happiness included the freedom of women to control their own bodies, while omitting the same document's references to the Creator and the right to life that precede the other two rights.[56]

---

50. Although Biden has characterized the Supreme Court's decision as extreme, he once voted 1n 1982 for a constitutional amendment that would have had the exact same effect of returning the abortion issue to the states. At the time, he cited his Catholic background (Lerer, "When Joe Biden Voted") Then he reversed his vote, indicative of a discomfort with the issue that no longer appears to exist to the same extent.

51. Ertelt, "Joe Biden Celebrates Abortion," §3–4.

52. Cusaac-Smith, "Abortion rights were on the ballot."

53. Ertelt and Bilger, "Montana Defeats Ballot Measure."

54. Wolf, "These are the states where abortion rights are still protected."

55. Bilger, "Kamala Harris Tells Pastors."

56. Bilger, "Kamala Harris Leaves God and the Right to Life Out."

Biden's first legislative victory was the passing (by the narrowest of margins in the Senate, with no Republican support) of a COVID-19 relief bill that included repeal of the Hyde amendment. The day prior to the bill's passing in the Senate, leaders of Pro-Life Evangelicals for Biden responded with an open letter to the effect that they felt "used and betrayed" but had "no intention of watching these things from the sidelines." The letter stated:

> As pro-life leaders in the evangelical community, we publicly supported President Biden's candidacy with the understanding that there would be engagement [with] us on the issue of abortion and particularly the Hyde Amendment. The Biden team wanted to talk to us during the campaign to gain our support, and we gave it on the condition there would be active dialogue and common ground solutions on the issue of abortion. There has been no dialogue since the campaign. . . . Many evangelicals and Catholics took risks to support Biden publicly. President Biden and Democrats need to honor their courage.[57]

That these prominent evangelical leaders should have felt "used and betrayed" illustrates the naiveté—matched only by the naiveté of right-wing evangelical supporters of Trump—of looking to government for support of an essentially religious agenda. It's not as if Biden hadn't publicly and frequently indicated his intentions.[58] It may yet prove to be the case that greater attention to the socio-economic issues that partly underlie the abortion issue may have a beneficial effect, but to put one's faith in the Biden presidency is at least as unwise as was unqualified support for Trump.

At a rally in Florida in November 2022, Biden spoke about being a practicing Catholic and added that he supported *Roe v. Wade*, giving as his reason "the most rational basis upon which confessional faiths can agree: No one knows precisely when does human life begin."[59] As we have seen, this may be true of some faiths such as variations of Islam and Judaism, but it is certainly not true of the Catholic faith,[60] nor is it scientifically true. Even if

---

57. Pro-life Evangelicals for Biden, "Open Letter."

58. At a gala hosted by the Democratic National Convention in Atlanta in June of 2019, Biden publicly announced that he no longer supported the Hyde Amendment, which he had previously supported. (Glueck, "Joe Biden Denounces Hyde Amendment.")

59. Bilger, "Biden Claims 'No One Knows Precisely.'"

60. A May 2022 poll by the Pew Research Center found that while "The Catholic Church in the United States has long been one of the foremost opponents of legal abortion . . . for U.S. Catholics, the abortion issue isn't so clear-cut. Like the American public as a whole, most Catholics think abortion should be illegal in some cases but legal in others" (Smith, "Like Americans Overall," §1.) See also, Smith, "US Catholic

there were doubt about when human life begins, one would think it would be prudent to err on the side of caution, as Ronald Reagan once said, as I recall, in his typically folksy manner—if you see a body lying at the side of the road, you check to see if it's breathing before you start shovelling dirt!

C. EVERETT KOOP

A pro-life evangelical who was a Republican but won the grudging respect of his previous critics on the left, while losing support on the right, was the late C. Everett Koop (1916–2013), Surgeon General in the Reagan Republican administration. In his autobiography, Koop recounts his brutal confirmation hearings as Surgeon General during which liberals attacked him viciously for his known anti-abortion views. His conservative supporters, on the other hand, seemed interested only in having him promote those views. When Koop adopted a more broadly pro-life stance by launching an anti-smoking campaign that took on the powerful tobacco lobby, and advocating sex education in schools and condom use by active homosexuals "foolish enough" not to practice abstinence in order to prevent the spread of AIDS, he found that former foes like Ted Kennedy became his staunch supporters, while previous admirers, like Jesse Helms of the Helms amendment, either dropped out of view (as in Helms's case) or became active critics. These included fellow-evangelicals.

Koop writes:

> Castigation by the *political* right, although disappointing and unpleasant, did not unduly upset me; after all castigation

---

bishops worry about abortion views." According to Dr. Patrick Whelan, a doctor and professor at the Institute of Advanced Catholic Studies at the University of Southern California, "In fact, many US Catholics' views on abortion are similar to Biden's. The vast majority of Catholics are pro-life and pro-choice. It's a moral issue but they don't think the government should be making that decision" (Vlamis "Catholic bishops' effort."). When a majority of US Catholic bishops voted to draw up a statement on what qualifies a Catholic to receive holy communion, prompted by Biden's publicly stated position, they were warned by the Vatican not to cause division. Despite the current Pope's frequent reference to abortion as murder, Biden claims that on a visit to the Vatican he was assured (presumably for other reasons) that he was a good Catholic and should continue taking communion (Rogers and Horowitz, "Biden: Pope said he should receive communion."). Like Biden, Nancy Pelosi received communion at a Papal Mass despite her Archbishop having banned her from communion and warning of the grave danger to her soul of her advocacy of abortion (Patterson, "Pelosi Received Communion in the Vatican.") Her response to the Archbishop of San Francisco's discipline was dismissive, pointing out that the Catholic Church "has not denied communion to lawmakers who back the death penalty—which also violates the church's Catechism." (Watson, "Pelosi responds to archbishop.").

seemed to be their business. But I did feel a profound sense of betrayal by those on the *religious* right who took me to task. . . . Everyone, or at least those who did not know me, said that I had changed. Conservatives said I had changed and they were angry. Liberals said I had changed, and they were pleased. But I had not changed at all. . . . My whole career had been dedicated to prolonging lives, especially the lives of people who were weak and powerless, the disenfranchised who needed an advocate: newborns undoubtedly who needed surgery, handicapped children, unborn children, people with AIDS.[61]

Koop includes a chapter on abortion, in which he gives some fascinating background on how he came to participate with Francis Schaeffer in the book and film series, *Whatever Happened to the Human Race?* This more than anything else was responsible for alerting evangelicals to the evils of abortion, infanticide, and euthanasia. Later, as Surgeon General, Koop was asked to prepare a report on the health effects of abortion on women. In the end, he concluded that there was not sufficient scientific evidence to support either the "pre-conceived beliefs of those pro-life or of those pro-choice."[62] The television networks, instead, reported that he "had issued a report confirming that abortion produced no evidence of negative health effects on women." Koop scrambled to correct this misinformation, but the damage was done. One pro-life leader was reported as saying that Koop had "buried the pro-life movement." Although he was in fact aware of anecdotal evidence of the negative effects on women's mental and emotional health (as well as physical on occasion), he believed that the entire focus of the proposed report was misguided. "The issue of abortion is not to be decided in terms of its effect upon the mother, but in terms of its effect on the unborn child. The effect upon the mother is unclear; the effect upon the unborn child is clear—and fatal."[63]

Koop was particularly stung by criticisms from fellow-Christians:

> People who should know better, people who knew that Jesus commanded our love for one another. And it takes more than just saying it. . . . My feelings of sorrow and disappointment increased because I was convinced that my fellow evangelicals had not only failed to understand my position, but had also refused to muster the intelligence and scholarship to try. I

---

61. Koop, M.D., *KOOP: Memoirs of America's Doctor*, 216.
62. Koop, *Memoirs*, 276.
63. Koop, *Memoirs*, 278.

believed, however, that no matter how they reacted, I had done the right thing.[64]

In *The Right to Life, the Right to Die*, Koop makes it clear that he was personally opposed to abortion, except in those rare cases (in Western society, that is) where a mother's life is genuinely in danger. He used to make exceptions for other hard cases such as rape, based on Christian compassion as he then understood it. But following a conversation with a nurse about rape and the sovereignty of God, he says that whether it was this conversation or "whether it was the slow pressure of what [he] had read in the Scriptures concerning the certainty of life," he found himself saying "My position on abortion is essentially Roman Catholic but for different reasons."[65] However, as a matter of public policy recorded in his autobiography, he saw room for compromise, in the interests of saving at least some unborn lives; a compromise neither side of the debate seemed to want:

> The rhetoric comes straight from the days of World War II. Both sides, pro-life, pro-abortion, are fond of using terms like "battle ground," "combat," "war," and "battle." Neither side seems to be winning any converts to its position. Sometimes I think both sides have forgotten why they are fighting. . . . I wonder if each side has not forgotten the human element that originally prompted the debate: the innocent unborn child, the agonized pregnant woman. . . .
>
> Anti-abortionists cannot simply rail against abortion; they must press for whatever legal, social, and economic changes are necessary to make childbearing equitable and fair. They should be willing to do anything they can to bring conceived children to birth. . . . Ethical compromise was impossible. But I did see the possibility for a practical compromise that would at least lower the numbers of abortions, lower the number of unborn children whose death was sanctioned by our laws and society. . . .
>
> I have always been surprised that liberals, usually so concerned about the underdog and the disenfranchised, have failed to champion the rights of unborn children. Nor did I understand some ardent feminists who see abortion as a weapon in the feminist struggle, a tool to oppose those traditionalist males determined to keep women in their place by denying them "control over their own bodies." The extremes of both sides, I realized, did not seek compromise; perhaps they did not even seek resolution. They were in it for the battle.

64. Koop, *Memoirs*, 279.
65. Koop, *Right to Life*, 14.

> But there were many others who were weary of confrontation and who might listen to a better way, who would welcome concentration on the root of the problem. . .[66]

On the occasion of Koop's death, Matthew Miller (not to be confused with Paul Miller, quoted earlier) wrote an article on "How the Evangelical Church Awoke to the Abortion Issue: The Convergent Labors of Harold O.J. Brown, Francis Schaeffer, and C. Everett Koop." In part, he was responding to a CNN Belief Blog by Jonathan Dudley which claimed that it was Jerry Falwell who "spearheaded the reversal of opinion on abortion in the late 1970s." There were several responses to Dudley which led him to quickly backtrack in a follow-up piece for the *Huffington Post* "in which he acknowledged, though somewhat dismissively, the 'right to life' work of Francis Schaeffer and a group called The Christian Action Council prior to Falwell's entrance on the political scene. Dudley discounts the impact of these early efforts, however."[67]

In seeking to set the record straight, Miller acknowledges that it is true that the evangelical church was slumbering for several years after the Supreme Court handed down the *Roe v. Wade* decision. "But it is not true that 'Falwell changed all that.' Instead, Falwell and the several other figures who took the lead of the pro-life movement in the 1980s were standing on the shoulders of three men whose paths and voices converged for a brief period of time in the mid-to-late 1970s, forming a powerful trio that finally awoke the evangelical church to the necessity of speaking up for the unborn."[68] These three men were Harold O. J. Brown, Francis Schaeffer and C. Everett Koop.

Brown (1933–2007) was a Harvard-educated historian and theologian who was working as the associate editor of *Christianity Today* when the *Roe v. Wade* ruling was announced. He wrote the lead article in the magazine's next issue, "Abortion and the Court." "Undeterred by initial and surprising indifference among evangelical to abortion, in 1975 Brown became the editor of *The Human Life Review*, founded by James McFadden. No story of the nascence of the evangelical pro-life movement is complete without reference to the influence of this review, which early on included such illustrious contributors as William F. Buckley and Malcolm Muggeridge (and eventually Ronald Reagan)."[69]

In 1975, Brown and Koop met in a meeting space provided by Billy Graham in Montreat, North Carolina, to launch the Christian Action Council

---

66. Koop, *Memoirs*, 280–82.
67. Miller, "How the Evangelical Church Awoke," §3.
68. Miller, "How the Evangelical Church Awoke," §4.
69. Miller, "How the Evangelical Church Awoke," §7.

(CAC) "which became the leading Protestant 'right to life' advocacy group on Capitol Hill" with Brown as chair. "It is true that the early efforts of the CAC ran up against a brick wall of evangelical indifference (and even suspicion), but it was not from Falwell that help would arrive."[70]

In 1961 Brown had met Francis Schaeffer, then a "relatively unknown 'man from Switzerland.'" Brown arranged for Schaeffer to give the second annual "Christian Contemporary Thought" lectures on Harvard's campus:

> As a result of this relationship, Schaeffer was introduced to the American evangelical scene and quickly achieved an unparalleled celebrity status that he would leverage to draw attention to the right to life issue.
>
> The film and lecture tour for *How Shall We Then Live?* (1976) served to awaken many evangelicals to the roots and implications of their own core convictions and concluded by connecting the right to life issue to those core convictions, as Schaeffer parsed the Supreme Court's Roe decision in terms of his famous "line of despair".[71] This pro-life material was considered risky, and Francis Schaeffer took some persuading to include it, as his son Frank has recounted in his controversial memoir (2007). But an old friend of the Schaeffer family took notice and soon joined them in what would become the tipping-point of this story.[72]

This friend was Koop who had treated the Schaeffer's daughter Priscilla in 1948 and subsequently developed a friendship with the Schaeffer family, leading to his participation in the film series and book *Whatever Happened to the Human Race?* Released in 1979, this project "did what no effort over the previous six years had succeeded in doing: it broke through."

In the years that followed:

> A "second generation" would take the helm of pro-life advocacy, and we are familiar with their names: Jerry Falwell, James Dobson, Tim and Beverly LaHaye, and a host of others....
>
> Schaeffer would die in 1982 [actually, it was 1984], Brown's Christian Action Council, of which he remained chairman, would shift its primary focus to founding Gospel-centered crisis pregnancy care centers with remarkable results [the organization is now known as Care Net]. Upon his death

---

70. Miller, "How the Evangelical Church Awoke," §8.

71. Schaeffer first introduced his "line of despair" in his 1968 book, *He is There and He is Not Silent*. It refers to the chaotic, irrational consequences of an existentialist philosophy in which there is no objective truth.

72. Miller, "How the Evangelical Church Awoke," §9b–10.

in 2007, Brown was remembered in *Christianity Today* as one whose "most prominent work was helping form and intellectually arm the pro-life movement." As a reward for his pro-life efforts, Koop would be appointed by Reagan to be his Surgeon General in 1981....[73]

Miller concludes:

> Perhaps it is because none of these three carried the mantle of the pro-life movement in the 1980s and 1990s that we hear relatively little of them as pro-life champions today.... But it is reasonable to suppose that without Brown, Schaeffer, and Koop, there may not have been a pro-life movement in the 1980s at all, nor in the years that followed. And while it's unlikely we'll see any monuments in the near future singling out these three remarkable individuals, we would not only be forgetful, but truly ungrateful, if we did not remember their courageous efforts to speak up for those who cannot speak for themselves.[74]

To sum up, the moniker "evangelical" has taken on a political meaning, especially in the United States, that is not part of its historic tradition. Because of this, there has been some concerning inconsistency in the way in which evangelicals have approached the abortion issue; namely the single-issue focus of opposing abortion as a moral issue which has resulted in supporting candidates of demonstrable moral failures and associating opposition to abortion with right-wing politics. As reported above, this has not always been the case, as evidenced by the existence of Pro-Life

---

73. Miller, "How the Evangelical Church Awoke," §18.

74. Miller, "How the Evangelical Church Awoke," §19. Schaeffer came under considerable criticism in later years from erstwhile admirers who had benefited from his countercultural critique in the past, especially during the 1960s, but now saw him as identifying with the right-wing fundamentalism of the Moral Majority. This was, in part, due to his subsequent books, *A Christian Manifesto* (1981), in which he seems to embrace a form of the Christian America myth about the Founding Fathers, and *Whatever Happened to the Evangelical Church?* (1984), which was a defense of biblical inerrancy against neo-evangelical views that the Bible is infallible but not inerrant in matters of science and history, and an attack on the moral decline in American society seeping into the evangelical church. However, William Edgar, who knew him well and had conversations with him about these things, interprets Schaeffer's later developments as consistent with previous ones. In *A Christian Manifesto*, Schaeffer was careful to point out that "we should not wrap Christianity in our national flag" and "Throughout he was concerned to show that the Christian faith should not be *conservative* but *revolutionary*. A conservative is just part of the status quo, whereas revolutionaries are a minority that must buck the tide." Edgar, *Francis Schaeffer on the Christian Life*, 76. Cf. *Complete Works of Francis A. Schaeffer*, 5:485–86.

Evangelicals for Biden, but this is a minority, and largely ignored voice. The late C. Everett Koop demonstrated a relatively rare commitment to conservative politics, while seeking to address a wider range of what are arguably pro-life issues. This led to opposition and loss of support from fellow conservatives, including evangelicals. Given that the effort to take control of the issue of abortion through politics has largely been unsuccessful and has led to several varying and opposing views on abortion, what position should evangelicals take when considering their position on pro-life issues? In the next chapter, I will draw our attention to the early church and beyond, shifting our focus from politics to theology where, I argue, abortion issues really should be addressed.

Discussion Questions

1. Considering Bebbington's quadrilateral (that evangelicals believe in the divine inspiration and authority of the Bible, in the need for personal conversion, the centrality of the cross of Christ for our salvation, and in activism), how do these concepts set evangelicals apart from other Christians or religions that you're familiar with?

2. Given the root word of evangelical is *evangel* (meaning gospel), how is being gospel or Bible-based still associated with the term "evangelical Christian" in North America today? How is this not the case?

3. How do the justice or the mercy aspects of the pro-life movement align with evangelicalism as the author understands evangelicalism, or as you understand evangelicalism?

4. Both "Christian Nationalism" and "evangelical Christianity" have many political connotations in America today. How does this help and/or hinder the evangelical Christian's pro-life position?

3

Lessons From the Early Church and Beyond

IF WE ARE TO TAKE "EVANGELICAL" IN THE BROAD SENSE of "New Testament Christianity" (as Packer and Stott did), this sends us back to the early church to consider how abortion was viewed then. The New Testament, like the Old, has nothing directly to say about abortion, but it is clear from history that abortion was common in the Graeco-Roman world of the time and before it. The Oath of Hippocrates (460–357 BC) which forbade the giving of "a pessary to cause abortion," in pre-New Testament times indicates an ancient opposition to abortion but, since an abortive pessary was seen as a poison, this appears to have been more for the protection of the mother than the unborn child.[1] Both Plato and Aristotle advocated abortion, Plato even mandating it in his ideal *Republic* for women over forty. Aristotle in his *Politics* "did distinguish between 'lawful and unlawful' abortions based on whether or not the fetus was alive," but "did not provide any criteria for determining this." In another of his works he wrote that "life is present in a fetus when distinct organs have formed: forty days after conception for males, ninety for females."[2]

---

1. Gorman, *Abortion & the Early Church*, 21.

2. Gorman, *Abortion & the Early Church*, 22. Marvin Olasky, referencing Aristotle's *History of Animals* and *On the Generation of Animals*, quoting from Jones, *Soul of the Embryo* (27), puts the formation of female fetuses at eighty to ninety days, adding that "Aristotle was a step back from Hippocrates (460–370 BC), whose followers saw the formation of limbs and organs as complete in about forty days, or six weeks. (As it turns

The Stoics held that the "fetus is part of the mother and that life begins only with the fully developed infant's taking it's first breath"—a rather modern-sounding position! However, contrary to what might have been expected, they opposed abortion but this was based on a common view (shared with Plato and Aristotle) that "the welfare of the family and state—not the rights of the unborn"—were "the foremost consideration in the question of the propriety of abortion." Michael Gorman observes, "Despite their antiabortion position, the Stoics' view of the beginning of human life, coupled with philosophical support for abortion, challenged Christian thinkers in later years."[3]

Roman law viewed abortion as an offense "against the husband and father." At the same time, "The earliest Roman law code, The Twelve Tables (circa 450 BC) permitted a father to expose any female infant he wished and any deformed baby of either sex. In the early Republic, exposure was probably more common and accepted than abortion, but neither was ever punished as a crime per se."[4] The Twelve Tables "proposed social and political censure for husbands who ordered or permitted their wives to abort without good reason, but no fines or penalties were exacted from them, and those outside the family who might have been involved were unaffected by the law."[5] "There is some evidence that the late Republic enacted a law to punish sellers of abortifacient drugs but not because they caused abortions. Roman law did not consider the fetus a person, so there could be no law to protect rights which did not exist."[6] During this time, Christians were known to rescue abandoned babies left to die.

Cicero (106–43 BC) "the greatest of Roman orators" called for capital punishment for deliberate abortion, but this was based on "its injustice to the father, the family name, the family's inheritance rights, the human race and the state. He makes no reference to harm to the mother or the

---

out, that's the furthest extent of legal abortion in today's pro-life 'heartbeat bills.')" See *Story of Abortion in America*, 27 and 27n6.

3. Gorman, *Abortion & the Early Church*, 23. Cf. Ovid *Fasti* 1.621–24; Hippolytus, *Refutation of All Heresies* 9.7; Origen, *Against Heresies* 9. "The later Stoics may have been influenced by the religious beliefs of the Orphics, who were the first Greeks to be concerned about the unborn's fate. This concern was prompted by an eschatology based on the idea that there is a normal cycle of life and death, and a subsequent bodiless existence of the soul. People who died prematurely—such as those aborted—are doomed to an evil fate after death. This belief led to a condemnation of abortion, exposure and infanticide" (22–23). Cf. Tertullian *De anima*, 25.

4. Gorman, *Abortion & the Early Church*, 25.
5. Gorman, *Abortion & the Early Church*, 25.
6. Gorman, *Abortion & the Early Church*, 26.

fetus; Cicero is reflecting a very Roman approach to abortion."[7] With rare exception, such as the Latin poet Ovid (43 BC–AD 17),[8] this approach continued more or less until the time of Constantine (emperor from 306–37 AD) and his "Christian" empire.

Michael Gorman's *Abortion & the Early Church* documents the early church fathers' opposition to abortion against this background. A chapter of Gorman's book is also devoted to "The Jewish World." He notes that "It is generally accepted that two Jewish views on abortion existed, the Alexandrian and the Palestinian. According to most scholars, the strict Alexandrian view required punishment for damage to a fetus according to its stage of development, whereas the more lenient Palestinian view, holding that the fetus was not a person, required punishment only for harm to the mother." However, "both schools confined their discussion to accidental or therapeutic abortions" and both "condemned deliberate abortion as disrespect for life and as bloodshed. . . . The Jewish abhorrence of deliberate bloodshed and its respect for life, including that of the unborn, formed a natural foundation for the Christian writings on abortion."[9]

Although the New Testament makes no explicit reference to abortion, Gorman believes it is "by no means far-fetched" to conclude that "the association of the use of drugs (*pharmakeia*) with abortion in pagan and later Christian writing suggests that there may be an implicit reference to abortion in such texts as Galatians 5:20 and Revelation 9:21, 18:23, 21:8 and 22:15, where words of the same group are used."[10]

The earliest specific written references to abortion are in the *Didache* and the *Epistles of Barnabus*, followed by the *Apocalypse of Peter*, Clement of Alexandria (circa 150–215 AD) in *Prophetic Eclogues* and *The Tutor* (*Padagogus*), and the Greek apologists, the best known of whom, Tertullian, wrote that "murder being once for all forbidden, we may not destroy even the foetus in the womb. . . . To hinder a birth is merely a speedier man-killing; nor does it matter whether you take away a life that is born, or destroy one that is coming to the birth. That is a man which is going to be one; you have the fruit already in the seed."[11] Following the "Christianization" of the Roman empire under Constantine, during the fourth and early fifth centuries "the first ecclesiastical laws against abortion were passed,

---

7. Gorman, *Abortion & the Early Church*, 26.
8. Gorman, *Abortion & the Early Church*, 28.
9. Gorman, *Abortion & the Early Church*, 44–45.
10. Gorman, *Abortion & the Early Church*, 48. Gorman also notes, 48n1, "Paul's use of *ektroma* in 1 Corinthians 15:8 may refer to abortion, but the usage is enigmatic."
11. Tertullian, *Apology* 7.1. Quoted in Gorman, *Abortion & the Early Church*, 55.

and five major church Fathers—Basil, Jerome, Ambrose, Augustine and Chrysostom—commented on the practice."[12]

The Council of Elvira (circa 305) was the first Christian body to enact punishment for abortion (or possibly infanticide), followed in 314 by the Council of Ancyra, which explicitly condemned women "who prostitute themselves, and who kill the children thus begotten, or who try to destroy them when in their wombs. . . " Basil of Caesarea (circa 330–79) stated that "She who has deliberately destroyed a fetus has to pay the penalty of murder." He also condemned as murderers those who helped women to abort.[13] Ambrose of Milan (circa 339–97) condemned especially the rich who "in order that their inheritance may not be divided among several, deny in the womb their own progeny. . . "[14] Jerome (circa 342–420) in one of his most famous letters condemns unmarried women who "when they learn they are with child through sin, practice abortion by use of drugs." Sometimes they die themselves and so are guilty of "three crimes: suicide, adultery against Christ, and murder of an unborn child." However, "like Tertullian before and Augustine after, Jerome distinguished between the formed and the unformed fetus and said that a certain stage of development is necessary before there is a person and, hence, before there can be a murder. This distinction received much more attention and approval in the West than in the East."[15]

A MATTER OF THE SOUL

To identify the point in time when a fetus become a person, some have considered the emergence of the soul. Augustine (354–430) "fluctuated on the question of the soul's origin. He seems to have thought at various times that it is pre-existent, that it comes from the parents like the body, that it is created and given by God at conception, or that it is infused at the point of formation." For Augustine "the destruction of a formed fetus was murder, but the destruction of an unformed fetus was not murder."[16] In *Enchiridion*, his handbook on the Catholic faith, he "admits that it is natural to think that an undeveloped fetus would perish" rather than be resurrected. "Immediately, however, he checks this assumption: 'But who, then, would dare to deny—though he would not dare to affirm either—that in the resurrection day what is lacking in the forms of things will be filled out. . . . What is not yet whole

---

12. Gorman, *Abortion & the Early Church*, 63.
13. Gorman, *Abortion & the Early Church*, 66–67.
14. Gorman, *Abortion & the Early Church*, 67–68.
15. Gorman, *Abortion & the Early Church*, 68–69.
16. Gorman, *Abortion & the Early Church*, 70.

will become whole."[17] "Augustine's method of handling abortion changed as his thought matured.... Speculation about the origin of the soul, about the human and nonhuman fetus now gave way to his long-held conviction that human life is 'God's own work.'... Augustine chose to emphasize the value of all life, whether actual or potential."[18]

Chrysostom (347–407) was emphatic in calling abortion murder or "something even worse than murder" that he associated with sexual immorality. He saw the fetus "as an object of God's care." (This is based on a "forceful sermon on Romans 13:11-14.")[19]

In the Middle Ages, St. Thomas Aquinas, influenced by Aristotle, estimated the time at which a soul entered a male fetus as forty days, with females following at eighty days. He associated this with quickening (referring to the first movements felt by the mother), following Aristotle's view that the unborn go through three stages: vegetative, animal, and human. This view influenced subsequent legislation. Klaas Runia, writing in 1971 says, "Thus in England after the fifteenth century, when common law declared that life began at the moment of quickening, abortion was a criminal offense only after the fetus was quick. This position has influenced present laws, which require a birth certificate only after the fetus is twenty weeks old." (But see Olasky's reservations below about this history.)

Runia continues:

> In 1588 Pope Sixtus V tried to change the position of the Roman Catholic Church by stating that the soul entered the embryo at the moment of conception. His efforts were undone by his successor, Gregory XIV, but finally in 1869 Pius IX reversed (*sic*) the Roman Catholic Church to the position of Sixtus.
>
> This is still the official position of the Roman Catholic Church. Ensoulment begins at conception and, therefore, every form of abortion, including therapeutic abortion, is sinful. Exceptions are made only in cases of an extrauterine pregnancy or a cancerous uterus, in which an operation directed to save the life of the mother leads indirectly to the death of the fetus; the point is that the fetus cannot be killed directly to save the life of the mother.[20]

---

17. Gorman, *Abortion & the Early Church*, 71.
18. Gorman, *Abortion & the Early Church*, 72.
19. Gorman, *Abortion & the Early Church*, 72–73.
20. Runia, "Abortion Perspective," 19–20.

REFORMATION AND POST-REFORMATION PERIODS

The Reformers, Luther and Calvin, both expressed strong anti-abortion views. Luther wrote in his *Commentary on Genesis:* "How many girls there are who prevent conception and kill and expel tender fetuses, although procreation is the work of God."[21] Calvin, in discussing a crucial passage, which he does in connection with the command not to murder, anticipates a more recent interpretation of Exod 21:22–25:

> This passage at first sight is ambiguous, for if the word death only applies to the pregnant woman, it would not have been a capital crime to put an end to the foetus, which would be a great absurdity; for the fœtus, though enclosed in the womb of its mother, is already a human being, (*homo*,) and it is almost a monstrous crime to rob it of the life which it has not yet begun to enjoy. If it seems more horrible to kill a man in his own house than in a field, because a man's house is his place of most secure refuge, it ought surely to be deemed more atrocious to destroy a foetus in the womb before it has come to light. On these grounds I am led to conclude, without hesitation, that the words, "if death should follow," must be applied to the *foetus* as well as to the mother...[22]

Abortion, with a few exceptions, was not much discussed in the post-Reformation period. The English Puritan Richard Baxter's (1615–91) thousand-plus-page *A Christian Directory*, covers a vast amount of human behavior, but does not mention abortion. John Flavel (1620-91) was likely reflecting a common understanding when he wrote in *The Mystery of Providence*, "Abortives go for nothing in the world, and there are multitudes of them. Some never had a reasonable soul breathed into them, but only the rudiments and rough draft of a body; these come not into the account of men, but perish as the beast does."[23]

John Owen (1616–84) condemned infanticide (as would all Puritans) in chapter 16 of *Indwelling Sin in Believers*, but the New England Puritans are said to have allowed abortion up till quickening in conformity with English common law. Marvin Olasky disputes this: "Justice Harry Blackmun in his 1973 *Roe v. Wade* decision asserted that English 'common law' accepted abortion. He relied on and repeatedly cited as authoritative two journal articles by Cyril Means Jr., who happened to be the top lawyer of the National Association for the Repeal of Abortion Laws. Surprise! Means cited two

---

21. Luther, *Lectures on Genesis*, 4:304.
22. Calvin, *Four Last Books of Moses*, 41–42.
23. Flavel, *Mystery of Providence*, 38.

English cases but left out numerous others that undermined his contention about abortion's acceptance."[24]

Olasky then provides carefully researched examples from both England and colonial America where perpetrators of abortion, sometimes by forcing a pregnant woman to drink an abortifacient, were charged with murder. In one case of a "man child about three months old," Olasky comments, "Justice Harry Blackmun in *Roe v. Wade* will say abortion prior to quickening was not a crime in English or colonial common law. If that's true, why a charge of murder upon the death of an unborn baby merely three months after conception?"[25] In a footnote referencing work by Philip Rafferty, Olasky notes that we "should distinguish between 'quicken' (the first felt movements) and 'quick': the latter meaning 'alive' in the sense of the old expression 'the quick and the dead.' In that sense an unborn child would already be quick from conception onward. Rafferty... notes that two centuries ago a *Supplement to Johnson's English Dictionary* defined 'quick' as 'pregnant with a live child.'"[26]

Later Olasky writes:

> To understand why abortion was so rare in early America we need to spend less time debating obscure 'common law' cases and more time entering the stream of church-going colonists walking to come and worship on a Sunday morning with the father carrying the family Bible. That was the one book in most homes. In an era of frequent Bible readings few missed God's creative involvement in human life from its beginning. Colonists read in Psalms, Job, Isaiah, Jeremiah, Luke, Galatians and other books not only that we are made in God's image but that he "knitted me together in my mother's womb," "formed me in the womb" and "formed you in the womb."[27]

As abortion became increasingly common in succeeding centuries due to several factors, including social and cultural changes, laws were passed to outlaw it. "While historians say the first American law against abortion emerged in Connecticut in 1821, New York City took action 105 years earlier. In 1716, the Common Council forbade midwives to aid in or recommend abortion."[28] In 1858–59, the American Medical Association, after giving mixed signals earlier in the decade, formed a Committee on Criminal Abortion. "Committees are often ways to slow down or kill

---

24. Olasky and Savas, *Story of Abortion in America*, 22.

25. Olasky and Savas, *Story of Abortion in America*, 26. See also 309.

26. Olasky and Savas, *Story of Abortion in America*, 26n4. Cf. Rafferty, *Roe v. Wade: Unraveling the Fabric of America*, 151 and Rafferty, "Roe v. Wade," 5–6.

27. Olasky and Savas, *Story of Abortion in America*, 35. Scripture references are to Ps 139:13; Job 31:15; Isa 44:22 and 49:1,5; Jer 1:5; Luke 1:15; and Gal 1:15.

28. Olasky and Savas, *Story of Abortion in America*, 54.

initiatives, but this time, with Christian revival in the air, more doctors showed concern for their smallest patients." Abortion should be seen "as no simple offense against public morality and decency, no mere misdemeanor, no attempt upon the life of the mother, but the wanton and murderous destruction of her child."[29]

Olasky notes that "Many doctors were both anti-slavery and anti-abortion.... These doctors influenced their churches."[30] However, "Some pastors after the Civil War risked backlash by speaking of slavery and abortion as twin evils."[31] The General Assembly of the Presbyterian Church in the United States of America declared that it viewed "the destruction by parents of their own offspring before birth with abhorrence," but "Most pastors during the last quarter of the nineteenth century were not so clear.... After 1900, more pastors spoke about the plight of the poor but were still quiet about abortion.... Dr. Walter Dorsett, at an American Medical Association convention, complained that 'the clergy do not seem to be at all concerned. Few sermons are preached from the pulpit for fear of shocking the delicate feelings of a fashionably dressed congregation.'"[32]

The attitude of the churches was much the same in Europe. Abortion did not become a major issue until the loosening of regulations in the 20th century. Some of the strongest anti–abortion statements came, not from traditional evangelicals, but from the followers and successors of Karl Barth (1886–1966) the father of neo-orthodoxy. Barth himself stated in the mid-twentieth century:

> Our first contention must be that no pretext can alter the fact that the whole circle of those concerned is in the strict sense engaged in the killing of human life. For the unborn child is from the first a child. It is still developing and has no independent life. But it is a [human] and not a thing, not a mere part of a woman's body.... Whatever arguments may be brought against the birth and existence of the child, is it his fault that he is here? What has he done to his mother and the others that they wish to deprive him of his germinating life and punish him with death? Does not his utter defencelessness and helplessness, or the question whom they are destroying, to whom they have denied a future before even he has breathed and seen the light of the world, wrest the weapon from the hand of the mother first, and then from all the others, thwarting their will to use it.[33]

---

29. Olasky and Savas, *Story of Abortion in America*, 139.
30. Olasky and Savas, *Story of Abortion in America*, 142–43.
31. Olasky and Savas, *Story of Abortion in America*, 159.
32. Olasky and Savas, *Story of Abortion in America*, 159–62.
33. Barth, *Church Dogmatics*, 3:415–16.

Likewise, Dietrich Bonhoeffer (1906–45): "Destruction of the embryo in the mother's womb is a violation of the right to live which God has bestowed upon this nascent life. To raise the question whether we are here concerned already with a human being or not is merely to confuse the issue. The simple fact is that God certainly intended to create a human being and that this nascent human being has been deliberately deprived of his life. And that is nothing but murder. . ."[34]

And more recently, Jurgen Moltmann (1926–): "Every devaluation of the fetus, the embryo, and the fertilized ovum compared with life that is already born and adult is the beginning of a rejection and a de-humanization of human beings. Hope for the resurrection of the body does not permit any such death sentence to be passed on life. Fundamentally speaking, human beings mutilate themselves when embryos are devalued into mere 'human material,' for every human being was once just such an embryo in need of protection."[35]

The themes that emerged in the earlier part of this brief survey evidence concerns (and confusion) that emerge again among evangelicals in the early years of the current abortion debate, including general opposition to abortion, modified by equivocation and uncertainty about the exact origin of the soul and thus of human life and the implications for certain stages of development. How are evangelicals in the twentieth and twenty-first century understanding these ongoing concerns? In the next chapter, we will bring our historical review up to the twentieth century.

Discussion Questions

1. Review Gal 5:20, Rev 9:21, 18:23, 21:8, and 22:15. Which word do you think suggests an implicit reference to abortion?

2. How can the evangelical understanding of the soul be used to support a pro-life position?

3. Given the evidence that abortion has sometimes been considered and condemned as murder, why do you think the rhetoric has shifted towards seeing an unborn child as less than human?

---

34. Bonhoeffer, *Ethics*, 174.
35. Moltmann, *Way of Jesus Christ*, 268.

4

Developing Evangelical Views in the Twentieth Century

WRITING IN 1987, RON SIDER found that what "seems confusing to many is to notice that religious people, including evangelical Christians, cannot agree on whether the fetus is a human being." He cited several examples of this uncertainty, adding: "In light of the uncertainty and disagreement about the status of the fetus as well as the strength of the arguments for abortion, one can understand why many compassionate people of good will consider abortion morally acceptable." Then Sider noted, "A decade ago, I found these arguments conclusive. But troubling doubts and disturbing questions have caused me to change my thinking."[1] Sider was not alone in coming to a change of mind in the decade of the seventies and early eighties, as this chapter will show.

R.F.R. Gardner

One of the earliest contributions to the current abortion debate from an evangelical Christian was *Abortion: The Personal Dilemma* by R.F.R. Gardner, published in 1972, five years after the 1967 Abortion Act in Great Britain and the year before *Roe v. Wade* in the USA.[2] This book exercised considerable influence on both sides of the Atlantic, being hailed by the

---

1. Sider, *Completely Pro-Life*, 38.
2. Gardner, *Abortion* (1972).

Philadelphia-based (evangelical) *ETERNITY* magazine as "The most thorough Christian analysis of abortion that exists. This refreshing and penetrating book presents us with a spiritual and thoughtful analysis of abortion ethics that can be of great practical help."[3]

As John Frame notes in his review of the book, "This *might* have been the ideal Christian book on the difficult question of abortion. For one thing, it would be hard to imagine anyone better qualified to write such a book. The author is not only a consultant obstetrician and gynecologist, but also an ordained minister of the United Free Church of Scotland."[4] Gardner was also a former missionary doctor in Africa. His book demonstrates a broad understanding of cross-cultural issues, not only in Africa but throughout Europe, Asia, and Latin America. He documents the liberalization of abortion laws in Europe, leading up to the 1967 change in British law. He also provides a detailed and compassionate understanding of the causes leading to such liberalization, including deformities caused by the thalidomide drug prescribed to pregnant women in the late 1950s and early 1960s for the relief of nausea.

Although somewhat dated now, there is a wealth of useful information in Gardner's book. He provides information on the history of abortion, the attitudes of the early and medieval churches and of a few contemporary denominations and theologians, socio-economic factors in the decision to abort, physical, spiritual and psychological risks, sterilization, the use of contraceptives by married and unmarried women and men, etc. Besides, as Frame rightly observes:

> Mr. Gardner's heart-commitment is particularly obvious in the profound Christian *compassion* which permeates this volume. That compassion is most infectious: it is hard to read this book without at some point being convicted of one's own lack of love. Many will come to this book with neat, precise ideas on how people requesting abortion should be 'handled.' But Gardner will lead them through case after case after case—laboring with, agonizing with, each sad woman. What will happen to the woman if abortion is refused? if it is granted? What of her other children? What of her husband? What of the economic situation? the psychological? the medical? What of the morale of the doctors and nurses? For the reader this can be an exhausting business. It is hard work to do so much thinking; but then *love* is hard work. The aforementioned comprehensiveness

---

3. Endorsement on the cover of the American edition, published in 1972 by Eerdmans. *ETERNITY*, founded in 1950, ceased publication in 1988.

4. Frame, "Book Review," 31.

of Gardner's scholarship is in a sense a measure of his love, and of the love he wishes to arouse in his readers. The reader of this book can expect to *experience* a certain amount of agony, if he reads with any seriousness; and in God's providence such agony can yield spiritual fruit.[5]

However, when it comes to the relevant biblical material, Gardner's treatment is disappointingly brief and questionable:

> For example, in discussing the crucial passage in Exodus 21:22–25, Gardner explains that there have been three basic interpretations of the passage, the second one being 'that the fine is payable for the blow, providing that no harm follow to mother or child' [118f]. After merely listing the three interpretations, with no analysis or discussion, he concludes: 'It would seem fairly obvious that in any case the text implies a difference in the eyes of the law between the fetus and a person' [118]. But that conclusion is precisely what the 'second' view *denies*. Gardner's treatments of other texts are equally cursory. Further, there is no mention in this book of what in my opinion is the most crucial Scriptural consideration, namely, the obligation of the believer to avoid even the *probable* taking of human life.
>
> On such a slender biblical foundation, Gardner declares his view that 'while the fetus is to be cherished increasingly as it develops, we should regard its first breath at birth as the moment when God gives it not only life, but the offer of Life' (p. 126). He therefore advocates abortion in a great many situations, though he is not an advocate of 'abortion on demand'. Just where he draws the line is a bit difficult to explain, but there are *some* cases where he clearly advocates refusal of abortion.[6]

Not only does Gardner advocate abortion in "a great number of situations," he also performed several himself, as well as refusing others. Situations in which he approved and/or performed abortions included socio-economic reasons and family concerns, as well as emotional and physical health.

Despite his openness to abortion in some questionable situations which did not involve direct risk to a woman's life, Gardner ends his book by recommending Birthright, a pro-life organization, originally founded in Toronto with the creed: "It is the right of every pregnant woman to give birth, and the right of every child to be born." Gardner concludes:

---

5. Frame, "Book Review," 31–32.
6. Frame, "Book Review," 32.

"The present writer, while convinced that there is a real place for abortion in some cases, nevertheless is sure that the approach of Birthright is essentially the right one, and would be applicable to the majority of women seeking abortion today."[7] Perhaps nothing illustrates better the dilemma with which Gardner wrestled than his advocacy of a strictly pro-life (anti-abortion) organization while taking what most evangelicals today would consider quite a liberal position himself.

It is rare these days to come across the viewpoint among evangelicals that life begins at birth. Evangelicals on the whole have never advocated such an extreme position, but they have differed over the question of when exactly human life begins, or more exactly when the soul enters the human body.

Lewis B. Smedes

Eleven years after endorsing Gardner's book, *ETERNITY* announced that *Mere Morality* by Reformed ethicist Lewis B. Smedes (1921–2002) was its evangelical book of the year. Sub-titled *What God Expects from Ordinary People*, this is an exploration of the last six of the ten commandments and their implications for modern life. Coming to the subject of abortion, Smedes rejects the view that biblical passages like Psalm 139, which speaks of being knit together in our mother's womb, are definitive for determining the origin of personhood. Psalm 139 is poetry. "Consider: if the words were meant as factual information, what would we make of being 'wrought' in the depths, not of the uterus, but of the earth?" The Lord told Jeremiah that he had known him before he was in his mother's womb (Jer 1:5). "Is this divine sanction for saying that a person is present the moment an ovum has 46 chromosomes, even before it clings to the uterine nest? Paul knew that God knew and chose us before the foundation of the world (Eph 1:4)." "The Lamb of God himself was slain before the world's foundations were laid (Rev 13:18)." Thus, statements such as these are confessions about God, "not the precise status of fetal life."[8]

After considering various views, Smedes indicates a preference for an understanding that the fetus "*develops into a person gradually, with no fixed turning point*" (emphasis original). But rather than erring on the side of caution, he considers other factors that come into the abortion decision, such as the welfare of the mother as well as of third parties, and the "social crisis," then proposes a gradual approach to abortion whereby the first six

7. Gardner, *Abortion*, 276.
8. Smedes, *Mere Morality*, 128.

weeks are unrestricted, since "no one can reasonably be sure that the fetus is a person during the first six weeks. Indeed, the most reasonable view is that it is not a person." Severe restrictions are imposed from the sixth week to the twelfth, and "*Abortion after the third month should be a crime*" (emphasis original).[9] It is interesting that Smedes's six-week limit should be the same as ones being implemented today in certain states.

ETERNITY Magazine

Moving back in time to 1971, the year before the publication of Gardner's book and two years before *Roe v. Wade*, ETERNITY devoted an issue to the questions raised by the increasing availability of abortion in the United States. After a helpful survey by Klaas Runia of the reasons being advocated for abortion, as well as the history of Christian responses going back to the early church, Runia joined with nine other men in giving their views on the issue. None favored unlimited access, but they differed on which exceptions should be allowed and on the question of whether an embryo or fetus should be considered human or potentially human. In introducing this discussion, the editors observed, "On certain issues, all of our contributors agree; but on many they do not, so that an overall evangelical consensus on abortion seems far from complete. Sometimes men who use nearly identical language apply their insights in significantly diverse ways."[10]

Then in summing up the discussion, "*ETERNITY's* analysis" notes:

> Our evangelical spokesmen are agreed on two major areas:
>
> 1. All of them admit that they would permit an abortion to a woman whose very life was at stake due to complications of a pregnancy. . . . Today, thanks to advances in modern medicine, abortion to save the life of the mother is rarely required. Yet the fact that all our spokesmen agree that it is permissible raises the possibility that it may be warranted for sufficiently grave reasons in other situations as well.
>
> 2. Our contributors also agree on the intrinsic value of fetal life. . . . But at what point must the fetus be guaranteed an unqualified right to life. Some say at conception or implantation of the zygote in the uterine wall. Some give the fetus increasing value as it approaches birth. Some focus on

9. Smedes, *Mere Morality*, 143–45.
10. "Fetal Life," *ETERNITY*, 18.

viability, the point at which the fetus could survive outside the womb...[11]

Other issues addressed include eugenic abortion for fetal abnormalities (where again opinions differed), the extent to which Christians should seek to influence public policy, and "Is Life Ever Cheap? A scathing attack on abortion-on-demand by Carl F. H. Henry." Nancy Hardesty, formerly on the staff at *ETERNITY*, then a faculty member at Trinity College, Deerfield, Ill, addressed the question of "When Does Life Begin?"[12]

Hardesty begins with the assumption that the only Scripture which "comes close" to addressing abortion is Exod 21:22–25, the same passage to which Gardner would later appeal.[13] Hardesty concludes from this passage that "It can be inferred here that the fetus was not considered a human life or 'life for life' would have been demanded as it was for the mother's life or at least a 'fetus for a fetus' as was done under Assyrian law."[14] The article proceeds from there. After reviewing different positions, Hardesty quotes Paul K. Jewett, then professor of systematic theology at Fuller Theological Seminary, to the effect that "The amount of scriptural data is neither sufficient nor is the direction in which it points so unequivocal that one can be dogmatic." She then addresses the question: "When does the fetus receive a soul?" The traditional Jewish position, she says, based on Gen 2:7, is that "the soul inhabits the fetus when it draws its first breath outside the mother's womb." However, this is "complicated by the equally biblical belief that life also resides in the blood, as illustrated by Deut 17:23: . . . 'the blood is the life.' A further complication is that both Hebrew terms for 'breath of life' and 'blood' are applied to animal life as well as human life."[15]

Hardesty moves on to consider the two major positions on when the fetus gets a soul. Traducianism says "that either the parents generate from inanimate matter both body and soul or that the mother's egg is the source

---

11. "*ETERNITY's* analysis," 24.

12. Hardesty, "When Does Life Begin?," 19, 43.

13. More recently Num 5:27 has been claimed in support of the idea that God visited miscarriage on an unfaithful wife. This is based on an idiosyncratic translation in the NIV. The word "miscarriage" does not appear in the original Hebrew and there is nothing to suggest that the woman is necessarily pregnant. The first edition of the NIV offered the miscarriage interpretation as a footnote alternative, but it has found its way into the main text of subsequent editions. It is not found in more literal translations such as the KJV, NKJV, NASB and ESV. Besides, even if God did cause a woman to miscarry as a form of judgment, just as he killed adults for other reasons, this does not mean he did not consider her to be carrying a living child.

14. Hardesty, "When Does Life Begin?," 19.

15. Hardesty, "When Does Life Begin?," 43.

of the matter and the father's sperm the source of the soul; or. . . that the soul of the child is derived naturally from the soul of the parents. Either way, the fetus receives the soul at conception." (But see Kantzer's position below.) On the other hand, creationism "contends that God creates each soul separately. In support of this, its proponents cite such Scriptures as Gen 2:7, Isa 42:5, Zech 12:1, Num 16:22, Eccl 12:7 and Heb 12:9. All of these verses seem to indicate that God is involved with the creation of spirits in a different way than He is with flesh. . . . Because of medical indications that the fetus develops steadily from conception to birth, most recent creationists have dated 'ensoulment' from conception."[16]

This differs from older views. "English common law, which strongly influenced U.S. abortion law or lack of it until the Civil War, was based on the theological belief that the fetus moved at quickening because it had received its soul." Then again, "Aristotle and some of his Christian followers such as Thomas Aquinas said that a male fetus got its soul at 40 days and the female at 80."[17] (See footnote 2 of chapter 3, where Aristotle is said to have put the formation of the female fetus at eighty to ninety days. Also, see Olasky's reservations noted above, about the common understanding of English common law.)

Hardesty believes that one of "the most cogent Christian positions" was proposed by Dr. Kenneth Kantzer (1917–2002) at the Christian Medical Society's 1968 Symposium on the Control of Human Reproduction. (Kantzer was at that time dean of Trinity Evangelical Divinity School, later to become editor of *Christianity Today* from 1977–82). Kantzer's position combined a traducian view of the soul's origin with the "potentially human" view of the fetus. He offered several observations:

> First, no biblical passage condemns abortion or speaks of man as fully human before birth. Second, Exod. 21:22–25 explicitly distinguishes between the destruction of a fetus and the killing of a person. Third, scriptural language has many kinds of "souls"—even animals sometimes have one. Fourth, traducianism seems more true to the biblical view that man is made of the "stuff" he receives from his parents; and further, when God created man in Genesis 2, He ceased His directly creative work. Fifth, the Bible portrays heaven as populated with people who went through a test in life on earth. Since one third of all fertilized eggs are spontaneously aborted, heaven would be filled with fetuses if they are human. Bible verses which speak of God

---

16. Hardesty, "When Does Life Begin?," 43.
17. Hardesty, "When Does Life Begin?," 43.

forming man in the womb do not imply that no process is necessary before man becomes fully and truly human.

Thus, Dr. Kantzer would sum up his position: "It is ordinarily wrong to kill the life of the fetus, but it is not manslaughter. It is wrong because the fetus is potentially human and because of the sacredness of human life. It is not manslaughter because the fetus is not yet man. The exact moment or point in development at which a fetus becomes fully human we cannot determine for this lies in the freedom of God."[18]

1968 Symposium on the Control of Human Reproduction

As noted, Kantzer shared his views at a 1968 Symposium on the Control of Human Reproduction. Twenty-five evangelical scholars participated in that symposium and *Christianity Today* devoted its November 8, 1968 issue to their findings. There are articles on contraception and birth control, one by Paul K. Jewett (1920–91) on "The Relation of the Soul to the Fetus," (referred to by Hardesty above), and "A Protestant Affirmation on the Control of Human Population." (Note that it is distinctly *Protestant* rather than Catholic.) This last document deals with a number of issues related to the purpose of sexual intercourse and contraception. On the issue of "Induced Abortion, the Fetus, and Human Responsibility," it states:

> We are left with the most perplexing questions of all: Is induced abortion permissible and if so, under what conditions? If it is permissible in some instances does this mean that the act of intervention is sinful? Can abortion then be justified by the principle of tragic moral choice in which one evil is chosen to avoid a greater evil? Whether or not the performance of an induced abortion is sinful we are not agreed, but about the necessity and permissibility for it under certain circumstances we are in accord. The Christian physician who is asked to perform an abortion will seek to discover the will of God in this as in every other area of his life. He needs divine guidance for himself. . . . The physician in making decisions should take into account the following principles:
>
> —The human fetus is not merely a mass of cells or an organic growth. At the most, it is an actual human life or at the least, a potential and developing human life. . . .

18. Hardesty, "When Does Life Begin?," 43.

—The Christian physician will advise induced abortion only to safeguard greater values sanctioned by Scripture. These values may be individual, familial, or societal.

—From the moment of birth, the infant is a human being with all the rights which Holy Scripture accords to all human beings; therefore infanticide under any name should be condemned.[19]

Later, a section dealing with "Induced (Therapeutic) Abortion" notes:

The sanctity of life must be considered when the question of abortion is raised. Regardless of what stage of gestation—including birth—at which one considers the developing embryo or fetus to be equivalent to an adult human, the potential of the developing intrauterine life cannot be denied. There could, however, be compelling reasons why abortion must be considered under certain circumstances. Each case should be considered individually, taking into account the various factors involved and using Christian principles of ethics. Suitable cases for abortion would fall within the scope of the American College of Obstetricians and Gynecologists Statement on Therapeutic Abortion. However, we believe that isolated sociological pressures that justify abortion rarely occur. We do not construe the A.C.O.G. Statement as an endorsement of abortion on demand or for convenience only.[20]

The A.C.O.G. statement is included in the article. It defines therapeutic abortion as a medical procedure that "must be performed only in a hospital accredited by the Joint Commission on Accreditation of Hospitals and by a licensed physician qualified to perform such operations." At least two licensed physicians "other than the one who is to perform the procedure" must be consulted. Their opinions should "state that the procedure is medically indicated." The criteria for determining the permissibility of a therapeutic abortion are:

1. When continuation of the pregnancy may threaten the life of the woman or seriously impair her health. In determining whether or not there is such risk to health, account may be taken of the patient's total environment, actual or reasonably foreseeable. 2. When pregnancy has resulted from rape or incest: in this case the same medical criteria should be employed in the

19. "Protestant Affirmation," 18.
20. "Protestant Affirmation," 19.

evaluation of the patient. 3. When continuation of the pregnancy is likely to result in the birth of a child with grave physical deformities or mental retardation.[21]

These criteria, approved by the evangelical leaders at the symposium are a far cry from permitting abortion only on those rare cases when the mother's life is genuinely in danger. Taking account of her "total environment, actual or reasonably foreseeable" allows for wide discretion in terms of determining risk not only to a pregnant woman's life but her health broadly defined. Rape and incest, as well as "grave physical deformities or mental retardation" of the prospective child also qualify as permissible conditions. This broad interpretation of the law gave way in 1973 to what has been called "abortion on demand" that did away with the requirement of multiple physician consultations and the requirement that these procedures take place in licensed hospitals.

Bruce K. Waltke

Of particular interest for our purposes is Bruce K. Waltke's article, "The Old Testament and Birth Control." Then professor of Old Testament at Dallas Theological Seminary (later Regent College and Westminster, Reformed, and Knox Seminaries), Waltke is sometimes regarded as the "dean" of Old Testament studies. He states as one factor in suggesting that abortion was permissible under Mosaic law that "God does not regard the fetus as a soul, no matter how far gestation has progressed." By way of contrast, contemporary Assyrian law "prescribed death by torture in cases of procured abortion" and in the case of accidental miscarriage caused by a man striking a pregnant woman "he shall compensate for her fetus with a life." The Old Testament, on the other hand, "never reckons the fetus as equivalent to a life." Here there is reference to the by now familiar Exod 21:22–25.

At the same time, "the Christian is aware that God is actively involved in fashioning the fetus" as demonstrated by Ps 139:13–18. Thus, "while the Old Testament does not equate the fetus with a living person, it places great value upon it."[22]

Waltke's view came to be widely quoted by pro-abortion proponents who argued with some justification, that evangelicals were not always as opposed to abortion as they appear to be now. See, for instance, "My take:

---

21. Quoted in "Protestant Affirmation," 19.
22. Waltke, "Old Testament and Birth Control," 3–6.

when evangelicals were pro-choice" by Jonathan Dudley[23] and "The Argument for Abortion as a Religious Right" by Leila Ettachfini.[24] Both of these writers (and others) reference Waltke in support of their views. What they fail to mention is that Waltke changed his mind, or at least modified his earlier position. Seven years after the publication of the above article, Waltke signaled a change of mind about the interpretation of the Exodus passage. In a lengthy footnote to a paper delivered to the 27th annual meeting of the Evangelical Theological Society on December 29, 1975, and published in March 1976, Waltke admits that the case he previously presented "is less than conclusive for both exegetical and logical reasons."[25] Despite criticisms received by J. W. Cottrell in a 1973 *Christianity Today* article, Waltke still thought his previous interpretation to be the proper one. However, he admits that "Cottrell makes a good case against it." He continues:

> The purpose of the decision recorded in this debated passage was not to define the nature of the fetus but to decide a just claim in the case of an induced abortion that may or may not have been accidental. If the miscarriage occurred accidentally, then it would have been regarded as manslaughter, a crime not necessarily punishable by death. However, in the preceding case law, the judgment did not apply the princiocf of lex talionis [law of retaliation] in the case of a debatable death of a servant at the hands of his master. But it does not follow that since "life for life" was not exacted here that therefore the slave was less than a fully human life.[26]

This time, Waltke announces as his thesis "that the inspired authors regarded the fetus as a human being" and concludes, "The fetus is human and therefore to be accorded the same protection to life granted every other human being. . . . Concerning the practical application of this conclusion . . . abortion can be justified only in those cases when the fetus presents material aggression against the mother."[27] How he may have arrived at this conclusion will be discussed later. For now, it is necessary only to indicate the movement from Waltke's previous position.

---

23. Dudley, "My take: when evangelicals were pro-choice."
24. Ettachfini, "Argument for Abortion as a Religious Right."
25. Waltke, "Reflections from the Old Testament," 3.
26. Waltke, "Reflections from the Old Testament," 3.
27. Waltke, "Reflections from the Old Testament," 13.

John Stott

Meanwhile, returning to the British Isles, John Stott, writing in the *Church of England Newspaper* in 1971, identified the view that human life begins at conception with the Roman Catholic position. He argued that the fetus was only a "potential human being" and interpreted risks to the mother's life as "perhaps including her physical and mental health." Abortion would be justified in such situations since "the choice is between an actual human being and a potential human being."[28] Nine years later, writing in the American publication *Christianity Today*, Stott had changed his view. Basing his argument on Psalm 139, he states categorically:

> The fetus is not a growth in the mother's body (which can be removed as readily as her tonsils or appendix), nor even a potential human being, but a human life who, though not yet mature, has the potentiality to grow into the fulness of the humanity he already possesses. We cannot fix criteria of humanness (like self-consciousness, reason, independence, speech, moral choice, or responsive love) and then conclude that, lacking these, the fetus is not human. The newborn child and the senile old person lack these also. Nor can we draw a line at any point and say that after it the child is human and before it, not. There is no "decisive moment of humanization," subsequent to conception, whether implantation, or "animation" (when some early fathers, building on Aristotle, supposed that the fetus receives a rational soul. . .), or "quickening" (a purely subjective notion, when the mother first feels the fetus move), or viability (which is getting earlier and earlier), or birth (when the child takes his first independent breath). All these are stages in the continuous process by which an individual human life is developing into mature human personhood. From fusion onwards the fetus is an "unborn child."[29]

By 1984 and the publication of *Issues Facing Christians Today*, Stott had clearly adopted the position he had previously described as "Catholic," stating that conception is "the decisive moment when a human life begins," a viewpoint that "should include all Christians."[30] In this later work, Stott references an interdisciplinary seminar of theologians and doctors that took place in 1983 jointly sponsored by the London Institute for Contemporary Christianity and the Christian Medical Fellowship. The keynote address was given by Canon Oliver O'Donovan, then regius professor of

---

28. John Stott, "Abortion, Deformity and 'Vegetables,'" 5.
29. Stott, "Does Life Begin Before Birth?" 51.
30. Stott, *Decisive Issues Facing Christians Today*, 314.

moral and pastoral theology at Oxford. His title, "And who is a Person?" took as its starting point Jesus's parable of the Good Samaritan and the question "and who is my neighbor?" O'Donovan argued for a three-step process leading to the acknowledgement of "the gradualness of development into personal encounter, while affirming the reality of personhood from the moment of conception." In an unpublished essay on "The Logic of Beginnings," the late Professor Donald MacKay (1922-87), formerly director of the Research Department of Communication and Neuroscience at Keele University, "took issue with Professor O'Donovan's argument." MacKay "agreed that from the moment of fusion the conceptus has biological life and a marvellous repertoire of potentiality, but added that it only becomes a person possessing rights and demanding care when brain development makes self-supervision possible."[31]

Stott (as was typical of him) sought to find common ground between these seemingly irreconcilable positions. "Donald MacKay emphasizes the development of the fetus, while not denying that already the fertilized ovum has a rich repertoire. Oliver O'Donovan emphasizes that from the beginning the conceptus has a unique and complete genotype, and indeed personhood, while not denying its destiny is to reach human maturity. Is this not at base the old tension (with which the New Testament has made us familiar) between the 'already' and the 'not yet'?" Stott then quotes Tertullian, "he also is a man who is about to be one; you have the fruit already in the seed." Later, among others, he quotes T.F. Torrance to the effect that "the potentiality concerned is not that of becoming something else but of becoming what it essentially is." For all of Stott's attempts to find common ground between O'Donovan and MacKay, this sounds decidedly like siding with O'Donovan against MacKay whom he proceeds to say makes him "uncomfortable" with his use of non-personal analogies (material artifacts, clouds, gases, plants and animals).[32]

TOWARDS A UNIFIED POSITION

So why the change in Waltke, Stott, and others from the sixties and early seventies to the eighties and beyond? Part of the answer may be suggested by Mark Galli, responding to Jonathan Dudley's CNN Belief Blog (referenced above), where he claimed that "The reality is that what conservative

31. Stott, *Decisive Issues*, 319–21.

32. Stott, *Decisive Issues*, 319–21, quoting Tertullian in Gorman, *Abortion & the Early Church*, 54–58, and Torrance in the Church of Scotland's Board of Social Responsibility 1985 report to the General Assembly. See also Torrance, *Test-tube Babies* (1984).

Christians now say is the Bible's clear teaching on the matter was not a widespread interpretation until the late 20th century."[33] Dudley, as noted earlier, references the 1968 issue of *Christianity Today* in which Bruce Waltke, argued that "the fetus is not reckoned as a soul." Dudley also notes that the Southern Baptist Convention passed a resolution in 1971 affirming that abortion should be legal, to protect the life of the mother and her emotional life as well.

In response, Galli acknowledges that Dudley is "certainly right about the Southern Baptist Convention at the time." (It has changed its position since then.) But he claims that Dudley has mischaracterized Waltke's views, failing to point out that Waltke also stated that the Old Testament nonetheless "protects the fetus." (This was even before Waltke's change of mind as noted above.)

Dudley also observes that Paul Jewett's article on "The Relation of the Soul to the Fetus" looked at "the theological, historical, psychiatric, and sociological dimensions of the abortion issue" and ends "Abortion will always remain a last recourse, ventured in emergency and burdened with uncertainty."[34] Galli admits that Dudley is "formally right in this regard." With regard to Jewett's conclusion, Galli observes that:

> this sounds to me very much like early apologies for slavery, when some northern Christians imagined slave owners as benevolent masters of an inferior people. Once the horrors of slavery became known and the humanity of African Americans became evident, northern Christians increasingly become *(sic)* single-minded in their opposition to slavery. That has more or less been the history of contemporary evangelicalism regarding abortion. When it was indeed a rare occurrence *(sic)*, most of us could imagine an exception here and there. When it turned into the wholesale slaughter of millions . . . we have naturally become a little less flexible about it.[35]

Galli then points to what he considers to be one of "the finer moments in CT history," the 1973 editorial, referenced in chapter 2, by Harold O.J. Brown, "clearly denouncing *Roe v. Wade*. . . . 'Christians should accustom themselves to the thought that the American state no longer supports, in any meaningful sense, the laws of God, and prepare themselves spiritually

---

33. Stott, *Decisive Issues*, 319–21.
34. Stott, *Decisive Issues*, 319–21.
35. Galli, "'When Evangelicals Were Pro-Choice,'" §5.

for the prospect that it may one day formally repudiate them and turn against those who seek to live by them.'"[36]

Galli is most likely right that when abortion turned into the wholesale slaughter of millions we have naturally become "a little less flexible about it." It is also true, as pointed out earlier, that the 1979 Schaeffer-Koop film series and book, *Whatever Happened to the Human Race?* galvanized evangelicals to join the pro-life movement. Schaeffer used to speak of "co-belligerence" with Catholics and others, and this was definitely a factor in greater evangelical–Catholic cooperation on abortion and other issues. But the change of mind among leading evangelicals of an academic bent had begun before 1979 and seems to have been due, as the next chapter will show, to a greater attention to biblical teaching on the issue, and in particular a revisiting of the Exod 21:22–25 passage.

Discussion Questions

1. What can we learn from R.F.R. Gardner's perspective on abortion as described by Frame on page 56?
2. Reflecting on Hardesty's descriptions of traducianism and creationism (including the referenced scriptural passages), which perspective aligns best with your understanding and biblical reading, and why?
3. Consider the questions presented on page 62: Is induced abortion ever permissible and if so, under what conditions? Can abortion be justified by the principle of tragic moral choice in which one evil is chosen to avoid a greater evil?
4. If the Bible is the key to shifting perspectives towards the value of human life from conception on, how then can we spread this message to Christians and non-Christians alike?

36. Galli, "'When Evangelicals Were Pro-Choice,'" §6.

PART II

Theological: Why Evangelicals Should Be Pro-Life

5

Changing Views

An Interpretive Review
of Exodus 21:22–25

A PARTICULARLY SIGNIFICANT DEVELOPMENT in regard to the interpretation of Exod 21:22–25 was the *Report of the Committee to Study the Matter of Abortion*, submitted to the thirty-eighth General Assembly of the Orthodox Presbyterian Church in 1971 and referenced frequently in subsequent publications. The principal author of the report was John Frame, then associate professor of systematic theology and apologetics at Westminster Theological Seminary in Philadelphia. Frame has reprinted the report as an appendix to his book on *Medical Ethics*.[1]

The report is quite comprehensive, but perhaps most significantly it argues persuasively for a different interpretation of the Exodus passage than what was common at the time. This section of the report begins with the statement that "There is *nothing* in Scripture which even remotely suggests that the unborn child is *anything less than a human person from the moment of conception*" (emphasis original).[2] The one possible exception was what up till then had been considered to be the traditional interpretation of Exod 21:22–25, on which view "the child is given a 'lesser value' than the mother and is therefore regarded as something less than a human person."[3] The report goes on to argue that, even if this interpretation were

1. Frame, *Medical Ethics*, 83–122.
2. "Report of the Committee," 6.
3. "Report of the Committee," 6.

correct, it "does not prove that abortion is ever justified."[4] The passage in question "clearly deals with a case of *accidental* killing. If even such a killing of an unborn child is punishable by a fine, we must surely assume that the *intentional* killing of an unborn child is at least as serious as (in all probability more serious than) the offense in view in verse 22."[5] Among the reasons given is the one Bruce Waltke later admitted to:

> The immediate (*sic*) preceding passage (Ex.21:20f.) ... presents a situation where a master who kills a slave unintentionally ... escapes with no penalty at all! To argue from this passage that slaves are regarded by God as less than human persons would be precarious indeed! To argue from Ex. 21:22–25 that the unborn child is not a person is even less plausible. Doubtless the unborn child, like the slave, had a lesser status in Israelite society than other persons. It cannot be demonstrated, however, that this lesser status was a status of non-personhood. And that is the point at issue.[6]

The report then turns to the adequacy of what was then the usual interpretation and finds it wanting for the following reasons:

> In the first place, the term *yeled* in verse 22 never refers elsewhere to a child lacking recognizable human form, or to one incapable of existing outside the womb. The possibility of such a usage here, as the interpretation in question requires, is still further reduced by the fact that if the writer had wanted to speak of an undeveloped embryo or fetus there may have been other terminology available to him. There was the term *golem* (Psm. 139:16) which *means* "embryo, fetus." But in cases of the death of an unborn child, Scripture regularly designates him, not by *yeled*, not even by *golem*, but by *nefel* (Job 3:16; Psm. 58:8; Eccl. 6:3), "one untimely born." The use of *yeled* in verse 22, therefore, indicates that the child in view is not the product of a miscarriage, as the interpretation in question supposes; at least this is the most natural interpretation in the absence of decisive considerations to the contrary....
>
> Further: the verb *yatza'* in verse 22 ("go out," translated "depart" in KJV) does not in itself suggest the death of the child in question and is ordinarily used to describe normal births (Gen. 25:26, 38:28–30; Job 3:11, 10:18; Jer. 1:5, 20:18). With the possible exception of Num. 12:12, which almost

---

4. "Report of the Committee," 6.
5. "Report of the Committee," 7.
6. "Report of the Committee," 8.

certainly refers to a stillbirth, it never refers to a miscarriage. The Old Testament term normally used for miscarriage and spontaneous abortion, both in humans and in animals, is not *yatza'* but *shakol* (Ex. 23:26; Hos. 9:14; Gen. 31:38; Job 2:10; cf. II Kings 2:19, 21; Mal. 3:11). The most natural interpretation of the phrase *weyatze'u yeladheyha*, therefore, will find in it not an induced miscarriage, not the death of an unborn child, but an induced premature birth, wherein the child is born alive, but ahead of the anticipated time.[7]

After providing further reasons from the text to support this position, the report concludes:

> To summarize the proper interpretation of this passage, we regard the following as an adequate paraphrase: "And if men fight together and hurt a pregnant woman so that her child is born prematurely, yet neither mother or child is harmed, he shall be surely fined, according as the woman's husband shall lay upon him; and he shall pay as the judges determine. But if either mother or child is harmed, then thou shalt give life for life, eye for eye, tooth for tooth, hand for hand, foot for foot, burning for burning, wound for wound, stripe for stripe."[8]

The report was approved after some debate, mainly about whether this was an issue on which the church should advise the civil government (as recommended elsewhere in the report). However, the late Paul Woolley (1902–84), who was then professor of church history at Westminster Seminary, wrote a minority report. He agreed with much of the majority, which he described as "very ably prepared and a very useful document." He indicated general agreement with the exegesis of Exod 21: 22–25 but questioned its relevance to the issue of voluntary induced abortion since the passage "should be translated in such a way as to make it clear that it refers to the premature, induced birth of a viable child."[9] In a strongly worded dissent, Woolley continued:

> A definition of "human person" in a sense appropriate to this context is, therefore, desirable. It is, however, very difficult to secure agreement upon such a definition. This is most ably set forth in sections 14 and 15 of the majority report with much of which sections the undersigned is in agreement.

---

7. "Report of the Committee," 8–9.
8. "Report of the Committee," 9.
9. "Report of the Committee," 22.

> However, the author finds himself compelled to differ with the proposition that a fertilized egg is, from the moment of fertilization, a human person. It may possess the potentiality of becoming a person. But to affirm that it is a person seems a piece of rationalistic folly. It is to be noted that the majority report is too wise to do this. But it affirms that the Christian is under scriptural obligation to act as though this were the case. This is even worse. It is at this point that the Christian is compelled to differ with the majority report. . . .
>
> It, therefore, appears to the author of this minority report that the Church is on the verge of . . . adding additional sins to the scriptural catalogue. That some instances of abortion are sinful is obvious. That they all are is not. Yet, with one minor possible exception, the report of the committee concludes that they are. This is quite illicit.
>
> The report accompanies this by an encouragement of the enforcement of religious principles by state legislation. Setting the feet of the church upon this path may perhaps be expected of people who have not known what it is to live under a denial of religious freedom. But it is a very dangerous course, nevertheless, and the study of history provides plenty of supporting evidence.[10]

Woolley's view that to affirm that a fertilized egg is to be equated with a human person is a "piece of rationalistic folly" seems consistent with much of the prevailing evangelical opinion at the time. However, the report's majority opinion had a significant influence on the gradually changing understanding of other evangelical scholars. For instance, H. Wayne House took a similar line in "Miscarriage or Premature Birth: Additional Thoughts on Exodus 21:22–25."[11] Curt Young, one-time director of the Christian Action Council, writing in *The Least of These*, follows the same basic argument and commends the OPC report as one of the most exhaustive treatments of the subject. He also references John Calvin and the nineteenth century commentators Keil and Delitzsch (evidence that the view was not entirely novel), as well as contemporary (in the 1980s) Old Testament scholars Gleason Archer and Meredith Kline. Jack Cottrell is also mentioned as one among others who on the strength of exegetical evidence "changed their understanding of this passage and adopted the stronger view."[12] Kline argued similarly in "Lex Talionis & the Human Fetus," reprinted in Volume

---

10. "Report of the Committee," 22–23.
11. House, "Miscarriage or Premature Birth," 108–23.
12. Young, *Least of These*, 220.

5 of *The Simon Greenfield Law Review* (1985–86). The then editor of the *Review*, John Warwick Montgomery, in commending Kline's article wrote that it "lays to rest (permanently we trust) the oft-recurring but utterly fallacious argument that Exodus 21:22–25 places a lesser legal value on life in the womb than on adult life."[13] Montgomery went on to reference his own examination of that argument in his book, *Slaughter of the Innocents*.[14] In 1990, R.C. Sproul quoted extensively from the OPC report as reproduced in John Frame's *Medical Ethics*.[15] John Jefferson Davis, in *Evangelical Ethics*, makes no mention of the report, but does reference several of the scholars mentioned above in his advocacy of the same position.[16]

This is not to say that all were convinced. Montgomery's hope that Kline's interpretation "lays to rest" the alternative interpretation, proved to be somewhat premature. For instance, Joe M. Sprinkle takes issue with this interpretation and argues that, "Although one might like to find definite answers to the abortion question from Exod 21:22–25, it is not possible to do so.... Contrary to the exegesis common among certain anti-abortion theologians, the most likely view is that the death of the fetus is to be assumed throughout the entire case."[17] More recently, Wes Granberg-Michaelson, a former General Secretary of the Reformed Church in America, in an article on "The Real Question in the Abortion Debate," states categorically that, "in Exodus 21:22 the injury of a pregnant woman in battle, causing a miscarriage, is subject to a fine, but the death of that woman is punished by death," without any acknowledgement or apparent awareness of alternative interpretations. (Granberg-Michaelson adds that "When Moses is ordered to do a census in Numbers 3:15, not only are pregnant women only counted as one, but children less than one-month old are not counted at all."[18] Are we therefore to conclude that human life, or at least personhood, begins at one month?)

CURRENT POSITION

What, indeed, are we to conclude? Although the OPC's report is unequivocal in its interpretation of this passage, it does equivocate in other areas. While it makes a compelling case for the relevance of such passages as

13. Montgomery, "Editorial."
14. Montgomery, *Slaughter of the Innocents* (1981).
15. Sproul, *Abortion*, 197–98.
16. Davis, *Evangelical Ethics*, 153n82.
17. Sprinkle, "Interpretation of Exod 21:22–25," 233–53.
18. Granberg-Michaelson, "Real Question in the Abortion Debate" §13.

Psalms 51 and 139, as well as Jesus's incarnation and John's leaping in his mother's womb, the report is careful to make qualifications—for instance that Psalm 51 describes the origin of David's sin, not of his life, and that while Jesus' human life began at conception, he had existed from eternity. The conclusion, therefore, is not that we can prove beyond a shadow of a doubt that human life begins at conception, but that we should operate on that assumption. Wooley took issue with this, saying it amounted to imposing extra-biblical standards.

Personally, I think the report was needlessly cautious. Granted, Jesus existed before his conception in his mother's womb, but that is when his *human* life began. As the Dutch theologian Herman Bavinck (1854–1921) put it, "the human nature formed in and out of Mary . . . from the earliest moment of conception was united with, and taken up into, the person of the Son."[19] Throughout church history, Christians have confessed their faith in the Christ who was "conceived by the Holy Spirit and born of the virgin Mary" (Apostles' Creed). The 1563 Heidelberg Catechism, in expounding this creed asks, "How does the holy conception and birth of Christ benefit you?" Answer: "He is our mediator, and with his innocence and perfect holiness he removed from God's sight my sin—mine since I was conceived."[20] Surely the implication is that this benefit began with Christ's conception and that my sin began with my conception, based on Ps 51:5. (The eccentric interpretation that David's mother conceived him by a sinful act is contextually untenable.) Besides as Koop points out: "Biologists seem to have no trouble believing that life begins at the time of fertilization when they talk about lizards, doves, or baboons. . . "[21] How much more the incarnate Son of God!

Elsewhere, Koop quotes a September 1970 editorial about a "quality of life" ethic replacing the traditional "value of life" one:

> Since the old ethic has not been fully displaced it has been necessary to separate the idea of abortion from the idea of killing, which continues to be socially abhorrent. The result has been a curious avoidance of the scientific fact, which everyone really knows, that human life begins at conception and is continuous whether intra—or extra uterine until death. The very considerable semantic gymnastics which are requited to rationalize abortion as anything but the taking of human life would be ludicrous if they were not often put forward under socially

---

19. Bavinck, *Reformed Dogmatics*, 3:291.
20. Heidelberg Catechism, q. 36.
21. Koop, *Memoirs*, 264.

impeccable auspices. It is suggested that this schizophrenic sort of subterfuge is necessary because while a new ethic is being accepted the old one has not yet been rejected.[22]

Likewise, at the first international conference on abortion, "a purely secular group of people said, 'We can find no point in time between the union of sperm and egg and the birth of an infant at which point we can say that this is not a human life.'"[23] It is difficult to think of a purely secular group of people saying this today, but it should not be difficult for evangelical Christians to do so. Thus, the viewpoint presented in the final section of this chapter will inform our continued exploration of the evangelical value of life. Defining the unborn as human, however, is not enough. Pro-lifers, whether evangelical or Catholic, frequently say that the unborn are persons made in the image of God. But what does this mean?

Discussion Questions

1. Reread Exod 21:22-25; what parts stand out to you now in light of what you have read in this chapter?

2. "There is nothing in Scripture which even remotely suggests that the unborn child is anything less than a human person from the moment of conception"—do you agree? Why or why not? How does this statement challenge you?

3. Considering the Hebrew words interpreted and described on page 74-75, does this change your understanding of the passage, and if so, how?

---

22. Koop, *Right to Live*, 46.
23. Koop, *Right to Live*, 43-44.

6

Abortion and the Image of God

As this book goes to press, shockwaves are reverberating throughout much of American media, medical, legal, and political circles, over the decision of the Alabama Supreme Court to find that embryos developed through in vitro fertilization (IVF) are considered to be children under state law, citing the image of God as the the basis of that law. This finding has been described as "bizarre" and as having "potentially drastic consequences."[1] The Alabama legislature moved quickly "to protect [IVF] providers and patients from criminal or civil liability if embryos they create are subsequently damaged or destroyed."[2] Questions have been raised about the relationship between church and state, and the perceived threat of theocracy.

Pro-lifers have mostly applauded the ruling, since they frequently assert that the unborn are created in God's image. But what does this mean? The phrase is seldom defined. This is not to say that theologians have made no attempts to define what the divine image means, but those attempts very seldom take into account the status of embryos or fetuses. This chapter reviews some of that literature and makes some connections between the evangelical understanding of the image of God and the pro-life position established in the previous chapter.

Our starting point is Gen 1:26-28 (ESV):

> Then God said, "Let us make man in our image, after our likeness. And let them have dominion over the fish of the sea and

---

1. Ziegler, "The twisted irony," §2, 3.
2. Hennessy-Fiske, "Alabama lawmakers pass legislation," §1.

over the birds of the heavens and over the livestock over all the earth and over every creeping thing that creeps on the earth."

> So God created man in his own image,
> in the image of God he created him;
> male and female he created them.

> And God blessed them. And God said to them, "Be fruitful and multiply and fill the earth and subdue it, and have dominion over the fish of the sea and over the birds of the heavens and over every living thing that moves on the earth."

Some of the early church fathers distinguished between "image" and "likeness." One view was that "image" referred to the body while "likeness" referred to the soul. Another distinguished between the intellectual ("image") and moral ("likeness") qualities of the soul. Later, in the Counter-Reformation period, Robert Bellarmine (1542–1621) postulated that "image" was a designation of mankind's natural gifts with "likeness" referring to supernaturally added gifts. The likeness of God was thus lost in the fall, but the image remains. This view has largely remained in Roman Catholic theology as a distinction between the *dona naturalia* and the *dona supernaturalia*.[3] Protestants, however, generally understand the divine image and likeness to be interchangeable terms (Gen 5:1; 9:6; 1 Cor 11:7; Col 3:10; Jas 3:9), or as John Murray puts it, "the words 'according to our likeness' are so co-ordinated with the words 'in our image' that we should take them as explanatory or definitive rather than supplementary."[4] But there the agreement seems to end.

One difficulty is that there are passages of Scripture which suggest that, even after the fall, humanity still possesses the image of God, while there are others that imply that it was lost and needs to be restored in Christ, the perfect image of God (Col 1:15). Some (mostly Lutherans) have tended to emphasize the qualities of knowledge, righteousness and holiness that were lost in the fall. Others (mostly Reformed) have distinguished between a broader (Gen 9:6; 1 Cor 11:7; 15:49; James 3:9) and narrower sense (Eph 4:24; Col 3:10) of the divine image. The narrower sense consists of what was lost in the fall and is regained in Christ, while the broader sense consists of those qualities that separate humans from animals: creativity, intelligence, language, a sense of right and wrong, a spiritual as well as a moral nature.

Further differences arise related to whether the dominion over the rest of creation granted to Adam and Eve in Gen 1:28 is part of the divine image

3. Berkhof, *Systematic Theology*, 208.
4. Murray, *Collected Writings*, 34.

or a consequence of it, and over whether *in* the image of God could be translated *as* the image of God or if only Christ *is* the image of God and we reflect that image to the extent that we are in Christ.[5] (In support of translating *as* the image of God, it has been pointed out that kings, and sometimes priests, were called the image of their god in Egypt and Babylonia/Assyria. The biblical concept of the *imago Dei* was thus an account of human culture such that all of humanity, not just kings and priests, are called in a functional, even a missional sense, to be "God's representatives and agents in the world, granted authorized power to share in God's rule or administration of the earth's resources and creatures")[6] Some insist that the image extends to our physical bodies, others that it applies only to our spiritual nature. One thing that is clear from Gen 1:27 is that both male and female equally share in the divine image. Karl Barth deduced from this that the image consists of our differentiation and relationships as male and female.[7] Given all these various views (and there are others), no wonder some writers simply say after referencing the image of God, "whatever that means!"

The difficulty with these definitions, especially the "broader" one, is that they can apply only in a potential sense to the unborn. Then there are those who are born with severe physical and mental disabilities so that their intelligence and other capacities such as creativity and language, even awareness of surroundings and the ability to control movements, are significantly compromised. Thus, Peter Singer could say, as he famously wrote in the July 1983 issue of *Pediatrics*:

> Once the religious mumbo jumbo surrounding the term "human" has been stripped away, we may continue to see normal members of our species as possessing greater capacities of rationality, self-consciousness, communication, and so on, than members of any other species; but we will not regard as sacrosanct the life of each and every member of our species, no matter how limited its capacity for intelligent and even conscious life may be. If we compare a severely defective human infant with a nonhuman animal, a dog or a pig, for example, we often find the nonhuman to have superior capacities, both actual and potential, for rationality, self-consciousness, communication, and anything else that can plausibly be considered morally significant. Only the fact that the defective infant is a member of the species Homo Sapiens leads it to be treated

---

5. Hughes, *True Image*, 3–9.
6. Middleton, *Liberating Image*, 27.
7. Barth, *Church Dogmatics*, 3:184–87.

differently from the dog or pig. Species membership alone, however, is not morally relevant...[8]

Sometimes pro-lifers like to point out that children born with significant handicaps can still have meaningful lives and accomplishments. For instance, *Whatever Happened to the Human Race?* features a young man born without arms who nevertheless grew up to become a theological student. There are other examples one could mention, but this, it seems to me, is to play into the hands of those like Singer who determine worth on the basis of accomplishments, whereas there are those to whom just breathing and digesting food that is spoon-fed to them over a lengthy period of time is all they can accomplish in a day. (Early in our marriage, my wife worked with such children at the Lynch Home in suburban Philadelphia.) Then, there are those at the other end of life who are in a comatose or so-called "vegetative" state. Their value resides not in their accomplishments or abilities, but in the fact that they are human beings who by that definition alone are made in the image of God. As John Frame has stated, "the image of God embraces everything that is human."[9]

I was encouraged to find a similar approach in a sermon by the late Timothy (Tim) Keller (1950–2023), founding pastor of Redeemer Presbyterian Church in New York. He references Singer and acknowledges that he would be right if human (and animal) worth is to be based on capacities rather than the image of God. Keller's description of a secular understanding of human worth sounds suspiciously like the broader definition of the image of God in traditional Reformed theology:

> The reason a human being deserves rights, protections, is because they have the capacity, they have the capacity to reason, they have self-consciousness, they have the capacity to make moral choices, they know right from wrong, they have the

---

8. Singer, "Sanctity of Life?," 129.

9. Frame, *Systematic Theology*, 796. Frame says this in the context of the fact that men and women share equally in the divine image. Prior to that, he discussed the image in terms of the biblical offices, or in his language: control (kingly office), authority (prophetic office) and presence (priestly office). His terminology may be original, but his descriptions do not differ much from traditional Reformed views of the broader image. He also takes the view that the image extends to our bodies, not in the sense that God has a body, (although Christ did take one on and God is sometimes described metaphorically as having ears etc.), but in that "Man's physical strength is a major aspect of his power to subdue the earth and take dominion of it" (787). However, given that some animals, such as elephants, have greater strength than humans, it is difficult to see how this sets us apart as those made in the image of God. But in terms of the later discussion on body-soul unity it may make some sense to say the body is part of who we are as image bearers.

capacity for what some professors call "preferences." And because they have reason, and the ability to make choices and they have preferences, they are moral agents and therefore they are capable, or they are worthy of protection; they have rights.

But Keller goes on to say, "there is a huge problem with this whole approach, the secular approach to rights. . . .":

> Because the life in the womb doesn't have capacities. They can't make choices. They can't reason, they can't tell right from wrong, they can't live apart from the mother. They don't have capacities and therefore they don't have rights. . . . But if that's true let's keep something in mind. Born infants don't have those capacities either. They can't reason; they have no preferences yet. They can't make moral choices and neither can senile old people. And neither can very mentally handicapped people. And therefore . . . if you believe abortion is alright, then you really can't protect the rights of any of these other people because their rights are based on capacities. . . .
>
> If you don't believe in the image of God, what are you going to ground human rights in? You're going to ground it in capacities. If you can't protect the unborn you can't protect the newly born, you can't protect the mentally handicapped, you can't protect old people. It's a fact. It's logical.
>
> If you go back to the beginning of the Christian church, here's what you saw: they came into a Greco-Roman world that also grounded the idea of rights on capacities. Aristotle said that some races are too emotional, they couldn't reason because they didn't have the capacity for higher reason. They deserved to be slaves. And in the Greco-Roman world you had slavery, you had terrible poverty, you had lots of abortion (it was very dangerous then, but it still happened), you had infanticide, it was perfectly legal, especially girl babies died of exposure. And you took the elderly and sick poor people and just let them die. And that was all legal; and it was done all the time.
>
> But the Christians came along and they believed in the Imago Dei. And because they believed in the image of God . . . well, first of all, they were totally against abortion, from the beginning. Because if you believe in the image of God you have to be. You have to be. You know, I mean, if human life is good, then nascent human life has got to be good. But they were also against infanticide. They were not one issue people. They cared for the poor. They cared for women. . . . They were champions of women; they were champions of orphans; they were champions

of the weak; they were champions of the poor. And they were against abortion. And they put the rest of the culture to shame because of their belief in the sanctity of life.

So that eventually, the whole Western world adopted the idea of the image of God. Because when you believe in the image of God, the circle of protected life expands. But if you don't believe in the image of God, if you only believe in capacities or some other trumped up approach to why we believe in human rights, the circle will continually contract. It will get smaller and smaller, and fewer and fewer people will be protected. You see how incredible, crucial, important, the image of God teaching is.[10]

As far as I can tell, Keller did not actually define what the image of God consists of, but he made clear (by implication, at least) what it is not and why it is important to understand that it does not consist of what he calls capacities (or abilities).

SONSHIP

Frame and others also point out that the image of God is closely linked to the concept of sonship. Thus, for instance, Herman Bavinck: "As a human being a man is the son, the likeness, or offspring of God (Gen 1:26; 9:6; Luke 3:38; Acts 17:28; 1 Cor 11:7; Jas 3:9)."[11] Adam was created as a son of God. That familial likeness has been marred, just as has the *imago Dei*, but not entirely lost.[12] It is fully restored in Christ, the perfect Son of God, and since the biblical concept of sonship includes inheritance (Rom 8:15-17), it also extends to redeemed daughters of God. One of the best definitions of the divine image, in my view, is provided by Curt Young in his book *The Least of These:*

> No other creature can claim the distinction of being created in the image of God. Because of that, human beings possess a

---

10. Bayly, "Tim Keller addresses abortion," §4.
11. Bavinck, *In the Beginning,* 186.
12. Carmen Imes, author of *Being God's Image* (2023) believes that "the *imago Dei* cannot be marred, lost, or destroyed in any way. An illustration that might be helpful is that of an estranged relationship between parent and child. The estrangement cannot change the basic identity of the child as a child of the *imago Dei,* the glory is lost at the fall, but not human identity. This is why the NT can speak of our conformity to the image of the Son. Jesus is the image of God, like all of us, but unlike all of us his life is congruent with his identity. He shows us how to faithfully live out the consequences of that identity. As we do so, we share in his glory" (personal correspondence, November 2, 2022).

> special dignity and value. The core truth . . . is fairly simple. We were created to be God's children.
>
> In Hebrew, the phrases "created in the image of" and "made in the likeness of" connote a filial . . . relationship. When God created man, He intended a creature who would relate to him and know Him as "Father which art in heaven." He also intended a creature who would resemble Him in holiness as a child resembles His parents. . . .
>
> Luke's genealogy of Jesus (Luke 3) also clarifies what it means to be made in the image of God. Everyone is the son of someone until we finally reach Adam, who is described as the son of God. This description is true because Adam was created in God's image.[13]

In Gen 1:26 God said, "Let *us* make mankind in our image" (emphasis added). It has been argued that he was thereby addressing his "heavenly court" of angelic beings. A parallel situation is found in Isa 6:8a where the Lord, surrounded by seraphim, asks "Whom shall I send? And who will go for us?" Likewise in Ps 8:5, we are told that man was created a little lower than the angels (ESV) or heavenly beings (NIV), where the Hebrew word in question is *elohim*, "the usual Hebrew word for God in the Old Testament," which "can also refer, depending on the context, to false gods or the angelic host (other 'divine' beings)." Thus, according to J. Richard Middleton, "It is thus possible that not only Psalm 8 but also Gen 1:27 and 9:6 may be comparing humans not just to the creator but to the divine/heavenly realm in general, thus suggesting a broad analogy between the cosmic king, his royal angel courtiers, and his earthy human vice-regent."[14] However, while Ps 8:5 tells us we were made a little lower than the heavenly beings, it does not say we were made in their image and likeness.

An alternative (and preferable, in my view) interpretation that goes back at least as far as Augustine is that Gen 1:26 is an early hint of the Trinity, a doctrine made explicit in the New Testament. An objection to this view is that the original readers of Genesis would not have understood it as referring to the Trinity.[15] Be that as it may, the Trinity is already present in Genesis 1 as God (the Father) creates the heavens and the earth by speaking his Word (vv. 3–24; identified as the Son of God in John 1:1 and Heb 1:1) and "the Spirit of God was hovering over the face of the waters" (v. 1). Thus in 1:26, God in his very being as a triune God defines the nature of relationship and he created humans to be uniquely in relationship with

---

13. Young, *Least of These*, 34–35.
14. Middleton, *Liberating Image*, 59.
15. Imes, *Being God's Image*, 35.

him and with one another as brothers and sisters in Christ. "God lives in, and is blessed in, relationships. He is blessed in the togetherness of Father, Son and Holy Spirit. If he made us in His image, then we, too, are made for relationship."[16] This relationship, both with God and with one another was broken by sin, but the potential still exists for renewal of those relationships in Christ. That potential exists for all who confess their sins and turn to Christ in faith and repentance. It also exists for those not yet born with the capacity to exercise such faith, as well as the handicapped who through no fault of their own bear in their bodies and minds the consequences of our human fallenness. To be clear, this is not to say that the unborn have the *potential* to be in the image of God; they *are* in the image of God with the potential of developing a relationship with their Creator who is also their heavenly Father. Besides, they also have the potential of being God's representatives in ruling over the rest of creation as in Gen 1:28, imperfectly in this life and perfectly in the renewed creation that awaits.

THE ORIGIN OF THE SOUL

At this point in our discussion, we will revisit the issue of when the soul enters the body (as discussed in chapter 3). Being made in the image of God and the union of the body and the soul are fundamentally related issues. Thomas Aquinas, as we saw, put this merger at forty days gestation for boys and eighty for girls. More recently, Gardner put it even later at the moment of birth. He notes that: "Embryologists now believe that anything up to half of all conceptions end in spontaneous miscarriage, usually very early on. . . . If all these early miscarried fetuses possess souls, the majority of 'humans' in heaven will have never even reached the stage of being organized into fetal human shape." With regard to *in vitro* conceptions, Gardner asks, "does this cell-mass, which is not the result of human intercourse, which has never occupied a human body since fertilization, possess a soul? When the experiment is over and the material is tipped down the sluice, is a soul being destroyed? To think so requires in my judgement a trivialization of the meaning of the soul."[17]

---

16. Macleod, *Faith to Live By*, 97. There has been considerable debate in recent years on the so-called "Social Trinity." Advocates of this view have been accused of remaking the Trinity in our image and manipulating it to justify endless social agendas (see e.g., Barrett, *Simply Trinity*, 2021). But it is not necessary to endorse all that comes under the label of "Social Trinity" to recognize that the concept of relationship is central to who the triune God is and that this is reflected in his human image bearers.

17. Gardner, *Abortion*, 123–24.

When the British government was debating the 1990 Human Fertilization and Embryo Act that allowed for embryo research up to the fourteenth day following conception, one argument made was that some cells of the blastocyst following implantation form the embryo while others form the placenta. The implication is that since the cells making up the embryo cannot be distinguished from those making up the placenta, these cells are disposable, but a counter-point is that "this is not a good argument for embryonic tissue experimentation since we don't know enough to distinguish between body and non-body tissue at the blastocyst stage and cannot obtain it without a threat to the embryo."[18] This pushes the argument back from the embryo to the status of the blastocyst formed by implantation, which is thought to take place eight or nine days after conception.

We have already been introduced to the two principal views on the origin of the soul, creationism and traducianism (chapter 4). According to Louis Berkhof, creationism "is more in harmony with Scripture . . . since the Bible throughout represents body and soul as having different origins, Ecc 12:7; Isa 42:5; Zech 12:1; Heb 12:9; cf. Num 16:22."[19] On the other hand, Bruce Waltke makes a compelling case for traducianism as the way in which the image of God (which he defines as being spiritual, rational and moral) is passed down seminally from generation to generation.[20] Creationism means that the soul could be created at any point in pre-natal development (although, as we saw, Hardesty pointed out that "most recent creationists have dated 'ensoulment' from conception"),[21] whereas traducianism generally ensures that it begins at conception.

Another related issue is whether humans are made up of body and soul (dichotomy as in e.g., Louis Berkhof)[22] or body, soul, and spirit, (trichotomy, as in e.g., James Boice).[23] Trichotomists base their argument on such passages as 1 Thess 5:23 and Heb 4:12. The soul is generally understood as the animating part of human life, with the spirit being the spiritual nature that connects to God. Dichotomists say that spirit and soul are used interchangeably in Scripture (along with mind, heart etc.) and there is no basis for distinguishing between them.

---

18. Richards, email correspondence, June 24, 2020.

19. Berkhof, *Manual of Christian Doctrine*, 125. Berkhof is less emphatic in his *Systematic Theology*, but still indicates a slight preference for creationism (199–201).

20. Waltke, "Old Testament Teaching," 10–13.

21. Hardesty, "When Does Life Begin?," 43.

22. Berkhof, *Systematic Theology*, 192–93.

23. Boice, *Genesis*, 1:97–98.

More recent scholarship has suggested that these distinctions between creationists and traducianists and dichotomists and trichotomists are not really necessary or biblical. To quote Frame again:

> The notion of soul and body as metaphysical components of human nature goes back to Greek philosophy. In Plato's thought, the body is material and emotional, the soul intellectual and immaterial. . . . Descartes, in the seventeenth century, also saw the soul as purely immaterial and the body as purely material and this dichotomy led to the mind-body problem in early modern thought. . . .
>
> Given this history, it is not surprising that Christian thinkers sometimes confused Plato's and Descartes's ideas with those of Scripture. But the Bible never says that the soul is entirely immaterial or that the body is purely material. Nor does it say that the soul must gain control of the body. Rather, in Scripture soul and body equally describe the whole person. Both, therefore are equally fallen, both equally in need of redemption.
>
> If we reject the idea that the terms spirit, soul, and body designate metaphysical components of the human person, then we can avoid taking sides on two theological controversies: dichotomy-trichotomy and creationism-traducianism. . . .
>
> As we have seen, the soul is not a separate part of a person. It is rather the person himself seen from a particular aspect. So there is no particular period in time when the body exists without a soul, nor any point in time when a soul is added to a soulless body. The soul exists from conception, for it is an aspect of the total person, who exists from conception.[24]

---

24. Frame, *Systematic Theology*, 800–1. The obvious question arises: what happens when soul and body are separated at death? Frame's answer is, "To say that a person's spirit or soul is in heaven is simply to say that he, the person is there. And to say that his body is in the grave is to say that he, the person, is there. . . . How can a person be in two places at once? I don't know. But that's the way Scripture presents the matter" (800). A more satisfactory answer is given by John Murray: "Even in death the body that is laid in the tomb is not simply a body. More properly, it is the person as respects the body. It is the person who is buried or laid in the tomb. How eloquent of this is the usage respecting our Lord. He was buried. He rose from the dead. In reference to Jesus the angel said: 'Come see the place where he lay'. . . .In and during death the person is identified with the dissolved material entity" (*Collected Writings*, 2:16). At the same time, "There is an aspect to (human) identity distinct from the body" that is "endowed with properties and qualities in virtue of which it is not subject to the disillusion which the body undergoes at death. This entity retains its identity and differentiating character after death. More properly, in virtue of spirit the person retains his identity, and continues to exist and be active in a realm and mode of existence consonant with and adapted to the disembodied state" (20-21). It is of this that the apostle Paul speaks when he writes of willingness to "to be absent from the body, and to be present with the Lord"

Here Frame is less cautious than in the OPC report, where he said only that we should operate on the *assumption* that human life begins at conception.

Frame's academic background is in analytic philosophy. The late Scottish theologian T. F. Torrance's (1913–2007) was in classics and general philosophy, but he developed an increasing interest in the philosophy of science, for which he became best known. One of the lesser-known examples of his attempts to integrate the natural sciences with theology is in a lecture he gave at a scientific symposium in Milan on "Medicine and the Unborn Child," later published in booklet form as *The Soul and Person of the Unborn Child*. He notes that "I was happy that my presentation in Milan met with a good reception from scientists and with only a little critical reaction from theologians."[25] Here, Torrance applies the scientific insights of Michael Polanyi, Albert Einstein, and a few lesser-known scientists to the medical science and theology of the unborn child. He makes relatively few biblical references, but these include the conception of Jesus, and John the Baptist's leaping in his mother's womb as supporting evidence.[26] He also

---

(2 Cor 5:8, KJV). Although Murray elsewhere (*Collected Writings*, 2:39) says that it is not possible to exclude the body "from the scope of that which defines (man's) identity, the image of God," he also states as a continuation of the earlier quote (p. 21) that "All that we are most characteristically as beings created in the image of God, has its seat, unity, and abiding meaning in this entity" (i.e., the spirit).

Murray does use the language of a "metaphysical" distinction between body and soul or spirit (20), while at the same time making it clear that he rejects the Platonic view Frame criticizes of the body as the prison-house of the soul and of the soul being incarcerated in the body (14). In his chapter on "Trichotomy," (where he implicitly defends dichotomy, which Frame says is unnecessary) he rejects "the tripartite construction," but adds, "We need not suppose, however, that soul and spirit are always synonymous and are interchangeable. . . . There is no hard and fast line of distinction. But it would appear that, in certain cases, 'spirit' views the principle of life as derived from God and returning to him at death, whereas 'soul' views the animating entity as life constituted in a body, and finds its prototype in Genesis 2:7" (32).

There we read that the Lord God formed Adam from the dust of the ground "and breathed into his nostrils the breath of life, and the man became a living being" (Gen 2:7). However, while this may be a prototype for the distinction between soul and body, it is also the case that prior to the breath of life, there was no animation at all. This was a unique occurrence and not in the sense that Gardner implies (*Abortion*, 126), a model for future human lives in terms of when the soul enters the already animated body. While soul and body are separated at death, as a consequence of human fallenness, there is no suggestion anywhere in Scripture that they are separated in time at the beginning of life.

25. Torrance, *Soul and Person*, 2.

26. Precisely how much the unborn John knew about the coming of Jesus as the Messiah when he leapt for joy at the sound of Mary's greeting in Luke 1:44 is an open question on which opinions differ. What can be said for certain, based on Luke 1:15

states that "The concept of *person* actually derives from the Christian doctrine of God as the Holy Trinity, that is of God as an eternal communion of three hypostatic realities or Persons, who are who and what they are in their eternal coinherent relations with one another." Applying this concept of personhood in a secondary sense to human persons, "It is in the light of this personal and inter-personal nature of human beings that we may rightly think of man and woman as imaging or reflecting God the Creator." Further application to the status of the unborn child means that:

> the essential nature of the person and of the inter-personal structure of human beings. . . bears upon . . . the fact that that their personal being begins with their conception and is nourished through interpersonal relations with the mother. The human embryo as an embodied soul and a besouled body, is already *in parvo* a personal being, begotten to reflect the Personal Being of God, and indeed as a creaturely spirit to resonate with the Holy Spirit of God. By spirit is not meant that man was created as body, soul, and spirit, but rather that as spirit, man as body of his soul and soul of his body, is given a transcendental determination of his human condition before God.[27]

This is supported by the scientific evidence of the "*personal* growth of the baby in the womb through *interpersonal relation* between the baby and his/her mother."[28]

Torrance credits Einstein with "his recovery of a biblical Jewish-Christian, way of thinking of man as body and soul, which I like to think of as *body of his soul and soul of his body*. It was that unitary, non-dualist, way of thinking . . . that governed his science, and determined for him the fundamental interrelation between relativity and quantum theory." Torrance believes:

> it is that non–dualist unitary way of thinking that we need to recover in our understanding of the conception and life of the unborn child. Jews and Christians believe that God created the universe, matter and mind alike, out of nothing—that is the all-important notion of contingent rational order upon which all our modern empirical and theoretical science rests. My concern here is with the fact that this applies in crucial ways to human being. In creating human being, body and soul . . . God did not give being

---

is that "in some mysterious manner, incapable of further analysis, the Holy Spirit was already actively present in the soul of Elizabeth's child" (Hendriksen, *Luke*, 97).

27. Torrance, *Soul and Person*, 17–18.
28. Torrance, *Soul and Person*, 16.

and life to the body by itself, or to the soul by itself, but to man/woman in whom body and soul form a living unity. The human being is an integrated whole, not as soul and body, but an embodied soul and a besouled body, as Karl Barth once expressed it.[29]

An important consequence of this is that "it is extremely important, in family and medical care, to give attention to the fact that that the embryonic child, male or female, is an embodied soul and a besouled body, and is such already, not a potential, but an incipient person."[30]

Here, Torrance references Christ's conception in the womb of the Virgin Mary and suggests that this is what led the early church to reject both abortion and feticide as well as infanticide. "Full consideration of this was given by St. Gregory of Nyssa, who held that since human being is one, consisting of soul and body, soul and body come into being at the same moment in the womb. And with other Greek theologians he held that each soul is created by God along with the body and grows together with the body from the moment of conception."[31]

Torrance nevertheless acknowledges that "difficult circumstances arise in which exception is called for in the prohibition of abortion." He does not specify what these exceptions are but laments the fact that "in a society rife with moral relativism, the exception tends to be turned into a rule, which would then be another and serious form of what Michael Polanyi called 'moral inversion', one which, alas, is now very widespread."[32]

As one of Torrance's many admirers has said, he was not one to use a single-syllable sentence, when a multi-syllable one would do! This can make him difficult to follow. He was, nonetheless, at times capable of a more popular approach when needed. In 2000, Torrance spoke at a luncheon of Presbyterians Pro-Life at the General Assembly of the Presbyterian Church USA. His talk was subsequently published as *The Being and Nature of the Unborn Child*. Although he draws quite considerably on the booklet discussed above, he does so in a much less technical, more popular and devotional style. There is also more explicit biblical reference, especially to the incarnation of Christ. Torrance notes that "leading theologians in the early Church, followed by John Calvin at the Reformation, rightly traced the root of our redemption, not only to the death and resurrection of Christ, but to his very conception and birth of the Virgin Mary." The virgin birth:

> is crucial to our grasp of the nature and status in Christ's eyes of the unborn child. The Son of God became a human being for us

---

29. Torrance, *Soul and Person*, 17–18.
30. Torrance, *Soul and Person*, 7–8.
31. Torrance, *Soul and Person*, 9.
32. Torrance, *Soul and Person*, 9.

in the womb of the Virgin Mary. . . . He became what we are. . . . In becoming a human being for us, he also became an embryo for the sake of all embryos, and for our Christian understanding of the being, nature and status in God's eyes of the unborn child. So to take no thought, or no proper thought, for the unborn child is to have no proper thought of Jesus himself as our Lord and Savior or to appreciate his relation as the incarnate Creator to every human being.[33]

Torrance also speaks movingly of our Lord's tears over Jerusalem, comparing the holocaust of the destruction of Jerusalem over which Jesus wept to the "fearful holocaust of millions and millions of Jews in our time. But what of the abortions of unborn children that have taken place and continue to take place throughout the world, even in 'Christian' countries? Is that not the most incredible holocaust being perpetrated even now, in counties where people have heard and believe the Gospel and . . . profess to follow the Lord Jesus."[34]

There is no concession here to the need for abortion in certain circumstances, and Torrance also does not hesitate to say that abortion is an act of murder and a grave sin against the Lord Jesus. I question the usefulness of this language, especially the Holocaust comparison, in public debate. Indeed, many more unborn children have been killed than Jews during the second world war, but it is understandable that Jewish leaders would take offense at the comparison. Abortion as it is legally practiced today is a relatively brief procedure in a sterile environment. Whatever short-term physical pain might be experienced by the mother and perhaps by the child—at which stage of fetal development this takes place is disputed—it does not compare with the years of torture and deprivation experienced by holocaust survivors. Some women undoubtedly experience long-term emotional pain, as has been pointed out, but this does not appear to be the case with all, and again, the comparison is questionable.[35] However, if in this popular lecture Torrance tended more to hyperbole, his passionate advocacy for the rights of the unborn as image bearers of God is certainly welcome, coming from one of the leading theologians of the twentieth century (and in to the twenty-first) who was respected in the widest of theological circles.

Frame and Torrance come (or came) at the theological enterprise in quite different ways, not least in their respective doctrines of Scripture. On this, I side decidedly with Frame rather than Torrance. However, I believe that in this instance, while approaching the subject of human personhood

33. Torrance, *Being and Nature*, 4.

34. Torrance, *Being and Nature*, 6.

35. See Biesel and Lipton-Lubet, "Appropriating Auschwitz," for a critical discussion of how this frequently used analogy is perceived.

and the divine image from different perspectives, they complement one another. I am deeply indebted to them both.

The positions of both Frame and Torrance have widespread implications for our consideration of the value of human life. In the next chapter, I look at some related implications of what it means to be made in the image of God.

Discussion Questions

1. What do you consider to be the differences, if any, between image and likeness?

2. If those born with severe physical or mental disabilities are made in the image of God, how does this affect our understanding of what that phrase means?

3. If worth isn't based on accomplishments and abilities, what is it based on? How would you defend your position?

4. What, in your opinion, is the difference between soul and spirit? Is it helpful to differentiate them? Why or why not?

5. In what ways do Frame's and Torrance's positions complement one another?

7

Some Related Implications of Life in the Image of God

WHEN THE LATE DONALD MACLEOD (1940–2023) was editor of the Free Church of Scotland's *Monthly Record* (now simply *The Record*), he wrote an editorial on "Embryo Research: Where Are the Fences?" in September 1984. He began: "Thirty years ago the issues involved in embryo research were of little concern to Christians. Such practices as artificial insemination, in vitro fertilisation, embryo transplantation and surrogate motherhood were safely confined to the pages of science fiction. Today they are matters of urgent practical concern." Despite the potential benefits of such research, Macleod noted mounting concern from an ethical point of view. The central issue, he wrote, is "What kind of entity is the embryo?" In discussing this question Macleod noted that there are those, including some Christians who "make much of the fact that many fertilised ova are wasted naturally." He quoted Dr R. J. Berry, then Professor of Genetics at University College, London, writing in the April 1984 issue of the *Journal of the Christian Medical Fellowship*. According to Berry, "Knowing as we do that in the natural process large numbers of fertilised ova are lost before implantation, it is morally unconvincing to claim absolute inviolability for an organism with which nature itself is so prodigal."

Macleod responded, "It is difficult to follow this argument. Nature is prodigal with more than embryos, Earthquakes, floods, storms and famines take a massive toll of human life. Are we to emulate them? In the last analysis, indeed nature is prodigal with all of us. One hundred percent of us are eventually 'wasted'.... The odds against any fertilised ovum surviving to maturity are indeed high. But surely the logical inference is not that we should side with the forces of destruction but that we should lend the embryo every possible support."[1]

This was in 1984. Macleod subsequently lectured on the subject in at least Vancouver, Canada, and Melbourne, Australia. However, he since changed his mind and argued for the position he once found "difficult to follow."[2] His later view is more in line with that of R. F. R. Gardner, as quoted in the previous chapter: "Human eggs have now been successfully fertilized outside the body.... As I write I look at the microphotograph of one of these embryos, grown in culture.... When the experiment is over and the material is tipped down the sluice, is a soul being destroyed? To think so requires in my judgement a trivialization of the meaning of the soul."[3]

We have already dealt with the issue of the soul as an aspect of the human person from the beginning. Interestingly, Gardner seems to agree with this and quotes James Barr to the effect that "Man does not have a soul, he is a soul."[4] However, Gardner does not draw the logical conclusion that the human embryo is a human soul, and neither does Macleod, representing something of a reversal of the general trend we have observed: a movement towards greater recognition of the sanctity of life from conception on. Does it matter?

If what is concluded in the previous chapter about the image of God is correct, it matters a great deal how the human embryo is treated. This applies not only to embryo research but to other issues related to reproductive medicine and human life, some of which will now be alluded to.

CONTRACEPTION

The official Roman Catholic position is that artificial contraception "contravene(s) natural law in several ways. First, it separate(s) sex from its natural purpose of procreation, Second, by attempting to prevent the formation of a new human life, it challenge(s) God's authority as the Creator. Finally, it treat(s) human life as something to be prevented rather than valued."[5] Until well into the twentieth century, this was also the evangelical

---

1. Macleod, "Embryo Research," 183.

2. See, Macleod, "Highlands are now a Labour-free zone," §7; a position confirmed by personal correspondence.

3. Gardner, *Abortion*, 124.

4. Gardner, *Abortion*, 124.

5. Williams, *Defenders of the Unborn*, 16.

Protestant consensus. There can be little doubt that the ready availability of artificial contraception in the 1960s contributed to the growth of sexual promiscuity and thus of abortion. However, to place contraception on the same level as abortion is to minimize the significance of the development of a unique human being that takes place at conception, and thus can undermine the case against abortion in public debate.

The US Supreme Court's 1965 *Griswold v. Connecticut* decision reversed an 1879 Connecticut law that had included a prohibition of "any drug, medicinal article or instrument for the purpose of preventing conception."[6] *Griswold* found in the fourteenth amendment to the US Constitution's "due process clause" an unstated right to privacy that permitted *married couples* to make their own decisions about the use of contraception. The Connecticut law had echoed a 1973 federal anti-obscenity statute (still technically in effect) that, among other things, prohibited the "selling, giving away or mailing any article or medicines for the prevention of conception or for causing abortion."[7] This linking of contraception with abortion would soon lead to the same right to privacy found in *Griswold* being used in *Roe v. Wade* to legalize abortion.

Marvin Olasky comments: "The Catholic Church had fought for decades to link contraception and abortion, and abortion advocates now linked the two."[8] Again, the linking of the two in the nineteenth century:

> had three eventual twentieth-century effects. The linkage made it seem to many liberals that the debate in such matters was about sex, not killing. It weakened the nineteenth-century connection of feminism and pro-life views: When a new wave of feminism rolled in during the 1960s the battle for contraception (seen as a liberating instrument for women) turned into a campaign for abortion. Finally, court decisions on contraceptives and privacy—first within marriage and then between unmarried men and women—paved the way to *Roe v. Wade*, which some portrayed as one more case about liberty rather than an assault on the voiceless.[9]

That said, as regards to artificial means of contraception as distinct from Vatican-approved (at least since Pope Paul VI's 1968 encyclical, *Humanae Vitae*) "natural family planning,"[10] Dr. Chris Richards points out,

---

6. Stacey, "How Griswold v. Connecticut Led to Legal Contraception," §3.
7. Olasky and Savas, *Story of Abortion in America*, 259.
8. Olasky and Savas, *Story of Abortion in America*, 310.
9. Olasky and Savas, *Story of Abortion in America*, 260.
10. Armstrong, "Defense of Natural Family Planning," §5.

"After over fifty years of oral contraception, it has become clear that the use of artificial sex hormones to separate procreation from sexual union is difficult to do effectively and precisely." Richards continues, "The so-called 'morning-after pill', taken to prevent the progress of pregnancy after unprotected intercourse, works in a number of ways including the prevention of implantation, and, therefore, the killing of the early embryo. Some contraceptives including the progesterone-only pill and the intra-uterine device (IUD) may sometimes work in the same way."[11]

One effect of the 2010 Affordable Care Act, signed into law by then President Obama, was that employers were obliged to provide employees with access to the whole range of contraceptives, including the morning after pill. This led some evangelical educational institutions to join with the (Roman Catholic) Little Sisters of the Poor in filing suit, finally receiving relief from the Supreme Court.[12] However, more recently, this oft-stated concern about the morning after pill has been challenged by the Food and Drug Administration (FDA) in the US. In a December 23, 2022 posting, the FDA stated that the current science supports a conclusion that Plan B One-Step (i.e., the morning after pill) "works by inhibiting or delaying ovulation and the midcycle hormonal changes. The evidence also supports the conclusion that there is no direct effect on fertilization or implantation."[13]

It is not clear what exactly the supporting "current science" is. Randy Alcorn's *Does the Birth Control Pill cause abortions?* (eight edition, revised 2007) contains numerous quotes from medical sources, including the FDA, asserting that not only the morning after pill, but various others that come under the general heading of "the Pill" can on occasion prevent implantation of the blastocyst in the uterus after conception has taken place.[14] The FDA does not specify what current science refutes this earlier position. Short of further clarification, the non-scientist is left either to take the FDA at its word or to heed Richards's caution that when there is doubt about how a particular contraceptive works, "In such circumstances we must surely follow the biblical principle of avoiding any potential threat to life (see, for example, rules about building a safe parapet in Deuteronomy 22:8)."[15]

---

11. Richards, "When Does Life Begin?," 13–14.

12. See Cline, "Standing for the Sanctity of Life," 60–62.

13. U.S. Food and Drug Administration, "Plan B One-Step (1.5 mg levonorgestrel) Information," §12.

14. See e.g., a statement by a former FDA president in Alcorn, *Does the Birth Control Pill cause abortions?*, 32.

15. Richards, "When Does Life Begin?," 14.

Richards offers some helpful advice also on in-vitro fertilization and miscarriage, which I simply quote here with kind permission.[16]

In-vitro fertilisation

The practice of IVF necessarily involves the laboratory handling of the early embryo after fertilisation. Inevitably this exposes the embryo to dangers that are quite different from those of a natural conception. Parents (and laboratory staff) must be at peace about this moral responsibility. The risk becomes greater if, as is often done, more than one embryo is produced either for immediate implantation or, with even greater risk, for long-term storage. Many contemporary Christian ethicists advocate minimising risk by limiting the use of IVF to married couples where only one (or perhaps two) embryos are created and implanted at each attempt.

Miscarriage

The reality of life in the womb from conception has a profound influence on how we understand miscarriage, even at a very early stage of pregnancy. Very little is known about the natural survival rates of the early embryo on the journey from the site of fertilisation in the fallopian tubes to implantation in the womb. This is a time of 'radio silence' when the mother has no symptoms of pregnancy and laboratory tests cannot detect the embryo. The moment that implantation occurs, a hormone is released from the early placental tissue. This gives rise to the first symptoms of pregnancy such as nausea and a missed period, as well as a positive pregnancy test. No doubt some embryos die before implantation without the mother knowing about it. God is gracious in hiding from us some of our losses.

Yet once a woman is aware of being pregnant and then goes on to miscarry, we can expect a grieving process. This is the experience of many, and in itself is a testimony to the reality of life in the womb. Such grieving is not simply for the disappointment of dashed hopes of raising a child nor an emotional response to a changing hormone environment, although both may contribute. Because life starts at conception, there has been an actual loss of a life. Such knowledge helps to make sense of

---

16. Richards, "When Does Life Begin?," 14–15.

the strong emotions of grief that many miscarrying parents feel. It also helps those supporting them to take their loss seriously and share lovingly in their grief.

EMBRYO RESEARCH

We now return to the vexed subject of embryonic stem cell research. David VanDrunen writes in *Bioethics and the Christian Life*:

> One consideration is that many of the touted benefits of stem-cell research are entirely speculative at this point. The beneficial results are easy to imagine, and it is plausible to think that they are attainable. But researchers and their advocates have made plenty of big promises in the past that never materialized. Experimenting on and destroying image bearers, and spending billions of dollars in the process are all the more hard to justify given the uncertainty of the evidence that the benefits will be realized. Another consideration is that embryos are not the only source of stem cells that may prove beneficial for medical research. Umbilical cord blood, for example, is a fertile and rather plentiful source of stem cells that has already been put to good medical use (for example, umbilical cord blood stem cells can be used in place of donated adult bone marrow for bone marrow transplants, with better results under certain circumstances). Perhaps even more significantly scientists have recently developed methods of attaining pluripotent stem cells without destroying embryos in the process. These developments may make embryonic stem-cell research unnecessary altogether.[17]

VanDrunen's book was published in 2009. Three years later, British scientist John Gurdon and Shinya Yamanaka of Japan shared the 2012 Nobel Prize in physiology or medicine for experiments separated by almost fifty years. Gurdon's research led to the cloning, first of a frog in 1962, then "Dolly the Sheep" in 1997, and other mammals. In 2006 and 2007:

> Yamanaka extended this insight by turning back time on individual cells from mice and humans. . . . Any cell, he found, could be reverted to an early embryonic state.
>
> These "induced" embryonic cells behave much like the ethically contentious stem cells gleaned from human embryos. Like embryonic cells, they can be grown into many other types of tissues but without having to destroy any embryos.

---

17. VanDrunen, *Bioethics and the Christian Life*, 168.

SOME RELATED IMPLICATIONS OF LIFE IN THE IMAGE OF GOD 101

> The breakthrough offered hope that someday skin cells could be harvested from a patient, sent back in time to an embryonic state, and then grown into replacement tissues such as heart muscle or nerve cells.
>
> A huge global research effort is working to develop pluripotent stem cells, as they're called, into treatments for heart disease, some forms of blindness, Parkinson's disease and many other disorders. . . .
>
> But the therapeutic potential of induced stem cells remains in question. Some experiments show that the cells may form tumors, prompting skepticism that they will ever be safe enough to treat heart disease, Parkinson's disease and many other conditions in which specific cells of the body break down.
>
> However, the Nobel committee in its citation said the dual "groundbreaking discoveries have completely changed our view of development and cellular specialization. Textbooks have been rewritten and new research fields have been established. By reprogramming human cells, scientists have created new opportunities to study diseases and develop methods for diagnosis and therapy."[18]

But is it still accurate to say, as VanDrunnen does, that "many of the touted benefits of stem-cell research are entirely speculative at this point"? According to the Society for the Protection of Unborn Children (SPUC) in the UK, it was in 2018: "To date, embryonic stem cells have not been used successfully to treat any illness. Yet the use of adult stem cells and stem cells from umbilical cords and placentas continues to prove effective in treating disease. Uncontrolled growth of embryonic stem cells can produce tumours. The use of stem cells from adults, placentas or umbilical cords may therefore not only be an ethical alternative, but also a safer and more successful one." An inquiry as to the current accuracy of this statement elicited the following reply from John Smeaton, Chief executive of SPUC on April 14, 2021:

> We are updating our website, having consulted an international expert in this field. Our new posting will read as follows:
>
> **To date, embryonic stem cells have not been used successfully to treat any illness.** Yet, the use of adult stem cells and blood stem cells from umbilical cords continues to prove effective in treating disease. Uncontrolled growth of embryonic stem cells produces tumours. The use of stem cells from adult tissues and umbilical

---

18. Vastag, "Nobel Prize for medicine," §7–17.

cords are therefore not only an ethical alternative, but also a safer and effective one.[19]

Further, according to SPUC: "Stem cells from umbilical cord and placental blood have been used successfully to treat leukaemia and anaemia patients. Adult stem cells have also been used successfully in trials to treat patients with severe heart failure. In the future stem cells could be used to replace cells or tissues destroyed by Parkinson's disease, heart disease, spinal cord injury, diabetes and Alzheimer's disease."[20]

A June 8, 2019 post from the Mayo Clinic reads:

> **Adult cells altered to have properties of embryonic stem cells (induced pluripotent stem cells).** Scientists have successfully transformed regular adult cells into stem cells using genetic reprogramming. By altering the genes in the adult cells, researchers can reprogram the cells to act similarly to embryonic stem cells.
>
> This new technique may allow researchers to use reprogrammed cells instead of embryonic stem cells and prevent immune system rejection of the new stem cells. However, scientists don't yet know whether using altered adult cells will cause adverse effects in humans.
>
> Researchers have been able to take regular connective tissue cells and reprogram them to become functional heart cells. In studies, animals with heart failure that were injected with new heart cells experienced improved heart function and survival time.[21]

The appeal of embryonic stem cells is their greater versatility than adult stem cells, but as indicated above, researchers can now reprogram adult cells to act similarly to embryonic stem cells. Further, Yanamaka's research has produced induced embryonic cells without destroying human embryos in the process, although progress appears to have been slow because of the risk of developing tumors.

For those who have no ethical issues with creating and destroying human embryos, all this information may be moot, but for those of us who do, it is vitally important. Besides, the fact remains that while embryonic stem cell research continues to be just that (research), lives have been saved and diseases treated by other means such as umbilical cord and adult stem cells. It follows that human beings made in the image of God

---

19. Smeaton, email correspondence, April 14, 2021.
20. SPUC, "Stem Cell Research" §3.
21. Mayo Clinic, "Stem Cells," §18–20.

should actively work to further science and medical research without the potential of destroying that human life.

VACCINATIONS

The COVID-19 pandemic brought to the fore ethical concerns that some evangelicals and others have about vaccinations. Several of these concerns are beyond the purpose of this book and some of those are based on conspiracy theories.[22] Others merit more serious consideration, including a relatively few rare side-effects of which I have some personal knowledge, and which I agree have been underreported, and downplayed by governments and "mainstream" media.

Nevertheless, our present concern is with the undeniable fact that certain vaccines have been developed using human cell lines from aborted fetuses. Before discussing the ones developed specifically for COVID-19, it might be helpful to take note of the development of the rubella (German measles) vaccine.[23] Between 1962 and 1965 a rubella epidemic started in Europe and spread to the United States. Although a relatively mild disease, children who contracted it *in utero* were at risk of being born blind, deaf, mentally disabled, or with heart and other defects. As a result, it is estimated that in the United States alone, 5,000 pregnant mothers chose to abort, and some 6,000 others had miscarriages. Meanwhile, some 20,000 babies were born with one or more of the disabilities listed. A vaccine was developed by Dr Maurice Hilleman and licensed in 1969, but it was later replaced by vaccines derived from Dr Stanley Plotkin and his team's more controversial RA 27/3 strain of rubella virus which did not receive government approval for another decade. They were, however, tested in the UK and Europe, as well as the US and other parts of the world before that, and the vaccines were found to have less side effects than Hilleman's. Since then, they have been used to cure or eradicate a number of other diseases.

Part of the controversy surrounding Plotkin's research was due to the fact that it involved fetal cell lines from women who had chosen to terminate their pregnancies because of their fear of rubella and its potential consequences, but no babies were aborted then or since for the specific purpose

---

22. At the height of the pandemic, Dr. Jeffrey Barrows of the Christian Medical Dental Association was quoted as saying, "There are various wild conspiracy theories that are out there that are just completely off the wall. I don't know how they even get started. And I don't even want to repeat them because they're just so wild." (Smietana, "COVID vaccines are moral to use.")

23. The above information is based on the YouTube video, "Stanley Plotkin—The Future of Immunization," September 20, 2022.

of developing vaccines. Because of this, the Vatican approved the use of the rubella and other vaccines not only for the benefit of the recipients, but as a means of demonstrating neighbor love to others. The same reasoning was later applied to COVID-19 vaccines, although preference was given to those (Pfizer and Moderna) that were not developed from fetal cell lines, though they were tested using these cell lines. The AstraZeneca vaccine developed at the University of Oxford uses cells originally derived from tissue from a fetus aborted in the 1970s. The cell line used in the Johnson and Johnson vaccine was derived from an elective abortion that took place in 1985.

A letter from the chairmen of the Committee on Doctrine and the Committee on Pro-Life Activities in the United States (USCCB) states that:

> the USCCB, in collaboration with other organizations working to protect human life, has been engaged in a campaign advocating for the development of a vaccine for COVID-19 that has no link to abortion. . . . Both the congregation for the Doctrine of the Faith and the Pontifical Academy for Life emphasize the positive moral obligation to do good and in so doing to distance oneself as much as possible from the immoral act of another party such as abortion in order to avoid cooperation with someone else's evil actions and to avoid general scandal, which could happen if one's own actions were perceived by other people to ignore or to minimize the evil of the action.

However, while "love of neighbor should lead us to avoid giving scandal . . . we cannot omit fulfilling serious obligations such as the prevention of deadly infection and the spread of contagion among those who are vulnerable just to avoid the appearance of scandal." There are "different degrees of responsibility in cooperating with the evil actions of others. . . . As for the moral responsibility of those who are merely the recipients of the vaccines. . . a serious health danger could justify use of a vaccine which was developed using cell lines of illicit origin, while keeping in mind that everyone has the duty to make known their disagreement and to ask that their healthcare system make other types of vaccines available."[24]

The example of the rubella vaccine is given and then the bishops go on to consider the relative merits or otherwise of the vaccines that became available for COVID-19. Finally, a caution is issued against becoming complacent about recognizing an action as evil and not doing all one can to oppose that evil, or of giving the impression to others that one does not regard the action as evil. "With this in mind, we should be on guard so that the new COVID-19 vaccines do not desensitize us or weaken our

---

24. USCBS, "Moral Considerations," §5.

determination to oppose the evil of abortion itself and the subsequent use of fetal cells in research."[25]

The evangelical world does not have a similarly authoritative voice, but the various voices that have spoken out are in more or less agreement with the Catholic position:

> The Southern Baptist Ethics & Religious Liberty Commission also said receiving the vaccine is morally permissible. The Center for Bioethics and Human Dignity (CBHD) housed at Trinity International University, suggests that the way to right the past wrong is to advocate for ethically derived cell lines or better production methods for vaccines. The Christian Medical and Dental Association [not limited to but including Evangelicals] joined three other pro-life associations in calling researchers to develop ethical COVID-19 vaccines free of abortive cells in any stage of development.[26]

Albert Mohler, president of the Southern Baptist Theological Seminary and one of the most outspokenly conservative and pro-life evangelical leaders in America, has stressed the remoteness of the original cell lines being used and also the responsibility of neighbor love. "There are third parties—people who cannot take the vaccine or do not yet have access to it that could still be infected by those who refuse to take the vaccine," he wrote. "The general principle of the common good comes down to benevolence, love, care for others, laying down personal priorities for the service of others. Christians thinking about the issue of the vaccine must weigh this key biblical principle as part of their thinking."[27] Mohler also recommended that taking the vaccine should be voluntary, not mandated.[28]

There are valid reasons, such as vulnerability to serious allergic reactions, for avoiding vaccinations. Nevertheless, those who oppose them because of concerns about their connection with past abortions should at least take into account that this is a complex issue and that they are going against the advice of not only "mainstream society" but of religious leadership, evangelical as well as Catholic (among others). Non-evangelical Protestants are much less likely to be concerned about the ethical issues raised here. Of course, all human life, not just human life in embryo form, is made in the image of God. Evangelicals are called to protect all human life and to love our neighbors. It is these conflicting values that many in Christian

25. USCBS, "Moral Considerations," §5.
26. Randall, "3 Bioethical Questions," §15.
27. Mohler, "Vaccines and the Christian Worldview," §23.
28. Mohler, "Vaccines and the Christian Worldview," §26.

leadership have been considering when taking a position on the use of vaccinations that have been developed using fetal cell lines.

CAPITAL PUNISHMENT

Moving on from medically related complications of the image of God, a charge sometimes brought against pro-lifers is that they are inconsistent in opposing abortion but supporting the death penalty for murderers. The late talk show host Larry King (1933–2021) apparently said he "would give no credence to pro-life supporters until they became more consistent in their two positions."[29] In response, first of all, it can be said that not all pro-lifers support capital punishment. The 1995 *Catechism of the Catholic Church* allows for capital punishment "in cases of extreme gravity."[30] However, in August 2018, Pope Francis "building on the teaching of Pope St. John Paul II and Pope Benedict XVI," changed this to:

> Recourse to the death penalty on the part of legitimate authority, following a fair trial, was long considered an appropriate response to the gravity of certain crimes and an acceptable, albeit extreme means of safeguarding the common good.
>
> Today, however, there is an increasing awareness that the dignity of the person is not lost even after the commission of very serious crimes. In addition, a new understanding has emerged of the significance of penal sanctions imposed by the state.
>
> Lastly, more effective systems of detention have been developed, which ensure the due protection of citizens but, at the same time, do not definitively deprive the guilty of the possibility of redemption.
>
> Consequently, the Church teaches, in the light of the Gospel, that "the death penalty is inadmissible because it is an attack on the inviolability and dignity of the person" and she works with determination for its abolition worldwide.[31]

The words in quotation marks are taken from an address given by Pope Francis on 11 October, 2017. In that address, he also said: "Here we are not in any way contradicting past teaching, for the defence of the dignity of human life from the first moment of conception to natural death has been taught by the Church consistently and authoritatively. Yet the harmonious development of doctrine demands that we cease to defend

---

29. Sproul, *Abortion*, 111.
30. *Catechism of the Catholic Church*, Section Two, Article 5, §2266.
31. *Catechism of the Catholic Church*, Second Edition, Section Two, Article 5, §2267.

arguments that now appear clearly contrary to the new understanding of Christian truth."[32] Thus Roman Catholic pro-lifers cannot be charged with inconsistency on this issue.

Mainline Protestants would be in general agreement with the new Catholic position. There are other branches of Christianity such as Mennonites who oppose all forms of violence, including war and capital punishment as well as abortion. This was arguably the position of the early church before Augustine introduced the concept of just war in the fifth century. However, most evangelicals have historically supported the death penalty on the basis of such passages as Gen 9:6: "Whoever sheds the blood of man, by man shall his blood be shed: for God made man in his own image," and Rom 13:4b, "For he [the governing authority or ruler] is the servant of God, an avenger who carries out God's wrath on the wrongdoer" (ESV).

It is debatable whether Gen 9:6 is a mandate for capital punishment or just a statement of fact. It could be argued that it is poetry in the nature of a proverb, like, "Those who live by the sword die by the sword."[33] After all, God himself did not demand capital punishment for Cain, the first murderer, but instead placed a mark of protection on him (Gen 4:15). See also Moses (Ex 2:11–15) who became a leader of God's people. Perhaps capital punishment is permissible in certain extreme circumstances, but not necessarily required. But those who insist it *is* a mandate point out that it is precisely because we are made in the image of God that murder of another human is in effect an attack on God himself and that is why the only appropriate punishment is to take the life of the murderer. As R.C. Sproul (1939–2017) put it:

> The biblical view of the overarching sanctity of life is the same principle that leads people to be both anti-abortion and pro-capital punishment. The biblical reason for the institution of capital punishment is that murder is an intolerable violation of the sanctity of life. The murderer who willfully and maliciously takes another person's life thereby forfeits his right to his own life. . . . Advocates of capital punishment cannot rightly be charged with espousing a principle of injustice. If a murderer is killed as a punishment for killing someone else, the punishment is perfectly just. The penalty may not be merciful, but it is not unjust. An injustice would be dealt the murderer if his penalty were more severe than his crime.[34]

32. Daniels, "Death Penalty Opponents," §11.
33. Smedes, *Mere Morality*, 121.
34. Sproul, *Abortion*, 112.

The late John Murray (1898–1975) is another who took the view that Gen 9:6 mandated capital punishment, although he acknowledged that the Hebrew text could be read differently. He based this on corroborating evidence such as Rom 13:4 which grants the civil magistrate the "power of the sword" which implies "express warrant for the infliction of death." Paul, who penned Romans 13, in his defense before Festus said in Acts 25: 11, "If therefore I do wrong and have committed anything worthy of death, I refuse not to die" (KJV). In other words, Paul recognized that there were conditions that warranted the death penalty. Capital punishment was mandated in the Old Testament for sins other than murder (e.g., adultery). These other reasons tied to the Mosaic law fall away in the New Testament, but it remains for murder since "only in this case is the divine image in man pleaded as the reason for the penalty afflicted; assault upon man's life is an assault upon the life of God." "There is no suspension of the fact that man was made in the image of God; it is as true today as it was in the days of Noah."[35]

It is interesting that in his book *Principles of Conduct*, Murray included a chapter on "The Sanctity of Life" that was almost entirely devoted to the subject of capital punishment. There is no mention of abortion or related issues. The book was published in 1957, based on lectures given at Fuller Theological Seminary in 1955. It is not that abortion was not an issue then, but it had not yet become legal, and it seems that it simply was not on the radar of evangelical theologians like Murray.

His view of capital punishment can be considered the standard position of most evangelicals in the 1950s. It was also the standard in most Western nations, something that is no longer the case. There has been a corresponding shift in views among evangelicals so that the issue is at least debatable. Charles Colson, founder of Prison Fellowship in 1976 was once a strong opponent of the death penalty, but later changed his mind for extreme cases. His initial reason for opposition was because as a lawyer he had witnesses the flawed justice system in the United States. Others have also pointed out that it is disproportionately biased against African Americans and other minorities. Colson said that his previous views were:

> very much influenced by Deuteronomy 17 and the need for two eyewitnesses. I questioned whether the circumstantial evidence on which most are sentenced today in fact meets this standard of proof. I still have grave reservations about the way in which capital punishment is administered in the United States, and I still do question whether it is a deterrent. (In fact, I remain convinced it's not a general deterrent.) But my views

---

35. Murray, *Principles of Conduct*, 112.

have changed, and I now favor capital punishment, at least in principle, but only in extreme cases when no other punishment can satisfy the demands of justice.[36]

My point has not been to engage in the capital punishment debate, but to point out that the traditional evangelical position, still held by some in the pro-life movement, of supporting the death penalty for murder is not necessarily inconsistent with a strong pro-life ethic. In fact, it is based on the same principle that humans are made in the image of God and therefore life is sacred—deserving of protection and justice.

Discussion Questions

1. How convincing is the author's view of embryo research?
2. Are there some contraceptives that are more moral than others? How does one identify the rightness of an option? When does the line between contraception and abortion blur?
3. Considering vaccinations, what is one's responsibility in identifying vaccines that are created ethically? Are there alternatives? How does one navigate this concern?
4. What are the similarities and differences between capital punishment and abortion? Can one be for capital punishment and anti-abortion?

---

36. Colson, "Why I Support Capital Punishment," §3.

PART III

Practical: Mainstream Society and the Evangelical Pro-Life Position

8

"Adoption, Not Abortion"

HAVING, I TRUST, ARRIVED AT an unambiguously pro-life position, I now turn to consider why pro-life arguments do not always resonate with society at large as we might expect and hope for, beginning with the slogan "adoption, not abortion." I explore why adoption does not appear to so many women to be the obvious alternative to abortion that it is presented as by pro-lifers. In the next chapter, after reviewing some of the backlash to the overturning of *Roe v. Wade*, I profile a few mercy ministries as the appropriate response. A final chapter answers the question as why legislative solutions alone are not the answer. First, though, abortion and adoption.

In ancient Rome of biblical times, adoption was practiced largely for the benefit of the adoptive parents among the upper classes, especially senators. Childless couples needed a son to inherit their estate, and so the choice of an adopted son was very important, although girls were also sometimes adopted but had no inheritance rights. Several of Rome's emperors, most famously Augustus Caesar, came to power through adoption.

The New Testament understanding of adoption is vastly different. Unworthy sinners with nothing to commend them become children of God through adoption and gain the right to call God "Abba" (Father), becoming heirs of God and joint-heirs with Christ (Rom 8:15-17). This was made possible by the atoning death and resurrection of the "natural" Son of God, such that, as the late J. I. Packer (1926–2020) put it, the message of the New Testament can be summarized as *"adoption through propitiation,"*[1] propitiation

---

1. Packer, *Knowing God*, 194.

being the removal of God's wrath against sinners that was absorbed by Christ on the cross. No wonder Packer could also say, "Adoption is the highest privilege the gospel offers."[2] For this reason, by way of analogy, the adoption of children, especially in Christian circles, is understood to be a blessing to the adoptive child, as well as to the parents. It is frequently promoted as a better alternative to abortion, as indeed it is.

Because of the high abortion rate in Western society, there are relatively few babies available for adoption and many couples turn to international adoptions, especially from underprivileged nations where unwanted babies, especially those with various special needs, are abandoned to orphanages by their birth mothers. For instance, following the fall of communism in Romania, world attention was drawn to the desperate situation in the orphanages there and a movement began in the West to adopt some of the children in these orphanages. China and Haiti have also become favorite nations in which to seek adoptive children. In some cases, the children are abandoned simply because the parents cannot afford another child. In China's case, the one-child policy that was in effect from 1979 to 2015 was a factor. (This became a two-child policy in 2015, then a three-child one in 2021.)[3]

In *Adopted for Life: The Priority of Adoption for Christian Families and Churches*, Russell Moore argues that adoption should be a Christian calling and mission. He begins by relating his and his wife's experience of adopting their oldest two sons from a Russian orphanage where they were "lying in excrement and vomit, covered in blisters and flies."[4] The Moores subsequently had children born "the natural way," and an important point made in the book is that "'Adopted' Is a Past-Tense Verb."[5] In other words, adoptive parents who also have biological children must resist the temptation to think or speak of their "adopted" versus "natural" children. All siblings are equally their parents' children, equally deserving of their love and attention.

Another option for adoptive parents is to adopt older children who are in foster care. It is to this that the controversial race relations activist, Michelle Higgins, was referring at an Urbana conference, when she said, "We can wipe out the adoption crisis tomorrow. But we're too busy arguing to have abortion banned. We're too busy arguing to defund Planned Parenthood."[6] However, such adoptions are not always as straightforward

---

2. Packer, *Knowing God*, 186.

3. Crossing Borders, "China's One Child Policy."

4. Moore, *Adopted for Life*, 12.

5. Moore, *Adopted for Life*, 193. "'Adopted' Is a Past-Tense Verb" is the title of a chapter.

6. Quoted in Tisby, *Color of Compromise*, 183; Cf. "Michelle Higgins—Urbana 15." Tisby slightly misquotes Higgins, without affecting her main point.

as Higgins suggested. As Frederica Mathewes-Green has pointed out, most recently in 2013:

> It is true that 90% of children in foster care will never be adopted. This is because [they] are not available to be adopted; the biological parents have not relinquished their parental rights. Foster care is not a baby store where couples can go and pick out the child they like best. For those 90% of the kids in the public welfare system, caseworkers are still hoping to reconstitute the biological family, a goal called "family preservation." The reluctance to terminate the rights of even abusive parents can "turn adoptable two-year-olds into ravaged and virtually unadoptable seven-year-olds," says Olasky.
>
> That minority children wait at all is partly due to official resistance to allowing them to be placed in white families.[7]

As indicated in the above quote, there has been a movement among adoption agencies in recent years to place black or aboriginal children in the families of the same ethnic background. Adoption of such children by Caucasian parents has come to be thought of as "cultural imperialism." The same charge has been made of international adoptions.

An added complication for at least some Christian adoptive parents is the increasing requirement, by some adoption agencies and the state of Oregon, not only to be pro-choice on abortion, but to "respect, accept and support" the "sexual orientation, gender identity [and] gender expression" of the child they intend to adopt.[8]

Coming to the subject of adoption as an alternative to abortion, the popular slogan "adoption, not abortion" seems an obvious and compassionate one, but again the issues are not as straightforward as at first appears. Consider this from a brief but hard-hitting chapter, based on available research, in Gabrielle Blair's *Ejaculate Responsibly*, titled "Adoption is Not an Alternative to Abortion":

> The vast majority of those interested in relinquishing their child for adoption *never seriously considered abortion*. And for those denied access to abortion, 91 percent still won't choose adoption. Related, the adoption rate today for those denied abortion is the same as the pre-*Roe* rate. . . .
>
> Adoption is held up as an easy fix for abortion. . . . Simply sacrifice your life for nine months, go through the gruelling

---

7. Mathewes-Green. *Real Choices*, 87. Cf. Olasky, "War on Adoption," 38–44.
8. Johnson, "Christians Must Take Children to Transgender Procedures," §3.

process of child birth, and you can smoothly do the heroic act of "giving up" the child for adoption....

As a culture, we're beginning to understand that this narrative is deeply flawed....

Though it's not commonly talked about, one of the biggest reasons pregnant women aren't interested in adoption is because relinquishing a baby can be a traumatic experience. In Ann Fessler's book *The Girls Who Went Away: The Hidden History of Women Who Surrendered Children for Adoption in the Decades Before Roe v. Wade,* women describe worrying every single day of their lives about the baby they were pressured/forced to relinquish and never feeling relief about the experience. One woman who had relinquished a child and then later had an abortion said that people who claim the abortion trauma is anywhere near as bad as the trauma of relinquishment have no idea what they're talking about.[9]

Again, R.F.R. Gardner quotes an American psychiatrist, Dr Rosen:

No one in the technical literature has stressed the heartlessness, the cruelty and the sadism that the pregnant woman so frequently senses—perhaps correctly, perhaps mistakenly—when the physician, minister, or lawyer suggests to her that she carry the child to term and hand it over, never to see it again, to someone else to rear. They object to 'farming the child out for adoption' and maintain '... Do you think I could give away my baby after carrying it for nine months?... A hundred years ago you could take babies away from slaves... You can't do that now! And you can't turn me into the kind of animal that would give my baby away.'[10]

Writing in 1973, but still relevant today, Gardner also says, "Adoption does not, unfortunately, guarantee that for the child all will be well. That the child born out of wedlock has no more than a 50% chance of growing up into a well-adjusted adult, whether adopted or brought up by his mother, is the judgement of Alexina McWhinnie, who has done a retrospective study of fifty-two adults in South-East Scotland who were adopted as children."[11] Reasons for successful or unsuccessful adoptions are then given, including the strength or otherwise of the marriage relationship, the support level of the entire family, whether the child is adopted out of love for children or to

9. Blair, *Ejaculate Responsibly*, 104.
10. Gardner, *Abortion: The Personal Dilemma*, 175.
11. Gardner, *Abortion: The Personal Dilemma*, 189.

meet a need in the adoptive parents, and whether or not comparisons are made with any biological children in the family.

If the above quotes come across as extreme and one-sided, Frederica Mathewes-Green is much more positive about adoption, but nevertheless in a chapter titled "Adoption: Grief and Grace," reports that in the summer of 1993, she:

> sent a survey to almost two thousand pregnancy care center directors, asking them to rank-order a list of possible problems a client might report. Respondents were asked to rate each item twice, indicating how frequently it occurred and how difficult it was to solve.
>
> Surprisingly, the same item rose to the top of both lists: adoption. The problem most frequently encountered when a woman was having difficulty continuing a pregnancy, the center directors said, was that "Adoption appears too difficult (practically or emotionally)." The same entry was rated the hardest to solve....
>
> The difficulty lies in helping the woman to consider the possibility, getting past the emotional hurdles and practical worries involved, without leading her to feel that the counselors are only using her to get to her child.[12]

More recently, in the arguments leading up to the reversal of *Roe v. Wade*, Justice Amy Coney Barrett, herself an adoptive parent, set off a firestorm of criticism by questioning why women could not simply choose adoption over abortion. One of several responses was an opinion piece in *The New York Times*, titled, "I Was Adopted. I Know the Trauma It Can Inflict." The author, Elizabeth Spiers, wrote that she was "floored" by Coney Barrett's suggestion. She:

> may not realize it, but what she is suggesting is that women don't need access to abortion because they can simply go do a thing that is infinitely more difficult, expensive, dangerous and potentially traumatic than terminating a pregnancy during its early stages.
>
> As an adoptive mother herself, Justice Barrett should have some inkling of the complexities of adoption and the toll it can inflict on children, as well as birth mothers. But she speaks as if adoption is some kind of idyllic fairy tale...[13]

---

12. Mathewes-Green, *Real Choices*, 83.
13. Spiers, "I Was Adopted" §2–3.

Matthewes-Green discusses the anti-adoption arguments of the pro-choice lobby, including referencing a 1993 article by Marvin Olasky called "The War on Adoption":

> Olasky believes that "three strategic needs of the pro-abortion mindset underlie the war on Adoption." The first is the need to paint the child as the property of its mother, so that in disposing of it her emotional needs come first. Second, the superiority of the two-parent family must be denied, so secure adoptive couples are presented as exploiters of helpless pregnant women. Third, happy adoption stories are a piercing reminder to post-abortion women struggling to stay connected with her (*sic*) choice. Unhappy adoption stories, on the other hand, can give her the kind of company that misery loves most.[14]

Mathewes-Green discusses the pros and cons of open adoption, where birth mothers are able to maintain varying degrees of connection with their children. She comes down firmly on the side of "the older system," noting that, "Though it now strikes many as cruel, closed adoption was actually intended to protect the best interests of all parties, including the birthmother. It was assumed that giving up a baby was terribly hard, and the brisker the separation the better: the less she had to remember, the less she would feel haunted."[15]

Russell Moore shows more openness to open adoption:

> Obviously, the secrecy and shame related to closed adoptions in generations past aren't fitting for a Christian ethic, but such aspects are almost never the case today. A relatively open adoption might be the best option for you. It could be entirely appropriate for you to keep in touch with a birth mother or grandparents via cards, letters, and photographs as the child grows up, when this is possible. Such contact honors the birth mother—an honor that is due, especially, in an age when she could easily have aborted the child—and adopting parents have nothing to fear from giving such honor where it is due.[16]

"Nothing to fear from giving such honor where it is due" may strike some as a little naïve. How does one determine when "such honor is due"? Complications can arise for the child who is conscious of a dual loyalty, especially if the birth mother is unnecessarily intrusive. However, it seems to

---

14. Mathewes-Green, *Real Choices*, 85. Cf. *Olasky*, "War on Adoption," 38–44. Olasky expands on this in chapter 29 (pp. 235–42) of *Story of Abortion in America*.

15. Mathewes-Green, *Real Choices*, 88–89.

16. Moore, *Adopted for Life*, 119–20.

me that whatever the advantages of closed adoptions, anything that makes it more palatable for a woman to choose adoption over abortion should be prioritized. I well remember, many years ago, when my wife and I attended a seminar provided by a Christian adoption agency. The organizers made it abundantly clear that their priority was not to find the best adoptive option for us, but to do what was best for the birth mother, whose choice was paramount. Perhaps that is as it should be.

Lest it appear that I am unnecessarily negative about adoption, let me hasten to add that the elder of our two sons (now an adult with children of his own) was adopted as a dearly beloved older child. However, I am not unaware of the challenges and sometimes heartache that adoption brings adoptive parents and children alike. Genetics play an important part in an adoptive child's makeup, as do early life experiences in the case of an older adopted child, and while with God all things are possible, no amount of loving nurture can by itself counteract this. I am decidedly pro-adoption and anti-abortion, but I believe that the pro-life "adoption, not abortion" slogan is often used without sufficient attention to the potential hardships involved and the pressure this brings to bear on birth parents, as compared with what at the time seems like the easier choice of abortion. I remember seeing a Facebook post stating that abortion is more ethical than adoption, since the pain of abortion is passing, but that of adoption is life-long. Such a view may be challenged, but the fact is that it exists and needs to be taken into account. Especially we who call ourselves evangelical Christians need to demonstrate greater sensitivity and compassion than is communicated by mere sloganeering.

Discussion Questions

1. How might the "adoption, not abortion" slogan be revised to seem more compassionate and understanding?
2. In your opinion, does adoption seem like a good alternative to abortion? How would you respond to someone who took the opposing view?
3. What are some of the challenges associated with adoption?

9

Evangelicals and Abortion in a Post-*Roe* World

IN HIS WIDELY DISCUSSED BOOK, *The Benedict Option*, Rod Dreher urges Christians to accept that "the culture war as we knew it is over. The so-called value voters—social and religious conservatives—have been defeated and are being swept to the political margins."[1] Dreher was writing during the Trump presidency, but before the emergence (or at least the prominence) of Christian Nationalism and before the reversal of *Roe v. Wade* which pro-lifers hailed as an answer to almost half a century of prayer. However, one only need consider the public reaction to *Roe*'s reversal, not to mention the changing sexual mores in terms of homosexual and transgender rights, to see that Dreher is right. (Dreher went from evangelical to Catholic to Eastern Orthodox, so he cannot properly be considered an evangelical. In April 2022, his wife served him with divorce papers and he moved to Hungary, which obviously tarnishes his reputation, but this does not affect the validity of what he wrote in *The Benedict Option*.[2] A friend suggested a better option for me might have been James Davidson Hunter's *To Change the World* [2010], which takes the position that rather than trying to change the world by political action, the church is most effective by simply being a "faithful presence" in society.[3] I can agree with much of

---

1. Dreher, *Benedict Option*, 79.
2. Dreher, "No One Gets Out of Here Unbroken."
3. Hunter, *To Change the World* (2010).

what Hunter has written, and disagree with some of Dreher's views, but I am sticking with the above quote from Dreher.)

Leaving aside the political turmoil caused by the *Dobbs* decision, with (most) Republicans and Democrats facing off against each other in Congress and in state legislatures, some states limiting abortion rights (which are often then challenged in court), others expanding them; the general result, according to polls, appears to have been a diminished trust in the Supreme Court which has come to be perceived as extreme.[4] As noted previously, a federal judge in Washington, DC, has suggested that the Supreme Court's ruling in *Dobbs* is only limited to the fourteenth amendment of the Constitution, but the thirteenth amendment which outlawed slavery might still grant a federal right to abortion.[5]

The internet frequently posts studies by "experts" claiming to debunk anti-abortion "myths," including the one that abortion can be psychologically damaging for women.[6] Comedians have had fun mocking the anti-abortion movement.[7] State imposed restrictions, such as Texas's six week "heart-beat law" have been labelled "draconian."[8] Even a proposed nation-wide fifteen-week ban, with exceptions for rape, incest and the life of the mother has met opposition and, in some cases, been labelled "extreme," even though the vast majority of abortions take place before that limit.[9]

On the other hand, a June 1922 Harvard-Harris poll found that while 55 percent of respondents disapproved of *Roe v. Wade* being overturned, 60 percent of Democrats as well as 84 percent of Republicans and 70 percent of independents thought abortions should not be permitted by states after fifteen weeks.[10] (This suggests some inconsistency, since *Roe v. Wade*, permitted abortion at least until viability, yet a majority of respondents opposed its overthrow.)

At the first Republican presidential candidates' debate on August 23, 2023, moderated by Fox News, former Vice-President Mike Pence proposed a national fifteen-week abortion ban. Former Ambassador to the United Nations, Nikki Haley responded that this was unrealistic as the Senate doesn't have the necessary sixty vote majority to enforce such a ban. Others insisted that abortion should constitutionally remain a states' issue. That a

4. See e.g., Carlisle, "Positive Views of the Supreme Court Drop Sharply."
5. Mangan, "Judge suggests abortion might be protected."
6. See e.g., Balevik, "10 Pieces of Common Abortion Misinformation."
7. See e.g., Wicks, "Loudest Political Voice on SNL."
8. Edelman, "'Insidious,' 'Draconian,' 'Cruel.'"
9. Wang and Kitchener, "Graham introduces bill."
10. CAPS (Center for American Political Studies), "Harvard Caps Harris Poll."

fifteen-week ban should be proposed by an outspoken pro-life advocate, and even this should be considered unrealistic, is indicative of how far removed a consistently pro-life position is from popular opinion on the issue.

Haley went on to ask, among other things "Can't we all agree that we should ban late-term abortions?" Others spoke of Democrats supporting abortion up to birth. Pro-choice Democrats take exception to such rhetoric, claiming that there is no such thing. For instance, Joe Biden's former press secretary Jen Psaki, now with MNSBC, lashed out at "entirely misleading claims," adding that, abortions past the point of fetal viability are "incredibly rare" and "involve agonizing, emotional, and ethical decisions."

Psaki cited Centers for Disease Control and Prevention data that shows 90 percent of abortions take place in the first twelve weeks of pregnancy. "No one is running on the platform of aborting viable babies," she said. "No one is selling late-term abortions. . . . No one. Not Joe Biden. Not Kamala Harris. Not Hillary Clinton. Not Nancy Pelosi or any other politician demonized by the right wing roots for more late-term abortions. None of them do."[11]

That may be, but it would be helpful if Democratic senators would make this clear by voting for legislation outlawing late-term abortions or what have been termed "partial-birth" abortions, where medication is used to stop the fetal heartbeat and an attempt is made to remove the child intact through the cervix. Pro-choice advocates insist that "partial-birth" abortion is not a recognized medical term and such procedures usually take place because of a need for medical intervention, such as a fetal abnormality or genetic anomaly.[12] It is because of this perceived need for medical intervention that so many are reluctant to support legislation that would provide some credibility for their claim that they do not support such abortions, relatively rare as they are.

Democratic representatives even voted against a bill called the Born-Alive Abortion Survivors Protection Act that passed the House of Representatives 220 to 210, but was not expected to be taken up by the Democrat controlled senate. The bill "would require health care providers to try to preserve the life of an infant in the rare case that a baby is born alive during or after an attempted abortion. . . Under the bill, health providers who fail to comply with the requirements for care could face fines or up to five years in prison. The bill would not impose penalties on the mother and would grant the mother protection from any kind of prosecution." Opponents have argued that "such measures restrict abortion access by threatening health

11. Moran, "Jen Psaki."
12. See Shiffer, "There's No Such Thing."

care providers. It is already considered homicide in the US to intentionally kill an infant that is born alive."[13]

However, *LifeNews.com* reported on a woman (Sarah Zagorski) who survived an abortion in 1990 at twenty-six weeks and was born alive. The abortionist "told her mother to just let Sarah die, but thankfully her mother experienced an immediate sense of urgency to protect her daughter and demanded that medical care be provided" and threatened to sue if it was not.[14] The same publication has reported "It is estimated that 85,817 infants have been born alive after failed abortions since 1973, and the average number of abortion survivors each year is approximately 1,734."[15] Such evidence suggests that the Republican backed bill was indeed necessary.

Vice-President Harris was pushed to set a limit for abortions when she was interviewed by Margaret Brennan on "Face the Nation." Harris repeatedly said that she and President Biden were not seeking anything more than a return to *Roe v Wade*, which guaranteed abortion access up to the point of viability, (which can fall anytime between twenty and twenty-four weeks given scientific advancements), but she refused to be more specific, even though she asserted that Republican claims of Democrats supporting abortion up to birth are "nonsense" and a "mischaracterization of the point."[16]

Brennan, in framing a question, stated that the charge of Democrats supporting abortion up to birth was not statistically accurate, since "less than 1% of abortions were performed after twenty-one weeks and a majority were performed before thirteen weeks, according to the Centers for Disease Control and Prevention."[17] Nevertheless, that less than 1 percent, if not exactly up to the point of birth, surely at least comes under the category of late term abortions and is not an insignificant number given the total number of abortions performed annually in the US (see comments by Dr. Aultman below).

President Biden has been a bit more specific than his vice-president. In June of 2023, he conceded that as a Catholic he's not "big on abortion" but he thought *Roe v. Wade* "got it right." Claiming that "the vast majority of religions have reached agreement on permitting abortion in the first trimester of pregnancy" (a highly disputable claim), Biden continued in a fundraising letter that, according to "all major religions," the decision to obtain an abortion in the first trimester is "between a woman and her

13. Foran and Zanona, "House passes 'born alive' abortion bill," §2–4.
14. Ertelt, "Woman Who Survived Abortion."
15. Ohden, "Over 85,000 Babies Have Survived."
16. Yilek, "Harris dismissed GOP claims," §8.
17. Yilek, "Harris dismissed GOP claims," §7.

family." The next three months are "between a woman and her doctor. The last three months have to be negotiated, because you can't—unless you are in a position where your physical health is at stake—you can't do it."[18] Perhaps there is some recognition here that when the vast majority of abortions take place (during the first trimester) there is seldom if ever any medical advice sought. This undermines the administration's claims that abortion is a medical necessity, unless stress caused by an unwanted pregnancy can be classified as a medical condition.

In an *Atlantic* profile of Dr. Warren Hern, who specializes in late term abortions, sometimes up to thirty weeks, Elaine Godfrey writes, "Hern is reluctant to acknowledge any limit, any red line. He takes the woman's-choice argument to its logical conclusion. . . . Abortions that come after devastating medical diagnoses can be easier for some people to understand. But Hern estimates that at least half, and sometimes more, of the women who come to the clinic do not have these diagnoses. He and his staff are just sympathetic to other circumstances." These other circumstances include younger women not being aware at first that they are pregnant, as well as more serious cases like sexual abuse victims who ignore their pregnancies or are too ashamed to see a doctor. One woman (a staffer) who opted for a late abortion because her husband had killed himself and "she was suddenly broke," said, "There isn't a single woman who has ever written on her bucket list that she wants to have a late abortion. There is always a reason."[19] Granted, but that reason is not always medical necessity.

Dr. Kathi Aultman, a former abortionist who is now pro-life, testified on Capitol Hill on behalf of an earlier version of the Born-Alive Abortion Survivors Protection Act and said this (in part):

> **There are those who say we don't need this law because late term abortions are so extremely rare that the law isn't necessary.**
>
> The data is incomplete, because not all states are required to report abortions or their complications, but we know from the CDC Abortion Surveillance Report that 1.3 % of abortions performed in 2015 were done after 20 weeks. That sounds like a small number, but 1.3% of 638,169 abortions represents 8,296 late term abortions.
>
> **We are told that Late Term abortions are only done in the most difficult and tragic circumstances where the mother's health is threatened, or she is carrying a baby with severe fetal anomalies.**

18. Yilek, "Harris dismissed GOP claims," §10–13.
19. Godfrey, "Abortion Absolutist," §6, 11, 22.

Julie Wilkinson is an RN who worked with Dr. Warren Hern for years in the 1980's. She assisted him with late term abortions through 26 weeks. I recently spoke with her about her work at the clinic and she told me that the vast majority of the abortions that they performed were done for convenience, not for fetal anomalies or maternal health problems.[20]

Given the above evidence, one has to wonder which side of the debate is providing "entirely misleading claims." When the Republican-controlled North Carolina legislature passed a twelve-week ban on abortion, with exceptions for rape, incest and the life of the mother, Democratic governor Roy Cooper vetoed the bill, in part because it also required three in-person visits with a physician before obtaining an abortion. The legislature was subsequently able to overturn the veto, but what is significant is that Cooper spoke in terms of creating a legacy of "doing what is right, saving lives and protecting women's reproductive freedom." It would be difficult to find a clearer illustration of the philosophical differences that underlie the abortion debate.[21] While some have characterized the North Carolina law as a compromise, Cooper saw it as a "compromise between the right wing and the radical right wing."[22]

Florida Governor Ron DeSantis, then a candidate for US president, signed a six-week abortion ban in his home state but demurred on a national ban, saying he lacked confidence that congress would "do anything meaningful" on the issue and that states would go in different directions. He was condemned by Susan B. Anthony Pro-Life America for expressing "a lack of will to enact national protections for unborn children." This seems hardly fair, given that DeSantis has also been heavily criticized for signing the Florida six-week ban and, as he pointed out in his own defense, "Nobody running [for President] has actually delivered pro-life protections. I have done that."[23] He also rightly pointed out that abortion will be solved from the ground up rather than by top-down legislation lacking popular support.

In Ohio, an attempt to raise to 60 percent the threshold needed to pass a proposed amendment to the state constitution enshrining abortion

20. This was reported in NRL News Today in 2019 and reposted on September 14, 2023, with this editorial comment: *An important note. Dr. Aultman uses CDC figures to calculate the number of late-term abortions. The Guttmacher Institute gathers more complete abortion numbers. It reported 926,200 abortions for 2020. 1.3% would be 12,041. But for a variety of reasons, this figure is likely considerably higher.*

21. Associated Press Video, "North Carolina governor discusses women's health."

22. Mueller, "Cooper calls North Carolina 12-week abortion bill," §1.

23. Maher and Mizelle, "DeSantis defends record on abortion."

rights met with "a crushing loss,"[24] and was one of several "devastating setbacks" for the "anti-abortion movement."[25] President Biden lost no time declaring victory: "Today, Ohio voters rejected an effort by Republican lawmakers and special interests to change the state's constitutional amendment process. This measure was a blatant attempt to weaken voters' voices and further erode the freedom of women to make their own health care decisions. Ohioans spoke loud and clear, and tonight democracy won."[26] The amendment later passed.

Companies of which Amazon is the best known have offered to pay for employees to cross state lines for an abortion.[27] Planned Parenthood has signaled its intention to provide mobile abortion clinics in the vicinity of states that have outlawed or severely restricted the practice.[28] Sheryl Sandberg, shortly after stepping down as CEO of Facebook (now Meta) donated $3 million to the American Civil Liberties Union "to fight abortion bans."[29]

The general consensus in mainstream media (other than right-wing stations like Fox and Newsmax, which don't consider themselves mainstream in any case) is that *Dobbs* is an attack on women's rights. Some prominent and respected women, like law professor Anita Hill (who famously opposed Justice Clarence Thomas's nomination to the Supreme Court in 1991, accusing him of sexual harassment) have characterized the Supreme Court's decision as evidence of chauvinism and misogyny,[30] despite the fact that one of the most outspokenly pro-life justices is a woman, Amy Coney Barrett. (No one seems to be concerned that an all-male Supreme Court gave us *Roe v. Wade* in the first place.)

Hotel heiress Paris Hilton revealed at the age of forty-two that she had an abortion in her twenties but had kept quiet about it because so much shame was attached to it. It was the *Dobbs* decision overturning *Roe v. Wade* that convinced her it was important to discuss the issue so many years later. "There's just so much politics around it and all that, but it's a woman's body. . . . Why should there be a law based on that?" she was quoted as saying: "It's your body, your choice and I really believe in that. It's mind-boggling to me that they're making laws about what you do with your reproductive health, because if it were the other way around with the guys, it

24. Ziegler, "Crushing Loss."
25. Rahman, "Anti-Abortion Movement."
26. Griffiths, "Biden spikes the football."
27. See e.g., Dastin, "Amazon to reimburse US employees."
28. Tucker, "abortion clinic on wheels."
29. See e.g., Dwoskin and Nix, "Sheryl Sandberg's next chapter."
30. As seen on "Alex Wagner Tonight," *MSNBC*, September 27, 2022.

would not be this way at all."[31] Hilton did not explain why she would have had so much shame over a procedure she believes to be so clearly a woman's rightful choice. Actress Anne Hathaway stated on the television program *The View* that "abortion can be another word for mercy," adding that "this is not a moral conversation about abortion, this is a practical conversation about women's rights, and by the way human rights, because women's rights are human rights."[32] Canadian novelist Margaret Atwood, author of the prize-winning *The Handmaid's Tale* (also a popular movie and television series) has claimed that the dystopian vision of her novel has been realized.[33] This is a vision of a patriarchal country, Gilead (clearly based on the United States), in which fertile women are reduced to child-bearing slavery. (One might think Atwood could have found a more appropriate model in some Islamic theocracies.) Such views may seem extreme, but they are in fact representative of mainstream feminist thinking.

A ten-year-old rape victim in Ohio had to leave the state for an abortion because she was past the deadline of Ohio's so-called "heartbeat law," when a fetal heartbeat is detected, usually at six week's gestation. This law was subsequently suspended by a court, but in the meantime the rape victim's case garnered international attention.[34] It has been stressed that poor black women in mostly Southern states are most affected by *Roe*'s reversal.[35] A few celebrities have now redefined their own previous miscarriages and/or ectopic pregnancies as abortions.[36] In this they may be technically correct. A miscarriage, for instance, is a spontaneous abortion, but there is a world of difference between that and a deliberately induced one. There has been confusion as to how new restrictive laws on abortion affect such things since medications used for postpartum hemorrhages can also be used for abortions.[37]

---

31. Suri, "Paris Hilton, 42, reveals she had an abortion."

32. Johnson, "Anne Hathaway tells 'The view,'" §1,6.

33. Atwood, "I Invented Gilead."

34. "If the United States was a country that valued women and girls, or that understood the moral gravity of misogyny, then there would be statues to people like Caitlin Bernard" (the doctor who performed the abortion.) Donegan, "She performed an abortion on a 10-year old rape victim," §1.

35. See e.g., Bose, "Roe v. Wade ruling disproportionately affects Black women."

36. See e.g., Kubota, "Cher recalls experiencing her first miscarriage at 18." Cher tweeted, "WHAT WOULD HAPPEN 2 ME TODAY." This is just one example of several celebrities who have felt it necessary to speak openly about their miscarriages, some of which happened years ago, and relate them to the contemporary situation.

37. Sellers and Nirappil, "Confusion post-Roe spurs delays."

There have been news accounts about women's lives being at risk because doctors were afraid of breaking the law by aborting their nonviable fetuses.[38] Five women (later to become twenty) sued the state of Texas, saying its abortion restrictions put their lives at risk,[39] and a judge subsequently lifted those restrictions temporarily in "cases of dangerous or complicated pregnancies. . . . The Texas attorney general's office, however, swiftly filed an appeal hours later, blocking the exemption from taking effect." Some months later, the Center for Reproductive Rights, which filed the suit on behalf of the women in Texas, did the same for eight women, four physicians, and a medical assistant across three states (Idaho, Tennessee, and Oklahoma), claiming that the women were denied access to abortion "while facing harrowing pregnancy complications that they say endangered their lives."[40]

A Texas woman, Kate Cox, left the state for an abortion after the child she was carrying was diagnosed with a rare and potentially fatal disease, but the state's supreme court denied her an abortion. She was invited as a guest of Dr. Jill Biden to the 2024 State of the Union address, where the president intended to use her story, among others, to highlight the perceived need to "Stop playing politics with the women's lives and freedom. Let doctors do their job."[41]

In other words, the attention has been focused on the few admittedly tragic hard cases, rather than on the vast majority of abortions that are performed for other reasons. As noted earlier, all abortion decisions are hard in that no woman positively desires one. There are women who for reasons of financial hardship, or because of pressure from husbands, boyfriends, parents, or other family members, make the tortured decision to abort, but there are also women who lead promiscuous lives and see abortion as a potential relief from a "mistaken" pregnancy. Typical of this mindset is the article, "I Had a Carefree Sex Life. The Next Generation Will Have Fear," in which a *Daily Beast* columnist who has not had an abortion herself reflects on how she grew up in a world where that option existed for her promiscuous lifestyle, but it now threatened.[42] I am reminded of an incident as far back as 1979 when I was attending a pro-life rally in Philadelphia. A few pro-choice women picketed us, and I got into conversation with one of them. She informed me of her preferred contraceptive, adding "with a back-up abortion." It would be unfair and inaccurate to

---

38. See e.g., Sharp, "Her baby was dying."
39. Kekatos, "5 women sue Texas over abortion bans."
40. Associated Press, " Women in Idaho, Tennessee, and Oklahoma."
41. Concepcion, "Kate Cox, Texas woman."
42. White, "I Had a Carefree Sex Life."

suggest that all pro-choice women take such a cavalier attitude to abortion, but it would be naïve to pretend that this attitude is not a factor in all too many cases. A sometimes-related issue is that unwanted pregnancies can interfere with a woman's education and job prospects. However, these are not the issues highlighted by those who seek to influence public opinion on the need to preserve abortion rights.

Some religious leaders and their supporters have come out in favour of abortion rights, a few understanding their calling to include transporting pregnant women to abortion friendly states.[43] Six religious leaders in Missouri filed a lawsuit against that state's anti-abortion law, arguing that "lawmakers imposed their religious beliefs on others through passing it," and that "The religious Christian right has co-opted language around religion and abortion and made it all about their own beliefs." One member of the group, a retired United Church of Christ minister, said she had prayed about what to do about the overturning of *Roe v. Wade* and this lawsuit was an answer to her prayers.[44] An unrelated report of another UCC minister quotes him as saying, "If you don't have faith for a person who's pregnant to make their own choices, then your faith is way too small. . . . If you're going to think that religion somehow says we need to restrict access because of God, then your god is way too small."[45] A progressive (Reform) Jewish synagogue sued the state of Florida for violating its religious rights since "under Jewish law, abortion 'is required if necessary to protect the health, mental or physical well-being of a pregnant woman.'"[46] Rep. Alexandria Ocasio-Cortez is reported to have said that "Our Jewish brothers and sisters are able to have an abortion according to their faith, and "abortion bans are based on 'fundamentalist Christian' beliefs." She "attacked pro-life laws as 'authoritarian' and 'theocratic,' claiming they violate the beliefs of other religions."[47] Three Jewish women in Kentucky also filed a lawsuit against the state abortion ban there, arguing that it is based on a "Christian understanding" of the value of human life.[48]

The Rev. Raphael Warnock, senior pastor of Atlanta's Ebenezer Baptist Church (of Martin Luther King Jr. fame) and Democratic senator from Georgia, has said that as a pastor he has a deep reverence for life and a deep respect for choice. Noting that "black women are dying three to four times the rate of white women in childbirth," he claimed that "find(ing) a way to

43. See, e.g., Vlamis, "Texas minister."
44. Fernando, "'It's time for us to be bold,'" §3, 11–13.
45. Mandelburg, "Christian Minister Says" §5, 7.
46. Fawcett, "Synagogue Sues Florida."
47. Bilger, "AOC Claims Abortion is a Religious Sacrament."
48. Shimron, "3 Jewish women file suit."

address the obvious bias in our health care system," is "exactly what Jesus would do." Perhaps, except that Warnock said this in the context of defending abortion as compatible with his Christian values.[49] (Despite its claim to have the most advanced medical system in the world, the US has a higher maternity death rate than other developed countries.[50] Racial disparity is one of several factors. Some studies claim a correlation with abortion restrictions beginning in 2020, but rather than a causal link it is more likely that some states with abortion restrictions "also have more limits on Medicaid coverage and fewer OB-GYNs and nurse midwives per capita.")[51]

As reported by the *Religion News Service*, a Presbyterian Church (USA) pastor, the Rev. Rebecca Todd Peters, told her congregation that abortion is "a moral good. . . an act of love, an act of grace, a blessing." Speaking of her own abortions in the past, she said, "I felt God's presence with me as I made the decision to end two pregnancies and I felt no guilt, no shame, no sin. A forced pregnancy or birth is not holy." She also reportedly said she believes abortion for any reason is morally justified, and the idea that abortion is wrong is "rooted in Christianity's patriarchal vision of womanhood." Peters spoke of the need to counter the message of Catholics and evangelicals that "abortion is a sin."[52]

In 2022, the PCUSA passed a resolution supporting "reproductive justice" and "abortion care."[53] The following year, the United Church of Christ General Synod overwhelmingly passed a resolution "Denouncing the *Dobbs* Decision and Proclaiming Abortion as Healthcare." The resolution proclaimed that "forced birth is an act of sexual violence and the choice to have and care for children is a sacred decision which should not be forced upon anyone."[54] The United Methodist Church withdrew from the Religious Coalition for Abortion Rights in 2016 and now claims to respect the sanctity of life of both mothers and unborn children.[55] However, its Council of Bishops bemoaned the reversal of *Roe v. Wade* as creating "a further divide

---

49. Ertelt, "Raphael Warnock: I Support Abortion." Warnock is theologically as well as politically liberal, and as pointed out in chapter 2, evangelicalism differs from theological liberalism in its view of the authority of Scripture, which includes the Hebrew (Old) Testament, but not extra-canonical Jewish writings on which Ocasio-Cortez and others are basing their assertions. They also fail to point out that most rabbinic writings on the subject refer to therapeutic, not unrestricted, abortions (see chapter 3).

50. Howard, "US Maternal Death Rate."
51. Madani, "States with more abortion restrictions."
52. Shimron, "Rebecca Todd Peters," §30, 10, 8.
53. Bilger, "Presbyterian Pastor Says."
54. DeLuca, "Abortion is health care," §1, 2.
55. "What is the UM position on abortion?" §1.

between persons of privilege who have the means to seek necessary health care and those who lack this privilege due to their current economic condition, their disproportionately affected lives, or the color of their skin."[56]

Joe Scarborough of MSNBC made a familiar argument when he declared, "As a Southern Baptist, I grew up reading the Bible. I may be a backslidden Baptist, but I still know the Bible. Jesus never once talked about abortion, never once, and it was happening back in ancient times. It was happening during his time. Never once mentioned it." Scarborough added, of "people who are perverting the gospel of Jesus Christ down to one issue," that "it's heresy." This prompted a number of responses, including one from Dr. Albert Mohler, president of The Southern Baptist Theological Seminary, who wrote, "It is insanity to go on national television and tell people that Jesus never said anything about abortion, therefore, we are making far too much of a deal about it." Mohler pointed out that when the angel Gabriel appeared to Mary, he announced that Jesus, the Son of God, would become human from the moment of conception. "That tells you a very great deal of the fact that from the very moment of conception, the scripture recognizes the humanity, even the personhood of the unborn child, even the unformed child."[57]

It is not only non-Christians and theologically liberal Christians who have opposed *Roe v. Wade*'s reversal. In chapter 5, I referenced Wes Granberg-Michaelson's article, "The Real Question in the Abortion Debate," in which he claims that the disputed Exod 22:21–25 passage involves a miscarriage that is punishable only by a fine. He also states that, while the argument might not be conclusive, Gen 2:7 suggests that life begins with birth (a position similar to that of Gardner, as seen in chapter 4). Certainly Granberg-Michaelson is sure that "there is no convincing biological, legal, or biblical justification for saying that [a full human life, deserving legal protection,] takes place at conception,"[58] and therefore other considerations, principally the needs and rights of the pregnant woman, must be taken into account. This article appeared in *The Reformed Journal*, a publication that serves the more progressive element of those confessionally committed to historic Reformed orthodoxy. Another article in the same publication on "Prayers for a Post Roe World" includes prayers by five women who are pastors in the confessionally orthodox Christian Reformed Church or the Reformed Church in America. One prayer focuses entirely on the "complex and painful" issue of adoption (a subject discussed in chapter 8, and on which the person submitting this prayer took part in

---

56. Council of Bishops, §1.
57. Mohler, "Briefing," §1, 2, 9.
58. Granberg-Michaelson, "Real Question in the Abortion Debate," §25.

a more extended discussion of the issue, "Adoption: Two Voices," in the same publication),[59] another expressed anger and vulnerability by someone who "never thought *Roe* would be overturned." One prayer, while taking no position on whether or not *Roe* should have been overturned, expresses love for those on both sides of the issue and asks for divine help to "honor all life, not only the lives of the unborn but also of mothers and fathers and immigrants and the impoverished and the neglected and abused and traumatized." These prayers, like Granberg-Michaelson's article, evidence some ambivalence about abortion mixed with genuine compassion for women with unwanted pregnancies, but two other prayers unambiguously oppose the Supreme Court's decision and its effects. One states that *Roe v. Wade* "gave women control of their bodies. . . . You did that Lord! A woman's body no longer dictated by others. But now allowing women the ability to choose their own fate is in jeopardy." Another expresses anger "that our right to end a pregnancy is no longer protected."[60] An earlier article, before the Supreme Court's decision but after the state of Texas (to be followed by others) passed its "heartbeat law," banning abortion after six weeks, is titled, "The Texas Abortion Law, the Antiabortion Movement, and the Politics of Cruelty."[61] More than one of these authors stated that they once took what would be regarded as a consistently pro-life position, something of a reversal of the development discussed in chapter 5.

David Owen Filson in "Living Pro-life in a Post-Roe World," notes that, following the Supreme Court's decision that the U.S. Constitution:

> never has and does not declare a woman's right to an abortion, sending the issue of abortion to the states, a tragic number of clergy across the country rushed to their keyboards to lament the unconstitutionality of the decision. . . .
>
> Through some real (*sic*) conceptual gymnastics, they've coopted the nomenclature of the pro-life community, reverse-thrusting with their own categories, redefining and spinning words and phrases to their own devices. Suddenly, pro-life people are actually the real killers because they *always* neglect the babies *after* they're born. . . .
>
> We even hear open claims in the media today by pro-abortion activists that they are the true pro lifers! After all, they tell us, it is pro-life to favor a woman's right to bodily autonomy, pro-life to want to see women not shackled down by having to raise a child instead of pursuing an education and career, pro-life

---

59. Roelofs and Helder, "Adoption: Two Voices."
60. The Editors, "Prayers for a Post-Roe World."
61. Vander Broek, "Texas Abortion Law."

to prevent children with Down's Syndrome from being born and having to face life with such a disability, pro-life to decrease the potential for minority babies to grow up in poverty, pro-life to fight against the "fact" that opposition to abortion arises from and perpetuates white supremacy. This last one would make Margaret Sanger proud. Sanger, founder of Planned Parenthood, desired a program of eugenics to help with what she saw as the problem of a growing black population. . .[62]

It is not clear to me why Margaret Sanger would have been proud to be associated with alleged *pro-life* white supremacists. Although she did not advocate abortion, nor did the Planned Parenthood organization she founded (originally the American Birth Control League) in its early days, when abortion was illegal and dangerous, Planned Parenthood has become the leading advocate and practitioner of legal abortion. Historically, it has attempted to distance itself from Sanger's history of eugenics, while praising her as a pioneer of women's rights. More recently, however, in an April 17, 2021 op-ed in the *New York Times*, its current president Alexis McGill Johnson wrote, "I'm the Head of Planned Parenthood. We're Done Making Excuses for Our Founder." She stressed that "We must reckon with Margaret Sanger's association with white supremacist groups and eugenics." Johnson's op-ed came over six months after a group of more than 120 black leaders urged Planned Parenthood to "confront the systemic racism of America's abortion practices and to publicly renounce the racist legacy of your founder, Margaret Sanger."[63]

There have been pro-life claims of an increase in government-approved arrests of pro-life protestors at abortion clinics for violating the Freedom of Access to Clinic Entrances Act (FACE), which makes it a federal crime to use force with the intent to injure, intimidate and interfere with anyone trying to access either abortion at an abortion facility or medical care at a pregnancy center, while less attention has been given to violent attacks on churches and crisis pregnancy centers. According to one report in December 2022, "At least 98 Catholic churches and 77 pregnancy resource centers and other pro-life organizations have been attacked since May," but the Department of Justice (DOJ) "has apparently not charged a single person in connection with these attacks. Meanwhile, the DOJ's Civil Rights Division has charged 26 pro-life individuals with FACE Act violations this year." (Other arrests have since been reported.)[64] Associate

---

62. Filson, "Living Pro-life in a Post-Roe World," 16–18.
63. McGill Johnson, "I'm the Head of Planned Parenthood."
64. Ertelt, "FBI Arrests Two Pro-Life Advocates"; Gillespie, "Wisconsin Man

Attorney General Vanita Gupta is quoted as saying that the overturning of *Roe v. Wade* was a "'devastating blow to women throughout the country' that took away 'the constitutional right to abortion' and increased 'the urgency' of the DOJ's work—including the 'enforcement of the FACE Act, to ensure continued lawful access to reproductive services.'"65 The newly minted Republican majority in the House of Representatives passed a bill in January 2023 condemning attacks on churches and pregnancy care centers, but it was thought to have no chance of passing the Democrat-controlled senate. Pro-choice advocates claimed it was disingenuous "arguing it ignores mounting violence and threats against abortion providers and people seeking abortion care."66 It might have been wiser to condemn violence on both sides of the issue.

The FBI did finally in January, 2023 offer a $25,000 reward for information leading to the "identification, arrest and conviction" of those who had violently attacked churches and pro-life centers in the previous year, while at the same time seeking information on the bombing of a Planned Parenthood facility. Conservative and pro-life media pointed out that this came only after, frustrated by the lack of action from the FBI, the New York pro-life organization CompassCare launched a private investigation into a June arson attack that caused more than half a million dollars in damage to its Buffalo facility and injured two firefighters. The Rev. Jim Harden, CEO of CompassCare, said it took the federal agency one hundred and sixty-one days and pressure from pro-life advocates to even include the arsonist on its Most Wanted list, and the FBI waited five months before releasing security footage showing the attack. Harden also accused the agency of ignoring numerous other arson and vandalism attacks on pro-life organizations.67 Then on January 24, 2023, *LifeNews.com* reported that, "The Justice Department has finally arrested and indicted abortion activists in connection with over 250 cases of violence against churches and pregnancy centers."68

Appearing before a U.S. Senate hearing, Attorney General Merrick Garland claimed his department applies the law "equally," and sought to explain the discrepancy in arrests by the fact that pro-choice activists tend to operate at night, whereas pro-lifers are photographed in broad daylight. As quoted in *LifeNews.com*, he said, "'Those who are attacking the pregnancy resource

---

Charged."

65. Olohan, "Biden Official Admits FBI Targeting," §2, 8.
66. Fernando, "GOP-led House passes 'born-alive' abortion bill," §21.
67. Barr, "FBI Offers $25,000 Reward."
68. Ertelt, "Two Abortion Activists Arrested," §1.

centers—which is a horrid thing to do—are doing this at night in the dark. We have put full resources on this. We have put rewards out for this.'"

"Garland said the people attacking pregnancy centers are clever and are doing it in secret, so it has been more difficult to find them; but he is 'convinced that the FBI is trying to find them with urgency.'"[69]

Perhaps one of the most egregious examples of government overreach involves the case of Mark Houk, a Catholic pro-life advocate and father of seven. On October 13, 2021, Houk was involved in an altercation outside a Planned Parenthood clinic in Philadelphia. He was charged with two counts of physically assaulting a seventy-two-year-old business escort at the clinic, in violation of the FACE Act. Houk's defence was that in the first instance he was trying to counsel two women across the street from the clinic (thus not physically blocking access) when he was verbally assaulted by the escort; in the second the escort was verbally harassing Houk's twelve-year-old son and when he refused to stop, Houk pushed him away such that he fell to the ground. When police declined to press charges, the escort did, but the charges were thrown out of court because he failed repeatedly to show up. Despite this, the Department of Justice decided to get involved nearly a year later and apparently sent up to twenty FBI agents to break into the Houks's home early one morning to arrest him in front of his wife and children, even though he had offered to appear voluntarily. (The FBI claimed this number is greatly exaggerated but did not provide an exact number.)[70] Houk was subsequently found not guilty by a Philadelphia jury. His attorney commented:

> The jury saw through and rejected the prosecution's discriminatory case, which was harassment from day one. This is a win for Mark and the entire pro-life movement. The Biden Department of Justice's intimidation against pro-life people and people of faith has been put in its place.... What in the world would possess the Department of Justice to send 20 or so heavily armed agents to this family's home, violate the sanctity of that home, frighten the children and then drag their father away instead of allowing us to present him peacefully—which we had offered to do?"[71]

---

69. Bilger, "Merrick Garland Says," §7–9.
70. Andros, "FBI Raids Home of Pro-life Christian."
71. Ertelt, "Jury Finds Mark Houk Not Guilty."

Houk later decided to sue the FBI.[72] Then he announced that he was running for Congress, saying it was "to further protect my family . . . and the Republic."[73]

Prior to the release of the actual *Dobbs* decision on June 24, 2022, a draft of the decision was leaked early in the previous month, creating a firestorm of criticism. Between this and the formal release of the decision, America experienced yet another school shooting, this time in Uvalde, Texas, where nineteen children and two adults were killed on May 24. (Sadly, there have been more such incidents since then.) This revived an ongoing debate about the availability of guns in America and the meaning of the Second Amendment on the "right to bear arms." Does it mean that this right is limited to a "well-regulated militia" or more generally to the "right of the people," a phrase that appears elsewhere in the Constitution, such as in the First Amendment? A majority of the same Supreme Court justices who overturned *Roe v. Wade* has taken the latter view, making it harder to limit the right to carry a concealed weapon.[74] Some of those who have been agitating for what many see as common-sense gun controls (like greater background checks and assault-weapon bans) similar to what exists in other countries, have seized on this issue to make the point that they are concerned to protect born children more than appears to be the case with conservatives who oppose abortion of unborn children but also oppose restrictions on gun rights.[75] This may be unfair, but there does appear to be a logical disconnect when pro-life gun rights advocates insist that laws against abortion will not eliminate the practice but can reduce the numbers, whereas they are not prepared to make the same argument about gun laws. As has often been pointed out, it is true that guns don't kill people, people do, and the underlying causes of why they do need to be addressed, but these underlying causes, such as mental illness, exist in other countries where guns are not so readily available as in the US. Laura R. Kerby reflected the views of many when she opined in the *Washington Post*, "The Christian right's version of history paid off on abortion and guns."[76]

As the first anniversary of the *Dobbs* decision (June 24, 2023) approached, pro-lifers claimed that it had saved over 25,000 or 60,000 babies from abortion, depending on the source.[77] However, the secular

72. Foley, "Pro-Life activist Mark Houk."
73. Mercer, "Pro-Life Advocate Mark Houck," §2.
74. Tucker, "Law Enforcement Officials."
75. See Greenfield, "Here's why people are connecting."
76. Kerby, "Christian right's version of history."
77. Mercer, "Dobbs Decision Has Saved Over 25,000 Babies"; Anderson, "Dobbs

media focused on how it has handed the Democrats a gift heading into the 2024 presidential election and that major pro-choice organizations have endorsed Biden,[78] that 61 percent of Americans were opposed to the Supreme Court's decision,[79] doctors were leaving states with abortion restrictions, women in these states were turning to an abortion hotline for advice on how to access abortion pills,[80] and that the "hidden harms of Dobbs are coming to light."[81] The National Domestic Violence Hotline later reported the troubling statistic that it had seen nearly a 100 percent increase in calls since the fall of *Roe v. Wade*, interpreting this as linked to an increased lack of "reproductive rights" and bodily autonomy.[82]

As Biden's poll numbers continued to be dismal into the late summer of 2023, his re-election campaign decided on an advertising campaign "highlighting former President Donald Trump and other Republican presidential candidates' hardline abortion stances"[83] (although Trump of late has been more ambivalent). The clear and consistent message has been that opposition to *Dobbs* is substantial and provides the Democrats with a winning election strategy. (Although it is widely believed that to be Democrat is to be pro-choice on abortion, that is not altogether true. There is an organization called Democrats for Life and another one named Progressive Anti-Abortion Uprising. The latter's founder, Terrisa Bukovinac, registered as a candidate to oppose Joe Biden for the Democratic nomination. Noting realistically that she was running, not to win but to be a voice for the voiceless, Bukovinac stated that "Pretending like millions of pro-life Democrats like myself don't exist isn't a strategy. The right to life must be protected at every age, everywhere. And that is why I am running for president of the United States."[84] Major issues on her platform include abortion, health care equity, economic justice, racial justice, criminal justice reform and environmental justice, according to her campaign website.)[85]

Has Already Saved" §2. A report released in August 2023 stated that in Oklahoma, following a May 2022 abortion ban from conception, the abortion rate dropped to zero (Ertelt, "Oklahoma Abortions Drop to 0"). The report doesn't say if women travelled to other states for abortions. Further claims of lives saved have since been made.

78. Long, "Planned Parenthood, Emily's List and NARAL Pro-Choice America."
79. ABC News, "Physicians, working within tight margins."
80. AFP, "After bans, American women turn to an abortion hotline."
81. Bultan, "The hidden harms of Dobbs are coming to light."
82. PBS, "The link between."
83. Sullivan, "Biden campaign spotlights abortion," §1.
84. Richardson, "Pro-Life Democrat," §1–3.
85. "Bukovinac for President, 2024."

It was noted earlier that a 2022 Harvard-Harris poll found that 55 percent of respondents opposed the overthrow of *Roe v. Wade*. Then a 2023 ABC News poll, referenced above, found 61 percent opposed. By way of contrast, a Rasmussen poll that first pointed out to respondents that "each state can now determine its own laws regarding abortion," then asked, "Do you approve or disapprove of the court overturning Roe v. Wade?" found that 52 percent approved, including 37 percent who strongly approved. Forty-four percent disapproved, including 36 percent who strongly disapproved. Pro-lifers understandably, if somewhat ingenuously, are tempted to seize on such evidence to suggest that the majority of Americans are really coming over to their side.[86] However, the reporting on the poll also recognized that "more voters identify as pro-choice than pro-life."[87] An AP-NORC poll found that, even in states with abortion restrictions, most Americans support abortion at least through the initial stages of pregnancy. "Overall, about two-thirds of Americans say abortion should generally be legal, but only about a quarter say it should always be legal and only about 1 in 10 say it should always be illegal."[88]

President Biden signed an executive order ensuring greater access to contraception declaring that "reproductive health care [not just abortion] is under attack." This was the third executive order he had signed related to reproductive health care. The first was on July the 8th, 2022 which expanded access to abortion and encouraged free legal representation for doctors and patients. The second was August 3rd, 2022, which expanded access to medicated abortion and provided support for providers navigating new restrictions.[89] However, it was Vice-President Harris who became the face and voice of abortion rights heading into the 2024 federal election.[90]

In a July 31, 2023 interview with ABC News while visiting Iowa where a six-week abortion ban had been signed into law, but blocked by a judge, Harris opined that "There's something underlying this approach that states like Iowa have taken that really suggests . . . that they don't trust women to be able to know what's in their best interests and make the decision accordingly." Claiming that restrictive abortion laws had led to "serious medical emergencies for millions of American women," she said she was concerned about what was happening, but expressed "faith in the people of

---

86. "So on this benchmark question this year's results showed a net gain of about 4% for the pro-life side. That is important to remember" (Andrusko, "Poll Show Majority of Americans," §17).

87. Rasmussen Reports, "Abortion: Half of Voters Approve," §1,2.

88. Mulvihill and Sanders, "Few US adults support full abortion bans."

89. PBS News, "The Abortion landscape."

90. Wright, "Kamala Harris found her voice."

America," encouraging them to get out and vote, noting that the American people have pushed back at the ballot box against states' implementation of the Supreme Court's decision. Later in the same interview, Harris said on the subject of an ongoing migrant crisis that "human beings should not be used as pawns in a political game."[91] Presumably, she does not regard the unborn as human beings in the same way.

ABORTION ABOLITIONISTS

Renewed attention has been given to those who call themselves abortion abolitionists who "(reject) incremental steps toward outlawing abortion and reserve strong criticism for those who accept anything other than a federal ban equipped with criminal penalties for all involved,"[92] including women and doctors. Although not directly related to issues of race (though poor black women are believed to be particularly affected), this minority of pro-lifers also invokes the legacy of William Wilberforce and the slave trade abolitionists. The abolitionist movement among Southern Baptists was strong enough that in 2021 its convention passed an anti-abortion resolution "that was so strident that a number of the convention's most prominent pro-life advocates voted against it." As written, the resolution says, "The murder of preborn children is a crime against humanity that must be punished equally under the law." It characterized an incremental legal approach to banning abortion as "appalling" and rejected "any position that allows for any exceptions to the legal protection of our preborn neighbors, compromises God's holy standard of justice, or promotes any God-hating partiality." This is a far cry from 1971 when the Southern Baptist Convention passed a resolution stating that abortion should be legal not only to protect the mother's life (which has been the traditional Protestant position), but also her emotional well-being (a condition difficult to define, and which has been used as a cover for so-called "abortion on demand"). In the end, the resolution only passed after it was amended to allow for the incremental approach it so strongly opposed.

These views have influenced some state legislatures and have fuelled fears that this is the real agenda of the pro-life movement. However, the National Right to Life organization on May 12, 2022, published a letter signed by over seventy pro-life allies that stated in bold type that:

---

91. ABC News, "Linsey Davis's exclusive interview with Vice President Kamala Harris."
92. Andersen, "When 'Pro-Life' Isn't Enough," §2.

> Women are victims of abortion and require our compassion and support as well as ready access to counseling and social services in the days, weeks, months, and years following an abortion. As national and state pro-life organizations, representing tens of millions of pro-life men, women, and children across the country, let us be clear: We state unequivocally that we do not support any measure seeking to criminalize or punish women and we stand firmly opposed to include (sic) such penalties in legislation.[93]

It could be argued that portraying women simply as victims of abortion undermines, and so demeans, their responsibility for their decisions, but to quote Marvin Olasky, "what I can say pragmatically is that arresting women is a sure way to arrest the progress of pro-life ideas in the twenty-first century."[94]

There is a certain logic to the abolitionists position. If indeed abortion is murder, then those who commit it (doctors) and their accomplices (attending medical staff and pregnant women) should be charged, just as they would be in the case of the deliberate killing of a two-year-old. But therein lies the rub. Those who perform abortions and women who subject themselves to them generally believe that they are aborting at most a potential life, not a legally defined person. Attempts to have the unborn declared to be persons have failed in the courts, except in the recent, highly controversial decision in Alabama. It would take a massive change in societal values to reverse this. Southern Baptist and other churches do not have the authority to enforce civil law. What they do have is authority to exercise godly discipline on their members, but that discipline always includes room for repentance and restoration.

As Ericka Andersen pointed out in a *Christianity Today* article on the subject:

> It's important to note that prior to 1973's *Roe*, state laws did not criminalize women who had abortions. Juries of that time considered them "victims" and sought only to punish abortion providers, so the view of abortive mothers as criminals is rather new.
>
> And though the country has seen more than 63 million abortions [now 65 million] since *Roe*, both grassroots

---

93. "An Open Letter to State Lawmakers." The letter was written as "Louisiana lawmakers were debating a law that would have permitted prosecution of mothers who obtained an abortion and had passed out of committee by a 7-2 vote. After the letter, the bill's sponsor removed it from the House calendar, effectively killing the legislation, at least for now" (French, "For Abortion Abolition," §17).

94. Olasky & Savas, *The Story of Abortion in America*, 442.

and political pro-life activists have helped lower the annual rate nearly every year since the early 1980s through incrementalist laws and tactics.[95]

David French, considered by some erstwhile colleagues to be an "accommodationist" on this and other matters, is I believe nonetheless correct when he says in a *Dispatch* column, "For Abortion Abolition, Against Abortion 'Abolitionists'": "Incrementalists aren't in favor of slow change in abortion laws for the sake of slow change, but rather accept attainable change even when you ultimately hope for greater regulation. . . . Abortion can only truly end when American culture changes, not just its law."[96]

ABORTION IN SOME OTHER PARTS OF THE WESTERN WORLD

Much more could be said, and further examples could be given. As indicated in the Introduction, abortion-related news seems to come out of the United States on a daily basis. This is where abortion is a politically contentious issue, especially since the reversal of *Roe v. Wade*. The rest of the Western world has shown no inclination to follow its direction and some national leaders have seen fit to criticize what is widely perceived as a setback for women's rights.[97] In England, Scotland, and Wales, abortion remains technically a criminal offense, but the Abortion Act 1967 made it legal as long as specific criteria are met. These criteria include "preventing grave permanent injury to [a woman's] physical or mental health," which is "typically interpreted liberally with regards to mental health to create a *de facto* elective abortion services (*sic*), and nearly all abortions—98% in 2019 and 2020—are performed to protect the woman's mental health."[98] It is possible to have an abortion up to twenty-three weeks and six days' gestation. There is no gestational limit for abortions if there's evidence of a fatal fetal abnormality or a significant risk to a woman's life if she continues with the pregnancy. The Society for the Protection of Unborn Children reports "a massive rise" in abortions in England, Wales and Scotland, in the first six months of 2022 compared to 2021.[99] In Northern Ireland, abortion

---

95. Andersen, "When 'Pro-Life Isn't Enough," §25–26. Actually, abortion rates rose from 2017 to 2020, reversing a thirty-year decline. (Belluk, "Abortion Increase.")

96. French, "For Abortion Abolition," §13.

97. Most notably Prime Minister Trudeau of Canada, President Macron of France, then Prime Minister Boris Johnson of the UK.

98. "Abortion in the United Kingdom," *Wikipedia*, §1–3.

99. John Deignhan, email message to author, August 1, 2023.

was decriminalised in 2019, and the new legal framework came into effect in 2020. Abortion is now unconditionally legal up to twelve weeks in Northern Ireland (as in the Republic of Ireland.) After twelve weeks, the law is essentially the same as in the rest of the UK.[100]

A particularly troubling case in England involved a forty-four-year-old mother of three who lied about how advanced her pregnancy was in order to obtain abortion-causing drugs under the "pills by post" scheme during the COVID lockdown in May 2020. Her unborn child was stillborn at an estimated thirty-two to thirty-four weeks' gestation. The woman was "initially charged with child destruction and pleaded not guilty, before pleading guilty to an alternative charge of administering drugs or using instruments to procure abortion. She was eventually sentenced to twenty-eight months in prison" on 12 June 2023, setting off widespread protests by abortion activists. However, the month following her conviction, three Appeals Court judges reduced her sentence to a suspended one of fourteen months, freeing her immediately from custody as it was a case that called for compassion rather than punishment and "no useful purpose was served by keeping her in custody." As reported in the *Daily Mail*:

> Campaigners hailed the decision a watershed moment in UK legal history, which prompted called for an "urgent" overhaul of Britain's archaic abortion laws. [The charge of which the woman was convicted was based on an "Offences Against the Person Act" dating from 1861.]
>
> The news was celebrated by human rights groups, with Amnesty International UK's women's rights director, Chiara Capraro, saying Ms Foster [the woman in question] should have never been put through "such a hideous ordeal in the first place."
>
> And the landmark decision sparked calls for Britain to update its abortion laws–which date back to 1861–with Chiara saying: "This is a deeply upsetting story, from beginning to end, and underscores the urgent need for abortion to be decriminalised in England and Wales."[101]

Pro-lifers, on the other hand, were encouraged to contact their MPs to say that abortion should not be decriminalized.[102] It is expected that by the time this book is published, the British parliament will have held

---

100. Calkin and Berny, "Legal and non-legal barriers," §16.

101. Cotterill and Chaudhary, "Enjoying her first taste of freedom" §4, 8, 10–11, 13, 15–16.

102. Williams, "Update on the Carla Forster Case."

a vote on removing criminal liability for abortions performed after the twenty-fourth week.[103]

Ms Foster was one of four women to be charged under the 1861 Act over a period of eight months, for seeking to procure the abortion of a viable child. The fourth was charged on August 15, 2023 with "administering a poison with intent to procure a miscarriage, between July 2 and July 7, 2020." A trial date was set but then charges were dropped.[104]

Then a former neonatal nurse was given a life sentence for the murder of seven babies and the attempted murder of six more. Noting that, according to a *Guardian* newspaper report, several of the babies were born prematurely, especially one, known as Child G born fifteen weeks early, who survived but is now severely disabled, David Robertson observed in the British publication *Christian Today* that "the tragedy itself and the coverage of it has revealed a great deal about our confused post-Christian society.... On the one hand we are outraged that a nurse attempted to kill a 23-week-old baby, but on the other hand, when Carla Foster was sentenced to jail for killing her thirty-four-week-old baby, our progressives were outraged that she should be punished at all! Abortion has become such a secular sacrament that to point out this inconsistency is almost regarded as blasphemy in our 'progressive' society."[105]

When Maria Caulfield, a Conservative MP in the UK was appointed minister for women in 2022, the response from women's groups and some charities was predictable because she had once called for debate on the current limit on abortions and voted against legalizing abortion in Northern Ireland. Harriet Wistrich, the director of the Centre for Women's Justice, said: "We are horrified that a clear opponent of abortion rights has been appointed minister for women." She added, "The vast majority of women want the right to choose," stating, "Her appointment signals a potential restriction on women's reproductive rights, which in turn is an attack on women's autonomy and freedom. We hope Maria Caulfield will keep her personal opinions on the issue of abortion to herself."[106]

Caulfield was subsequently condemned for tweeting her support of a woman who was arrested for praying outside an abortion clinic. She wrote, "People told me I was exaggerating when I said Christians would be arrested on the streets of England with the buffer zone legislation." The woman in question was arrested for violating buffer zone legislation

---

103. Hayward, "Parliament poised to decriminalise abortion."
104. Brown, "Teesside Woman Cleared."
105. Robertson, "What does the case . . . tell us about our society?" §1, 5.
106. Murray, "Tory MP who backed cutting abortion time limit."

that was intended to make it an offense to "interfere, intimidate or harass women accessing or people providing abortion services."[107] Charges were later dropped.[108] However, a subsequent arrest of a British army veteran reinforced Caulfield's prediction.[109]

Other European countries are sometimes held up as examples of nations with stricter abortion laws than the UK or US, but exceptions are made sufficiently often that the difference is virtually meaningless.[110]

In what has been generally understood to be a direct response to the US Supreme Court's *Dobbs* decision, France's parliament has now enshrined abortion as a constitutional right, possibly it has been suggested, paving the way for other European nations to follow.[111] A development that is not limited to Europe, but has been particularly "effective" especially in Iceland has been screening tests intended to prevent the birth of babies with Down Syndrome. According to a 2017 CBS News report, "With the rise of prenatal screening across Europe and the United States, the number of babies born with Down syndrome has significantly decreased, but few countries have come as close to eradicating Down syndrome births as Iceland. . . . Other countries aren't lagging too far behind. . . . According to the most recent data available, the United States has an estimated termination rate for Down syndrome of 67 percent (1995–2011); in France it's 77 percent (2015), and Denmark, 98 percent (2015)."[112] This could be construed as a form of eugenics in the womb, long after others forms of the practice have been condemned by society at large.

Canada has had no abortion law since the existing law was struck down by its Supreme Court in 1988. The Conservative government of the day attempted twice to introduce fairly restrictive abortion bills, in 1988 and 1989. The first was defeated by a combination of pro-abortion MPs and those who thought the law was too lenient; the second passed the House of Commons but was defeated in the Senate by a tied vote, thus giving us the current situation. Although provinces set their own gestational limits, abortion is technically legal nationwide at all stages of pregnancy, and there are documented, if relatively rare, cases of abortions up to 35 and 38 weeks gestation, for both medical and social reasons.[113] But the overall national limit

107. Nsubuga, "Tory minister criticized," §5, 11.
108. Ertelt, "Charges Dropped Against Pro-life Woman."
109. ET staff writer, "Ex-Soldier Charged."
110. See e.g., Serwer, "Myth That America's Abortion Laws."
111. Associated Press, "As France guarantees the right to abortion."
112. Quinones and Lajka, "What kind of society?" §1, 6.
113. After one of these in Montreal, the Quebec College of Physicians changed

is similar to that in the UK. Much the same applies in English-speaking countries on the other side of the world.[114]

The Rev. Peter Barnes, Presbyterian minister and author of the booklet, *Abortion: Open Your Mouth for the Dumb* has kindly supplied the following:

> The various Australian states have removed abortion from the criminal code and treated it as a form of health care. From early 2023 the Australian Capital Territory will provide abortions for free, even for those without a Medicare card. The ACT government claims this will provide access to 'safe, accessible and affordable abortion services.' The situation in New Zealand is comparable. Since 2020 an abortion up to 20 weeks—described as 'a minor operation'—are allowed, and with more consultation, after that time. Live births are treated as something of an embarrassment, and no law offers them any protection.
>
> Much of this recent legislative activity has been window dressing because abortion has long been accepted in practice. Moral courage is not a feature of a decaying West.[115]

It is reported that in the Australian states of Queensland and Victoria, between 2010 and 2020, 724 late term abortions resulted in live births of babies who were left to die. Other states apparently don't keep such statistics.[116]

The World Health Organization (WHO) defines health as:

> a state of complete physical, mental and social well-being, and not merely the absence of disease or infirmity. Making health for all a reality, and moving towards the progressive realization of human rights, requires that all individuals have access to quality health care, including comprehensive abortion care services—which includes information, management of abortion, and post-abortion care. Lack of access to safe, timely, affordable and respectful abortion care poses a risk to not only the physical, but also the mental and social, well-being of women and girls.
>
> Induced abortion is a simple and common health-care procedure. Each year, almost half of all pregnancies—121 million—are unintended; 6 out of 10 unintended pregnancies and

---

its abortion guidelines to "for pregnancies of more than 25 weeks, abortion services are offered in certain Quebec hospitals, when it is performed for a medical reason or because of a very specific social condition." Previously, abortions after 23 weeks were only permitted for "serious congenital anomalies" or "exceptional clinical situations." Farrow, "Whistleblower claims," §14, 15.

114. Melville, "Abortion care in Australasia."

115. Barnes, email correspondence, December 20, 2022.

116. Stoker, "'Babies Born Alive' bill."

3 out of 10 of all pregnancies end in induced abortion. Abortion is safe when carried out using a method recommended by WHO, appropriate to the pregnancy duration and by someone with the necessary skills. However, when women with unwanted pregnancies face barriers to obtaining quality abortion, they often resort to unsafe abortion.[117]

According to WHO, 45 percent of abortions worldwide are unsafe, mostly occurring in the developing world. Accordingly, "Upon request, WHO provides technical support to countries to adapt sexual and reproductive health guidelines to specific contexts and strengthen national policies and programmes related to contraception and safe abortion care. A quality abortion care monitoring and evaluation framework is also in development."[118] Countries in the so-called developed world contribute financially to these efforts.

It is thus apparent, that whereas a conservative majority on the US Supreme Court reversed *Roe v. Wade*, thereby not outlawing abortion, but simply sending it back to the states to decide, it did not do so based on a cultural consensus, and this consensus is even more lacking in the developed world outside the United States. Meanwhile, some Latin American countries with large Roman Catholic populations have been going in a different direction from their northern neighbor, legalizing or expanding abortion rights.[119] In particular, just over a year after the *Dobbs* decision in the US, the Mexican Supreme Court decriminalized abortion nationwide. Although some twenty out of thirty-two states still criminalize abortion and "further legal work will be required to remove all penalties," the ruling "will require the federal public health service and all federal health institutions to offer abortion to anyone who requests it."[120] Coincidentally, it also has the potential of making Mexico an increasingly attractive option for abortion seeking women in southern US states with significant restrictions—rather than the other way around.

CHRISTIAN ADVOCACY

Some have mistaken *The Benedict Option* as a call to withdraw from the world of politics but that is not what Dreher is advocating. "To be sure,

---

117. World Health Organization, "Abortion," §1–2.

118. World Health Organization, "Abortion," §22.

119. Rogin, "Why a growing number of Latin American countries are Legalizing Abortion."

120. Associated Press, "Mexico decriminalizes abortion," §2–4.

Christians cannot afford to vacate the public square entirely. The church must not shrink from its responsibility to pray for political leaders and to speak prophetically to them."[121] This involves advocating for religious freedom, as well as the establishment of "parallel structures" modelled on the political activism of Vaclav Havel (1936–2011) under communism, before he became the last president of Czechoslovakia (1989–92) and the first president of the Czech Republic (1993–2003). What all these "parallel structures" are need not concern us here but, without necessarily agreeing with all of Dreher's suggestions, we can surely agree on the importance of crisis pregnancy centers (now more often known as pregnancy care centers) both as a means of broadening the pro-life message and saving "countless unborn lives."[122]

It is noteworthy that the evangelical Christian Action Council, founded in 1975 as a political and educational lobby, subsequently crystallized its mission into:

> establishing pregnancy centers and equipping them to empower women to make life-affirming decisions in response to an unplanned pregnancy. The organization subsequently adopted the name "Care Net".
>
> Today, Care Net is an expansive network, advocating for 1,200 independent, affiliated pregnancy centers across North America, as well as operating Pregnancy Decision Line to reach women and men at their point of need.
>
> Care Net works to end abortion, not primarily through political action but by building a culture where woman and men receive all the support they need to welcome their children and create their own success stories.[123]

This change of direction was the result of coming to believe "that we can no longer hope that the courts and legislatures will protect women from the abortion system."[124]

Care Net and other similar organizations have come under attack as part of the post-*Roe* backlash. They have been accused of operating under false pretences with false advertising.[125] This is part of the ironic conundrum of being pro-life. Pro-lifers are accused of having a "fetus fetish" and caring only for the unborn, but when it is pointed out that they also

---

121. Dreher, *Benedict Option*, 82.
122. Dreher, *Benedict Option*, 98.
123. "Care Net History," §3–5.
124. Guy Condon, quoted in Zielgler, *Abortion and the Law in America*, 142.
125. See e.g., Montoya et al., "Problem with Crisis Pregnancy Centers."

serve women with crisis (unwanted) pregnancies, they are accused of false advertising and deceitful practices. Care Net in 2022 found it necessary to respond to these unfounded charges. Its report acknowledges that there may be unaffiliated centers that do not conform to Care Net's rigorous and transparent guidelines:

> In rare cases, these unaffiliated or noncompliant centers may engage in practices that organizations like Care Net publicly condemn. Moreover, if a Care Net-affiliated center chooses to ignore our standards, they are disaffiliated. However, to use that minority as an example of how most pregnancy centers operate is false and misleading. For example, it would not be fair to use imprisoned abortion provider Dr. Kermit Gosnell, who murdered newborn infants, as the example of how all abortion providers operate. Therefore, in the name of fairness, it is appropriate to judge the work of pregnancy centers based on the practices of the vast majority of them, which operate under the professional standards of national networks such as Care Net's.[126]

Care Net's publication, *Guidelines for Life Advocates: 10 Things Not to Do When a Woman Tells You She Wants an Abortion* includes this advice, "Effective Life Advocates avoid potentially manipulative tactics like over-emphasizing abortion procedure terms, exaggerating abortion risks, or introducing words like kill or murder. Instead remember how Christ reached out to us in love before we knew we needed Him."[127]

It is difficult not to feel some frustration at the charges made about these centers when one knows real stories of women who have reached out to them for help. The Director of the Pregnancy Care Centre in the Canadian city where I live tells of fifty- and seventy-year-old women wanting to talk about abortions they experienced decades ago but have carried in secrecy and isolation since. She shares stories as well of women seeking emotional and material support, women who perhaps want to carry their child to term but just don't know how they could do it on their own. These supports empower women to make the decision they actually desire rather than feeling cornered into a situation where they feel they have no option except abortion.

In Canada in 2021 the prime minister of the day (a professing Roman Catholic) instructed the finance minister to introduce amendments to the Income Tax Act "to make anti-abortion organizations that provide dishonest counselling to pregnant women about their rights and options

---

126. Care Net, "Unaffiliated Pregnancy Centers," 10.
127. *Guidelines for Life Advocates*, Care Net, 7.

ineligible for charitable status." I am not aware of any organizations having lost their charitable status to date on this basis, and it is clear from the websites of reputable pregnancy care centres that they do not provide dishonest counseling, but the Council of Canadian Christian Charites has expressed concern about how this mandate may be interpreted and implemented going forward.[128] In the US to date, the state of Illinois has passed a law permitting crisis pregnancy centers to be penalized if they appear to be, have been, or are planning to engage in "[a deceptive] method, act, or practice."[129] The law is being challenged in the courts.

Charges of false advertising and dishonest counseling did not begin after the *Roe* reversal, they simply intensified. Marvin Olasky reports that Ron Fitzsimmons, executive director of the National Coalition of Abortion Providers, visited key figures of ABC's *Prime Time Live*. He said they "immediately agreed to do an 'exposé' on the issue of crisis pregnancy centers." Fitzsimmons also urged Ron Wyden, an Oregon Democrat then in the house of Representatives, to hold hearings on whether pro-life centers told the truth. Wyden in 1991 "gave megaphones to abortion advocates and refused to let pro-life center leaders testify. Not only ABC, but CBS and NBC as well, decided to run stories attacking the centers, using the hearings as a hook."[130]

Further examples of this approach are then given. Earlier, in the 1980s, according to Olasky:

> Public relations expert Amy Sutnick, working with Planned Parenthood of New York City, planned an anti-CPC campaign featuring both a populist and an elite strategy. She was proud of her handiwork: She told me that to increase awareness with a "dramatic" account she handed the story to the *New York Daily News*, and then went to "The *New York Times* (sic) for influence on a decision maker." Sutnick's subsequent step was to plant an article about "deception" with a *USA Today* reporter who obediently said she was "overwhelmed by the brainwashing techniques and the lies." Among the "lies" typically offered by the counseling centers: information about when unborn children had beating hearts and fingers, and warnings that abortion scarred women psychologically.[131]

128. The Evangelical Fellowship of Canada, "Charitable status of pro-life organizations."
129. Campisi, "Lawsuits: Pregnancy Centers Are Being Targeted," §3.
130. Olasky, *Abortion at the Crossroads*, 103.
131. Olasky, *Abortion at the Crossroads*, 99–100.

Olasky provides an example of a 1985 "hit piece" in the *Austin American-Statesman*, using "Sutnick's Planned Parenthood template." This was an attack on a CPC that Olasky and his wife had co-founded. Susan Olasky, by means of tape recording was able to show that "twenty-four of the thirty-eight paragraphs in the story had misquotations, inaccuracies, or violations of standard journalistic ethics. The editor finally offered a grudging semi-apology and offered an equal space to tell the center's side of the story." In reality, Olasky observes, "CPCs were pro-life in hoped-for ends, but pro-choice in means. The volunteers . . . were not campaigning to make abortion illegal. . . . They were saying to young women: If you want what you need to make an informed choice, come here and then decide."[132] Several examples are given of women who changed their minds about seeking an abortion after seeing the evidence of fetal life on sonograms.

Care Net's policies, regulations, and procedures can be found on its website. Its mission statement reads: "Acknowledging that every human life begins at conception and is worthy of protection, Care Net offers compassion, hope, and help to anyone considering abortion by presenting them with realistic alternatives and Christ-centered support through our life-affirming network of pregnancy centers, churches, organizations, and individuals." Its vision is of "a culture where women and men faced with pregnancy decisions are transformed by the Gospel of Jesus Christ and empowered to choose life for their unborn children and abundant life for their families."[133] It is difficult to see how this could be more transparent.

In 2016, Care Net launched Making Life Disciples, described as "a curriculum that will equip churches to minister to women and men considering abortion."[134] It also now describes its ministry as "Pro-Abundant Life," based on John 10:10b where Jesus says, "I came that they may have life and have it abundantly," interpreted as a life that is "both physical (temporal) and spiritual (eternal)." As explained by Care Net's president and CEO Roland C. Warren:

> we have to not only prevent abortions from happening but also holistically serve women and men by addressing the societal issues and spiritual issues that contribute to them considering abortion in the first place. . . .
>
> Care Net educates and equips our more than 1,200 affiliated pregnancy centers on how to effectively serve women and men, build strong families, and discuss the importance of forming

---

132. Olasky, *Abortion at the Crossroads*, 100–1.
133. "Our Mission, Our Vision," *About Care Net*.
134. Dicaro, "Care Net Launches First-Ever Program," §1.

healthy marriages. We do this because 86% of women who have abortions are unmarried. We do this because in the two national surveys we conducted, we found that both women who have had abortions and men who have participated in them stated that the father of the child was the most influential in a woman's abortion decision. We do this because there is a father-absence crisis in our nation in which a quarter of children live in father-absent homes. . . . So, not focusing on engaging the father of the unborn baby would be an enormous strategic misstep in trying to prevent abortions in our nation.[135]

Among several videos produced or shared by Care Net, is a clip of pastor Tim Hawkins of Hill Country Bible Church, Austin, Texas, pointing out that whereas pro-lifers tend to focus on the nine months of a woman's pregnancy, a survey by Planned Parenthood shows that women facing an unplanned pregnancy focus more on the eighteen years that follow. They say:

1. **The baby would interfere with school, employment, or the ability to care for dependents** (74%). In other words, "I've got plans... How am I going to do school? How am I going to get my GED or get through college? What am I going to do? I've got people to take care of in my life. I've got dependents. How can I make a living?"

2. **I can't afford a baby now** (73%). "How will I pay for this child coming into the world?"

3. **I don't want to become a single parent or have relationship problems** (48%). "What about the husband or the father that is involved in this? How is that going to go down? Is he going to be accepting? Is he going to be part of this? Is this the person I want to spend my life with?"

4. **I've completed my childbearing or I'm not ready to have a child** (33-40%). "Am I ready to be a mom? Am I ready to become a mom again? Can I do this? Am I ready to be a be a father again? Can I be a father again?"[136]

These are among the concerns ministries like Care Net seek to address. It also provides videos for pro-choice Christians, challenging them to rethink their position.

As noted previously (chapter 1), a 2015 study by LifeWay, sponsored by Care Net reported on a nationally balanced survey of women who had

135. Warren, "Why the Pro-Life Movement Must Be Pro-Abundant Life" §1, 3.
136. Also available at Carpenter Theologian Blog, "Why Women Have Abortions."

experienced at least one abortion. The study was based on 1,308 completed returns. Among its findings:

- More than 4 in 10 women who have had an abortion were churchgoers when they ended a pregnancy.
- But only 7 percent of women discussed their abortion decision with anyone at church. Three-fourths (76 percent) say the church had no influence on their decision to terminate a pregnancy.
- Two-thirds (65 percent) say church members judge single women who are pregnant.
- A majority (54 percent) thinks churches oversimplify decisions about pregnancy options.
- Fewer than half (41 percent) believe churches are prepared to help with decisions about unwanted pregnancies.
- Only 3 in 10 think churches give accurate advice about pregnancy options.[137]

There is some slight room for encouragement in that self-described evangelicals are more likely than others to say that it is safe to talk with a pastor about abortion (71 percent compared to 38 percent).[138] On the other hand, there is the troubling statistic that 15 percent of self-identified evangelicals said that a local church paid for their abortion and 10 percent said the church referred them to an abortion provider.[139] Six percent of self-identified evangelicals said a local church encouraged them to have the procedure, and only 8 percent said the local church referred them to a pregnancy care center.[140] The challenge for churches is to be grace-filled, compassionate and non-judgmental, while at the same time "speaking the truth in love" (Eph 4:16) when teaching on the sin of abortion, rather than avoiding the subject until faced with a crisis situation. Indications are that the church needs to set its own house in order before addressing society at large.

If Care Net evolved from a political action group (Christian Action Council) into one that mainly focuses on pregnancy and family care, there are other organizations which were founded with explicitly non-political intents. Avail NYC, based in New York, is one such organization that provides both pre-and-post abortion services for women and men facing an

---

137. LifeWay, "Women Distrust Church on Abortion," §2–5.
138. LifeWay, "Women Distrust Church on Abortion," 77.
139. LifeWay, "Women Distrust Church on Abortion," 60, 64.
140. LifeWay, "Women Distrust Church on Abortion," 66.

unexpected pregnancy or abortion loss. Avail networks with over three hundred different community partners to provide an array of services including insurance, a medical provider, housing, and family support. According to its founder and CEO, Chris Whitford, this ministry in 2022 had served women and men from twenty states and fourteen countries. It was founded in 1996 and is strictly non-political.

Based on the question, "Who is my neighbor?" and Jesus's parable of the Good Samaritan, Whitford asks, "What does it mean for me to love the pregnant, distraught neighbour in front of me—or her boyfriend or husband? And what does it mean for her to love me as I help her? Or for each of us to love the tiny neighbour in her womb? What does it mean for us to love each other when we answer these questions very differently?" Whitford reports, "Our clients usually come to us believing abortion is their best or only choice, and we don't lecture them or refuse to deal with their mounting pressures.... If we fail to respect our neighbours despite any differences, why should they trust us? But if we embrace the vulnerability of being a faithful presence, a guide and not someone who seeks to control, then we can earn trust.... Each year, 68 to 78 percent of Avail's reporting clients change their minds and carry their pregnancies to term."[141]

New York City and State are predominantly liberal politically, with liberal abortion laws. If a ministry such as Avail's is needed there, how much more so in more conservative states with restrictive abortion laws that have been legitimately criticized for also offering fewer services for mothers and children.[142]

ProGrace, based in Wheaton, Illinois, is another organization that offers what it calls "a third option for approaching the abortion debate," one that does not use "pro-life" or "pro-choice" language. Its focus is on the need for churches to become safe places for women whether pre-or post-abortion. This approach is based on Jesus's conversation with the woman taken in adultery, recorded in John 8. (Most recent translations have this section in brackets as it is not found in the "best," i.e., earliest, manuscripts, but there is general consensus among most New Testament scholars that

---

141. Whitford, "Deep Wells of Mercy," 81–82. Whiford provides three stories of women with crisis pregnancies, one who made the choice to keep her child, another who was forced by family pressure to abort hers against her will, and a third who made the choice to abort. What is common to all three stories is unstable or abusive relationships with boyfriends or other family members. This, with countless other examples, gives the lie to the popular perception and propaganda that abortion is always a woman's right to choose.

142. See Badger, Sanger-Katz and Martin, "States With Abortion Bans."

the incident itself is authentic.)¹⁴³ ProGrace offers seminars and online courses for individuals, small groups and churches based on its "vision for the future":

> We consistently see that when a church begins to embrace and communicate a grace-centered response, women and men who have experienced unintended pregnancy and abortion open up about their experiences—sometimes for the very first time. We can make our churches safe by extending the same grace Jesus extends to all of us.
>
> Grace also paves the way for us to have new conversations outside the church with people **at all different points** on their beliefs about abortion. In fact, when I [CEO Angie Weszley] share about Pro Grace, the Gospel often flows naturally into the conversation. That's because this is all based on the Gospel—the good news that God extends grace first—then keeps extending grace, day after day, so we can become more like Him.
>
> When we are out in the community, having these conversations, our churches then become known as a safe place for women facing unintended pregnancy or after an abortion. When that happens, we can bring restoration to this issue and individuals impacted, as we create communities where women and children are thriving.
>
> Because that paints a picture of a different option than abortion or overwhelming struggle as a mom: a picture of hope. This is what women need to see if we are ever going to truly make a difference and see fewer women choosing abortion. We have to create for them a pathway where both they and their children can thrive.¹⁴⁴

In answer to the question of how *Roe*'s reversal might affect ProGrace's ministry, Angie Weszley, wrote that "three key realities haven't changed." These are:

1. Christians need a response to abortion that involves the Kingdom, not a political party.

2. The realities of unintended pregnancy that cause women to believe their only options are abortion or overwhelming struggle still exist.

---

143. See e.g., Morris, *Gospel According to John*, 779.
144. Weszley, *ProGrace: A New Christian Response to Abortion*, 22.

3. No abortion law will change the fact that only 7% of people approach Christians for help before an abortion, citing fear of judgment and lack of visible support.[145]

The evangelical approach to abortion should be one filled with the gospel and full of love, grace, and mercy. Avail, Care Net, and ProGrace are examples of ways in which evangelical Christians can advocate for and promote life-giving options, while continuing to be accessible and Christ-centered in their missions.

MEN AND ABORTION

In the previous chapter, I quoted Garbrielle Blair on adoption. She is a Mormon mother of six, and thus not an evangelical but someone who shares evangelical values on abortion, who has written a best-selling book with the provocative title *Ejaculate Responsibly*. Her point is that men need to take responsibility for their sexual activity and thus reduce the abortion rate. Her main point, backed up with research studies is that 99 percent of abortions are caused by unwanted pregnancies and men cause all unwanted pregnancies. "Men have two options for birth control: condoms and vasectomies. Both are easier, cheaper, more convenient, and safer than birth control for women."[146]

According to Blair, "We've put the burden of pregnancy prevention on the person who is fertile for 24 hours a month, instead of the person who is fertile 24 hours a day, every day of their life."[147] That may be an overstatement, but the point is clear enough. Men need to start taking responsibility for their fertility. Part of the problem is the perception that men dislike condom use. "Every few months, I see another viral tweet/TikTok from a woman talking about how many men try to talk women into having sex without a condom."[148] Given the risk of unwanted pregnancies surely condom use is a small sacrifice. Besides, it also protects against sexually transmitted diseases.

To be fair, pro-lifers have always stressed male responsibility. Blair is just being more blunt about it in a way that may make us uncomfortable but underlines an obvious truth. It is the pro-choice side that puts all the emphasis on women and their right to choose. One would have thought

---

145. Weszley, "Does the Roe decision impact the ProGrace strategy?," §2-3.
146. Blair, *Ejaculate Responsibly*, 29.
147. Blair, *Ejaculate Responsibly*, 2.
148. Blair, *Ejaculate Responsibly*, 37.

that a movement so linked to radical feminism would want to see men being held more accountable for their actions, but the stress on a woman's right to control her own body has had the related effect of minimising men's responsibility for abortion. Besides, as noted earlier, male support has been actively recruited by the pro-choice side.

The LifeWay study cited above found that 38 percent of the women interviewed said the father of the baby had the most influence in their abortion decision. Anecdotal evidence supports these findings. Certainly, in my experience of participating in Life Chain events (an annual silent protest against abortion), it is almost always men who are most vocally opposed to what we are doing. While there is evidence that some men experience grief after a partner's abortion, and others have actively tried to prevent one, for many men it is an escape from responsibility.

The indiscriminate advocacy of condom use may run the risk of the kind of opposition Everett Koop faced for recommending that promiscuous gay men wear condoms. However, given the reality of life in a fallen world, surely condom use is preferable to the taking of a human life that might have been otherwise avoided. Interestingly, and perhaps significantly, there have been multiple news reports (as a google search will show) of increased numbers of men having vasectomies as a result of the reversal of *Roe v. Wade*. In part, this may have been prompted by extravagant and unlikely claims of birth control now being outlawed (which, to be fair, Justice Clarence Thomas hinted at),[149] but the primary motivation appears to be the potential loss of abortion as a backup for failed or no birth control.

This can be indicative of a genuine concern for men's female partners. But for far too many men, I am afraid that Blair's advice will go unheeded because they are not interested in being responsible and caring with their sexuality. The #MeToo movement that began with the downfall of movie mogul Harvey Weinstein in 2017 has exposed the sexual abuse rampant among the powerful and previously admired celebrities in Hollywood, the media and elsewhere. What has happened there takes place every day among the less privileged of society. The conventional wisdom is that such abuse is about power not sex, but it is surely about both, placing personal gratification before all else. Both power and personal gratification make abortion an easy option over responsibility. More than that, it is about an old-fashioned concept, sin—which leads to my last point.[150]

149. See e.g., Neidig, "Thomas calls for overturning precedents."

150. Some feminists have interpreted the reversal of *Roe v. Wade* as just another form of male dominance, even as "punishment" for the #MeToo movement. What this fails to reckon with is that both the prevalence of elective abortion and the normalization of "free sex" with its attendant abuses by men are fruits of the sexual revolution

THE NEED FOR REVIVAL

In discussing the eighteenth-century movement to abolish the slave trade (see chapter 2), it was noted that the slave trade was only one of several moral evils in British society. Wilberforce and others fought and prayed for its abolition, while also addressing other social and ethical issues of their day. Likewise, being consistently pro-life in our day involves not only opposition to abortion, but concern for other issues such as endemic poverty and racism as well as sexual ethics. (John Piper is an example of someone who, when pastor of Bethlehem Baptist Church in Minneapolis, used to preach annually on racism as well as abortion, quipping that this made him a Democrat one week and a Republican the next, adding "Which is just the way I want it, because I am neither.")[151] But another factor that contributed to the abolitionists' success was the Evangelical Revival or Great Awakening that swept both Britain and America, under the leadership of Whitefield and the Wesleys, resulting in a spiritual and moral transformation that carried over into the nineteenth century. This is the factor that is missing in our day and without it no amount of political and legal action will succeed in abolishing, or at least decreasing, the evil of abortion. Prayer for spiritual renewal and revival accompanying the proclamation of the biblical gospel (*evangel*), with its attendant effect on society at large must be our greatest evangelical priority. I may not agree with all of Michael Brown's theology of revival, but I do agree with the title of his book, *Revival or We Die: A Great Awakening is Our Only Hope* (2021).[152]

---

radical feminism unleashed in the 1960s. Of course, sexual abuse existed before then. Feminism at its best was a corrective to a patriarchal social order that limited and demeaned the roles of women. Much has changed for the better since then. But to the extent that "sexual freedom" has been "liberated" from the restraints of marital relationships and joint parenthood it has had a damaging effect on both women and men. The answer is not to go back to the 1950s, but to move forward in the way suggested by journalist and public policy analyst Andrea Mrozek in her thoughtful article, "Whither Feminism?," 86–92.

In a subsequent issue of the same periodical, Kurt Armstrong reflects on the "serious business" of sex without the constraints of committed matrimony: "Without ignoring some of the historical problems with the institution of marriage, it's worth stating some of its basic social value. . . . [T]he fact is that most men contend with thoughtless, unloving, animal sexual impulses and desires that, unchecked, can be harmful to others, especially women. It should be abundantly clear that we cannot unleash sex from the narrow, restricting, repressive bonds of marriage without real personal and social consequences." ("Serious Business," 92.)

151. Piper, "Jesus Died to End Abortion and Racism."

152. Russell Moore in *Losing Our Religion* devotes a chapter to "How Revival Might Save Us," but warns against an identification of revival with winning the culture war (209). He quotes A.W. Tozer to the effect that "the need of the day is not simply

Discussion Questions

1. Does the reversal of *Roe v. Wade* appear to be a pro-life win? What are some of the challenges that the pro-life position is now facing as a result?

2. Why do you think that some religious leaders have stepped out in support of abortion rights after the reversal of *Roe v. Wade*?

3. What are some of the potential consequences of an Abortion Abolitionist position?

4. If our greatest defence against abortion is a spiritual awakening, what can those in the pro-life movement do to engage in Christian Advocacy? Is this "if" a given for all evangelical Christians?

---

revival, but a radical reformation that will go to the root of our moral and spiritual maladies and deal with causes rather than consequences, with the disease rather than the symptoms." Tozer concludes, "It is my considered opinion that under the present circumstances we do not want revival at all. A widespread revival of the kind of Christianity we know today in America might prove to be a moral tragedy from which we would not recover in a hundred years" (212). Tozer wrote this in the mid-twentieth century ("No Revival Without Reformation," 2.) How much more relevant might his words be today. However, a true God-sent revival such as has been experienced in the past would not be one of "the kind of Christianity we have in America today," but one of both genuine reformation and spiritual renewal.

10

Evangelicals, Abortion, and the Politics of the Cross

My intention had been that the previous chapter should serve as my conclusion, but a critic of an earlier draft wrote that:

> we get the impression (only an impression) that you are not bullish on political action—except for the continuing biblical obligation to pray for our leaders. And yet I find myself dissatisfied because I feel that your vague negativity toward the political approach is not well explored. If evangelicals, in the main, agree that life in a human womb is important to God, then why would we have any less right than liberals and leftists to fight in the political arena for our view? All laws, after all, are reflections of someone's morality. Why shouldn't it be *our* morality? Why should we acquiesce to theirs?

In commending, in modified form, the approach of *The Benedict Option*, I note in chapter 9 that it has been misunderstood as a complete withdrawal from political life: "To be sure, Christians cannot afford to vacate the public square entirely. The church must not shrink from its responsibility to pray for political leaders *and to speak prophetically to them*" (emphasis added). The question is how this is to be done. I do agree with calls for more Christians to run for political office (e.g., by Franklin Graham), but that is not enough, or even primary.

In Volume 1 of his 1984 volume *Involvement: Being a Responsible Christian in a Non-Christian Society,* John Stott asks rhetorically, "Should We Impose Our Views" on a pluralistic society? He offers three possible approaches which he terms imposition, laissez-faire, and persuasion. For imposition, he gives the examples of the Inquisition and (more relevantly for our purposes) Prohibition in the United States which, although codified in a constitutional amendment, resulted in the liquor trade going underground, with an accompanying rise in crime, such that a further amendment to the constitution voided the previous one.

For a laissez-faire approach, Stott offers the disastrous example of German Christians' (other than in the Confessing Church with its Barmen Declaration) acquiescence in Nazism. The approach he favors is persuasion by argument. This includes political arguments that ideally find their way into legislation by building a consensus in society at large.[1]

As Daniel Williams writes in *The Politics of the Cross,* "A law is most effective when it reflects widely shared views in a society. When a societal consensus no longer supports a particular law, it usually becomes a dead letter." After giving some historical examples, Williams adds, "White evangelical Christians who entered politics in the late 1970s for the purpose of changing the law in order to create cultural renewal had their priorities reversed; they should have attempted to change the culture, and if they had, changes in the law would have followed suit."[2]

I can do no better than to commend a careful perusal of Williams's book, subtitled *A Christian Alternative to Partisanship,* addressing the highly polarized political partisanship in the United States today, where neither party can claim the whole-hearted allegiance of the Christian, but there are policies of both to which a Christian can and should subscribe. The book was published in 2021 before the overturning of *Roe v. Wade,* but much of what Williams writes on that subject has proved to be prophetic. For instance:

> Pro-lifers have the votes to pass increased restrictions on abortion in many states. . . . But because they have not succeeded in creating a changed cultural consensus on unborn human life, any gains that they will make will probably lead to a political backlash that will hurt the movement. If they overturn *Roe v. Wade,* there is no question that the Democratic Party will be even more committed to mandating federal funding for abortion, which is already a promise in its platform. If they ban

---

1. Stott, *Involvement,* 1:73–93.
2. Williams, *Politics of the Cross,* 13.

abortion in some states, other states with a pro-choice majority will likely expand services. And the increasing availability of chemical abortions will make the debate over surgical abortions largely obsolete. We are probably not far from the day when any woman who wants a first-trimester abortion will be able to order abortifacients over the internet without a prescription, because that is already the case in other countries.[3]

Despite the greater access to chemical abortifacients that now exists, prescriptions are still required in the US, so the scenario envisaged by Williams has not quite yet arrived, but the Department of Justice has authorized mail orders to states where the procedure is illegal. The FDA had decided in 2021 to remove the drug's in-person dispensing requirement during the pandemic, which broadened access by allowing the drug to be prescribed via telehealth and sent in the mail. Then it permanently lifted a requirement that patients obtain mifepristone (used both for miscarriages and self-medicated abortions) in person from a health provider,[4] thus paving the way "for telemedicine abortion services which conduct medical consultations with patients by video, phone or online questionnaires and then arrange for them to receive the prescribed pills by mail."[5] This has the potential of making mail-order chemical abortifacients the equivalent of liquor sales in the Prohibition era in those states where they are still technically illegal and will have a modifying effect on reports of greatly reduced abortion rates in these states. However, at this time of writing, a case is working its way through the courts that could potentially reverse the federal government's approval of mifepristone.

In November 2022 a lawsuit was filed by the Christian legal group Alliance Defending Freedom (ADF), arguing that the FDA exceeded its regulatory authority and ignored safety concerns when it approved mifepristone. A pro-life federal judge in Texas, Matthew Kacsmaryk, sided with the plaintiffs, issuing a preliminary injunction on April 7, 2023 suspending the FDA's 23-year-old approval of mifepristone. He also endorsed the plaintiffs' views that a previously dormant, one hundred and fifty-year-old anti-vice law called the Comstock Act "plainly forecloses mail-order abortion."

Reaction from the pro-choice lobby was predictable. Vice-President Harris announced that she and President Biden would stand with the women

---

3. Williams, *Politics of the Cross*, 115–16.

4. This was by means of a narrow interpretation of an 1873 law still on the books that, on a straightforward reading, made it illegal to mail "drugs, medical instruments, and 'every article or thing designed, adapted, or intended for producing abortion, or for any indecent or immoral use...'"

5. Belluck, "Abortion Pills," §6.

of America and that to attack women's access to the abortion pill was to attack fundamental American rights. Documented side effects were dismissed as based on "junk science." Kacsmaryk's decision was partially based on two medical studies that were later withdrawn by the publisher, stating, "we made this decision with the journal's editor because of undeclared conflicts of interest and after expert reviewers found that the studies demonstrate a lack of scientific rigor that invalidates or renders unreliable the authors' conclusions." Lead author of the studies, Jim Studnicki, disputed this: "To date, [the publisher] has advanced no valid objection to their findings and shown no evidence of any major errors, miscalculations, or falsehoods."[6]

The Biden administration took the decision to the fifth circuit court of appeals, where two judges blocked the part of the ruling overturning the FDA's initial 2000 approval of mifepristone, but reimposed restrictions on the drug previously lifted by the FDA. They include limiting mifepristone use after seven weeks of pregnancy—previously approved through ten weeks—and banning delivery by mail.

This ruling was then appealed to the Supreme Court, which temporarily blocked the lower courts' decisions, returning the case to the fifth circuit. It also issued a stay while the issue continues to proceed through the courts, meaning that access to the pill would remain unchanged for the duration of the suit, with polls suggesting increased distrust in the court's ability to decide "reproductive health cases."[7]

A three-judge panel on the fifth circuit appeals court upheld parts of Kacsmaryk's decision, noting that the FDA "failed to adequately take into account safety concerns when it loosened access to mifepristone in 2016." The Justice Department, which strongly opposes the ruling, vowed to once again appeal to the Supreme Court, but because of that court's previous ruling, this "temporary pause has allowed the drug to remain widely available."[8] The maker of mifepristone has also asked the Supreme Court for a ruling in 2024.[9] Meanwhile, the state of Vermont passed legislation which, according to Alliance Defending Freedom, censors the ability of two pregnancy centers it is representing to "advertise their services and precludes the ability of centers to offer even non-medical services, information, and counseling unless provided by a licensed health care provider." In particular, the legislation classifies as "unprofessional conduct" pregnancy centers that offer abortion

---

6. Christensen, "Journal publisher retracts studies," § 8, 16.
7. Weixel, "Poll: most don't trust Supreme Court to decide."
8. Gregorian et al., "Appeals court upholds some restrictions," §2–4.
9. de Vogue. "DOJ and Mifepristone maker."

pill reversal (which apparently has documented successes) and this could result in "denial of a license or other disciplinary action."[10]

On the other hand, Walgreens, the second largest pharmacy supplier in the US, under pressure from pro-life attorneys general agreed not to sell mifepristone in nearly two dozen conservative states, in four of which abortion remains legal.[11] These developments could have a significant impact on the availability of "abortion pills" in the US. However, there are ways around legalities.

Leah Savas reports that by February 2022 (before the Supreme Court's ruling) Texas's "heartbeat law" had "survived a number of count challenges," but its:

> effect on abortion numbers was less clear. That month, the state reported that abortions in Texas in September 2021 had fallen to 2,197, down from 4,511 the previous September. [More recent post-*Roe* reports are of a 99 percent drop.][12] But other reports showed requests to the European abortion pill website AidAccess had skyrocketed in September, as had the numbers of Texas women traveling to out-of-state abortion facilities. News outlets told of abortion pill networks that helped women get abortion pills from Mexico.[13]

Another outcome would be a rise in surgical abortions (involving travel if need be) in those states where they are readily available. For instance, a study by researchers at Brigham and Women's Hospital in Boston found that there had been a 37 percent rise in "abortion care" for out-of-state clients at Planned Parenthood facilities in the first four months after the *Dobbs* decision, as well as use of charitable funding to pay for medical and travel expenses. One of the studies' authors is quoted as saying, "We've always had abortion travelers from New England, but now we see that we have people coming from much farther away like Texas, Louisiana, Florida, or Georgia."[14] (That said, data from the CDC showing that in Texas in 2022 the birthrate increased by 4.7 percent, the largest percentage increase in the country, does support the claim that abortion restrictions are saving lives.)[15]

Overall, it would appear that at least some of what Williams has predicted is coming to fruition in the United States currently. The political

10. Campisi, "Lawsuits: Pregnancy Centers Are Being Targeted," §8–9.
11. Ziegler, "Opinion: Walgreen's abortion pill decision."
12. Bilger, "Texas Abortions Drop 99%."
13. Olasky and Savas, *Story of Abortion in America*, 411–12.
14. Umholtz, "More out-of-state patients are traveling to Mass. for abortions."
15. Ertelt, "Texas Has Just 17 Abortions."

left is working very hard to oppose and thwart any legislation enacted by pro-life politicians. Without a cultural and societal change, the legislation does little to change the hearts and minds of those working tirelessly to provide and/or access abortion.

LIMITATONS OF LEGISLATIVE CHANGE

Marvin Olasky and Leah Savas's much anticipated *The Story of Abortion in America*, referenced occasionally in previous chapters, was released in January 2023, originally intended to coincide with the fiftieth anniversary of *Roe v. Wade*. It has rightly been termed a *tour de force*, detailing what it calls a "street-level history" of abortion in America from 1652 to 2022. The first forty chapters are written by Olasky, the last ten by Savas. These are bookended by an introduction and an epilogue, both by Olasky. The introduction states: "For 370 years, this book shows, laws and their enforcement have depended on public opinion. . . . This book reports on shifting public sentiment over the centuries and the sentiment in crucial subsets: journalists, pastors, doctors, and others. We also look at records of private opinion, since the views of a woman and her boyfriend or husband are still more influential than any law"[16] Olasky demonstrates how politicians from Ted Kennedy to Jesse Jackson to Clinton and Gore, who once opposed unrestricted abortion changed their views, or at least their rhetoric, when it became politically convenient to do so.[17]

Referring to the founding of Operation Rescue by Randall Terry, Olasky notes that Operation Rescue's vision was that "Protestors would block entrances to abortion businesses. Police would haul them away. Massive press coverage with video of the arrests would let pro-lifers gain sympathy similar to what civil rights activists in the 1960s received."[18] That this did not happen, I would surmise, is because most of the press, which was sympathetic to the civil rights movement, proved to be decidedly unsympathetic to Operation Rescue's tactics and to the pro-life movement in general. After one particular incident in Wichita, Kansas, "A poll by the local *Wichita Eagle* and television station KAKE asked city residents, 'How do you feel about Operation Rescues tactics?' One in five was positive, four in five were negative. Of those who said Operation Rescue changed their views of abortion, two-thirds said it had made them more 'in favor of abortion rights.'"[19]

16. Olasky and Savas, *Story of Abortion in America*, 1.
17. See chapter 38, "Pro-life Frustration," (313–22).
18. Olasky and Savas, *Story of Abortion in America*, 326–27.
19. Olasky and Savas, *Story of Abortion in America*, 327–28.

Olasky continues, "When Operation Rescue did not achieve what pro-life activists had hoped for, a few turned from non-violence to killing. In 1993 Michael Griffin murdered David Gunn in Pensacola, Florida, and Shelley Shannon wounded George Tiller in Wichita. . . . In 1994 Paul Hill in Pensacola murdered John Britton and Britton's bodyguard. Matt Waters of CareNet, the umbrella group for pro-life pregnancy centers, said Hill's action was 'absolutely negative' for the pro-life cause and positive for abortion advocates who 'raise money off of bulletproof vests. It's a fundraiser for them—a tragedy for us.'"[20]

To be clear, Operation Rescue joined other pro-life groups in roundly denouncing violence and murder. However, it has been argued that those who resorted to violence were taking to its logical conclusion, not only Terry's language of wanting to start a civil war,[21] but his and others' comparisons of abortion with the holocaust, and Terry's emulation of Dietrich Bonhoeffer, who was executed for participating in an attempt to assassinate Adolf Hitler. "Pro-life murderers did not invent the Holocaust analogy to justify their attacks on abortion providers. They simply capitalized on a metaphor that had been refined and elaborated by abortion opponents for decades."[22] This characterization may be unfair, but it is one that was pushed by various media outlets and so influenced public opinion. As Olasky writes, "The difference between Operation Rescue's nonviolence and those these killings was huge, but conservative activist Connie Marshner witnessed media lumping them together as extremist activity: 'Operation Rescue combined with shootings that were happening at the same time gave the pro-life movement such a black eye that many people became afraid to be pro-life.' Congress passed the Freedom of Access to Clinic Entrances Act (FACE) that turned into a federal crime any interference with an abortion center's normal operations."[23]

A more recent movement, based in part on Operation Rescue, and also on the example of Mary Wagner, a Canadian pro-lifer whose peaceful occupation of abortion clinics around Toronto had been covered by pro-life websites, is Red Rose Rescue, taking as its biblical mandate Prov 24:11, which is rendered as "Rescue those being dragged to death, and those tottering to execution withhold not. If you say 'I know not this man!' does not He who tests hearts not perceive it?" (This is from the 1970 edition of

---

20. Olasky and Savas, *Story of Abortion in America*, 328.
21. Olasky and Savas, *Story of Abortion in America*, 327n10.
22. Biesel and Lipton-Lubet, "Appropriating Auschwitz," 45.
23. Olasky and Savas, *Story of Abortion in America*, 328.

the New American Bible. My thanks to Karl Cooper for identifying it.)[24] According to its website:

> During a Red Rose Rescue a team of pro-lifers enter the actual places where the innocent unborn are about to be *"dragged to death."* . . . Red Rose Rescuers peacefully talk to women scheduled for abortion, with the goal of persuading them to choose life. They offer to them red roses as a sign of life, peace and love. Should the unborn still "totter to execution" Red Rose Rescuers stay in the place of execution in solidarity with their abandoned brothers and sisters performing a non-violent act of defense through their continued presence inside the killing centers remaining with them for as long as they can.
>
> The Rescuers stay with the abandoned unborn, as the manifestation of our love for them recognizing that unborn children, as members of the human family, have a right to be defended. The rescuers will not leave the unwanted, but must be "taken away."[25]

In other words, Red Rose Rescuers allow themselves to be arrested, tried and, if need be, imprisoned. Paragraph 15 of the organization's "Code of Conduct," states, "Unjust imprisonment is a spiritual extension of the rescue and an opportunity to continue to witness to the unborn whom Red Rose Rescuers sought to defend. In jail, the Red Rose Rescuers will pray, fast, serve fellow inmates, and offer reparation for the sin of abortion."[26] Whatever one thinks of such tactics, or of some of the underlying Roman Catholic theology ("offer reparation for the sin of abortion") one cannot but be impressed with the dedication that leads to seeing imprisonment as an extension of the movement's witness to the sanctity of life.

Olasky and Savas do not mention Red Rose Rescue, but by way of contrast with the tactics and reputation of Operation Rescue, they commend the work of pregnancy care ministries. Olasky notes that one of the first such centers "opened in Toledo in 1971, two years before *Roe. v Wade*" and ten years before Care Net's first pregnancy care center opened in Baltimore.[27] He also records the nineteenth-century work of homes for unwed mothers

---

24. The citation is actually from Proverbs 24:11–12.

25. Red Rose Rescue, "Mission Statement," §2–3. Cf. Sargeant, "Red Rose Rescue," 74–84. A separate pro-life organization with a more educational focus, going by the name of "The White Rose Resistance" is modeled on a movement of that name that opposed Nazism in Germany. See *White Rose Resistance—A Voice for the Unborn* (thewhiterose.life).

26. Red Rose Rescue, "Code of Conduct," §15.

27. Olasky and Savas, *Story of Abortion in America*, 331–32.

and the like where from the Civil War to the Great Depression, "women managed and volunteered at a huge variety of pro-life organizations that helped pregnant women and children without parents."[28] At a time when abortion was often associated with prostitution and male promiscuity, attention is also given to the alternatives provided by such organizations as the Young Men's Christian Association: "With enforcement largely unsuccessful in reducing the supply of abortionists what about decreasing demand? As specialist providers of abortion emerged, what about specialist providers of ways for young men to spend time in evening pursuits other than pressuring women for sex?"[29]

Since the relatively recent availability of ultrasound images at pro-life pregnancy centers Leah Savas documents several examples of how this has been used to convince women not to abort. However, when ultrasounds have been required in abortion clinics, the results have been substantially less. One woman in Birmingham, Alabama, "who looked at the ultrasound before aborting her baby told *The New York Times* in 2010, 'It was really the picture of the ultrasound that made me feel that it was O.K.' She said her eight-week-old baby 'looked like a little egg, and I couldn't see arms or legs or a face.' Another woman at the facility for her second abortion shared her tactic for having a less emotionally fraught procedure: 'You almost have to think of it as an alien.'" Savas surmises, "Such a stark difference between the effectiveness of ultrasounds at abortion facilities and at pregnancy centers makes sense: women who are already at an abortion facility are more invested (perhaps even financially) and more likely to feel it's too late to back out, no matter what they see on the screen. Meanwhile, ultrasounds at pregnancy centers generally cost the patient nothing and take place in an environment where the woman faces no pressure to abort."[30] Does this perhaps suggest that it is not the biological evidence so much as the state of mind (open to persuasion or not) women bring to these experiences that is determinative of the outcome?

In the epilogue, Olasky concludes:

> the need for compassionate help amid crisis pregnancies will remain. Some tiny humans will survive, but most who would have faced a death sentence will still face it, sometimes in New York, California, Illinois, or other abortion strongholds, sometimes in a lonely room where a desperate woman ingests a pill or portion, much as her predecessors in colonial America would

28. Olasky and Savas, *Story of Abortion in America*, 211.
29. Olasky and Savas, *Story of Abortion in America*, 122.
30. Olasky and Savas, *Story of Abortion in America*, 346.

have. Life or death for unborn children will still depend on the willingness of their mothers to protect them. . . .

We need to remember the historical reality: Even when public opinion concerning abortion was more negative than is now, enforcement of abortion bans was difficult. . . .

American abortion history has also shown me that social and economic pressures are strong: When abortion pressure grows the only fundamental thing stronger than that is love. Punitive attempts backfire. Harsh measures don't change hearts. Knowledge of fetal anatomy helps and ultrasounds are great tools. Knowledge of the Bible helps, but many are resistant. Community pro-life sentiment is crucial not only in prevention but in enforcement as well: Without it, district attorneys won't prosecute and juries won't convict.

This doesn't mean law is irrelevant: Laws can reduce the supply of abortionists and affect beliefs about right and wrong. Laws will not end abortion but they can reduce the body count, similar to the way laws against drunk driving today cannot end the practice but can save lives. Child-friendly public policies and corporate practices can also help. . . . We need more career and work time flexibility. Governments and corporations should have child support stipends and generous maternity leave policies. . . .

Besides those top-down changes comes the question of helping those who provide one-to-one help to women in crisis. Such states as Mississippi, Missouri, and Arizona are helping to reduce abortion demand by creating tax credits for contributions to pregnancy-resource centres. Tax credits could also help adoption nonprofits, but that will require more trust in God among women who sometimes choose abortion over "giving away" a child. As long as the only two choices for many women are abortion or becoming a single mom pressure to allow abortions legally or illegally will remain. . . .

Now that success on the supply side is possible we hope pro lifers will expand efforts on the demand side by helping young parents visualize their unborn children and by showing compassion in regard to material and spiritual needs.[31]

As Stott argued in the 1980s, persuasion is preferable to imposition. But who is to do the persuasion? While I applaud the practical legal suggestions made by Olasky, I suggested in the previous chapter that it is not insignificant that the Christian Action Council (CAC) with its legislative focus found it more effective to transform itself into Care Net with

---

31. Olasky and Savas, *Story of Abortion in America*, 439–43.

an emphasis on pregnancy care centers and related ministries. Although having a voice politically can produce meaningful change, the impact of intentional, empathic, and supportive care for women and men facing a crisis pregnancy is paramount. This is where lives are being saved and the life-changing gospel is being proclaimed, as the only basis of a transformed life-affirming society, practicing the politics of the cross.

Discussion Questions

1. What approach has the pro-life movement historically taken—imposition, laissez-faire, or persuasion (see p. 160)?
2. What evidence do you see of Williams's predictions (p. 160–61) in our society today?
3. If we prioritize the persuasion approach, how can the average pro-lifer respond in a compassionate, intentional, and empathetic way to the tragic reality of abortion? Do you find the author's approach convincing? Why or why not?

APPENDIX

The Prolific Deceivers at the Heart of *Roe v. Wade*

Daniel K. Williams

Reprinted with permission of the author and Christianity Today, *December 6, 2021.*

The life of "Jane Roe" of *Roe v. Wade* was not what it seemed.

When Norma McCorvey, using the alias "Jane Roe," sued Dallas district attorney Henry Wade for the right to an abortion that Texas law prohibited, she won plaudits from pro-choice feminists throughout the nation. Years later, in the late 1980s, McCorvey abandoned the anonymity of her alias and became a public advocate of abortion rights and a sought-out speaker on the pro-choice lecture circuit.

But in 1995, McCorvey took an action that made her a hero to a very different group of people: pro-life Christians. She renounced most of her earlier support for abortion rights and converted to evangelical Christianity. A photo that was widely reprinted in many evangelical publications showed an ecstatic Flip Benham—the director of Operation Rescue and the pastor of a Free Methodist church—baptizing a beaming McCorvey. Three years later, McCorvey converted to Catholicism, an action that may have linked her even more strongly to the pro-life cause. Yet in the last two years of her life, McCorvey distanced herself from organized religion, said that she supported abortion rights in at least the first trimester, and told a documentary filmmaker that her work for the pro-life movement had merely been an act.

So, which version of McCorvey was the real one? What does her complicated story tell us about the fifty-year political battle over abortion rights in America? And what does it tell us about the Christians who have been caught up in that struggle?

Joshua Prager's *The Family Roe: An American Story* is a masterpiece of journalistic research that uncovers the story not only of McCorvey but also her entire family, as well as a number of other Texans whose lives were caught up in *Roe v. Wade*.

(Full disclosure: Because I am a historian who has written about the pro-life movement, Prager reached out to me for help in locating a few archival sources, and at his invitation I offered comments on a few chapters before publication, but the research, interpretation, and storyline are entirely his own).

A tragic story

If McCorvey always remained somewhat of a shadowy figure—with neither pro-choice nor pro-life activists knowing for sure what she really believed—her extended family is even more obscure. Yet Prager, an award-winning journalist and best-selling author, spent more than a decade tracking down every member of the "Roe" family he could find, including McCorvey's three children, her mother and half-sister, and some of her long-term partners. In the process, he uncovered a tragic story of poverty, deceit, exploitation, and copious amounts of illicit sex and drugs.

McCorvey was an alcoholic, a chronic drug abuser, and a lesbian, but she was also a mother. Despite her landmark lawsuit, she had never had an abortion, even though she had wanted one. Two years before the Supreme Court ruled on her case, the child that she wanted to abort was instead given up for adoption—which meant (Prager knew) that the child could be located. Prager did locate her, along with her two older sisters, each of whom had been fathered by a different man and adopted by a different family. In addition, Prager interviewed many of McCorvey's associates, including the lawyers who represented her in *Roe v. Wade*, along with numerous others associated with the legal battle over abortion in the 1970s.

APPENDIX: THE PROLIFIC DECEIVERS AT THE HEART OF ROE V. WADE

McCorvey, he found, had grown up in a broken home, with an abusive alcoholic mother. For a short time, when McCorvey was in elementary school, her father tried to reform the family through religion: They were strict Jehovah's Witnesses for a few years. But eventually, the family left religion, the father left the family, and the mother went back to drinking. McCorvey, in turn, came of age with a determination to try her parents' vices, her father's cigarettes and her mother's alcohol. That, in turn, led to harder drugs—first marijuana and then cocaine and barbiturates. She began sleeping promiscuously with men but found relationships with women much more satisfying. McCorvey had many such same-sex relationships, and in between, she occasionally had trysts with men, some of whom she met in the bars where she worked or drank. Three of those relationships produced children.

The first child, Melissa, was raised partly by McCorvey's mother and partly by an aunt. Her family was so dysfunctional—with so few sober drivers among her relatives—that the state of Texas gave her a "hardship license" in her early teens so that she could legally drive and take care of her family. The experience gave Melissa a determination not to drink or be like her relatives. What she longed for more than anything else was a stable home. Despite—or perhaps because of—her family's drug abuse and promiscuity, she was drawn to the moral rectitude and assurance of a Southern Baptist church.

"Everything Norma stood for," she said, "I didn't want to be." She did lapse in her standards a little, sleeping with three different men during her late teens, but then she got married and found joy in raising a child. And despite the abuse she had received from her mother, she was the only one of her sisters to care for McCorvey during her later years and to remain at her bedside when she passed away at the age of sixty-nine. Yet Melissa's dream marriage ended in abuse and divorce, and at the end of the book, she is found postponing a hoped-for second marriage after her fiancé shocked her by downing four beers at a barbecue, an action that reactivated her deeply rooted fear of alcoholism.

The second daughter, Jennifer, was adopted at birth by an unrelated family and never knew about Norma McCorvey until she was an adult. Yet she developed an uncanny (and tragic) resemblance to her mother: She discovered in her teens that she was gay and loved alcohol. Like her biological mother, her own adult life became a life of heavy drinking and lesbian flings, mixed with unhappy relationships with men and two failed marriages. When she finally learned that both her mother and her biological father were bisexual, it all made sense, she thought; no wonder she was attracted to women. Today she is recovering from years of alcohol and drug abuse.

Shelley, the youngest, was adopted by a Lutheran family in the Northwest that started out looking like a picture-perfect Christian home but was eventually torn apart by her adopted father's alcoholism and subsequent divorce. She was 19 when she learned that Norma was her mother—at which point she was aghast. She was pro-life, she said; she wanted nothing to do with a woman who had tried to abort her and was completely unapologetic about it. But over time, Shelley's views moderated. She became pregnant out of wedlock herself, and though she ultimately decided to keep her baby, the experience made her more sympathetic to women like her mother who did want to terminate the pregnancy.

But that sympathy did not extend to McCorvey. At the end of the book, even after her mother's death, Shelley states that she is unable to forgive her mother for first wanting to abort her and then wanting to exploit her in the tabloids after tracking her down many years later. And yet her bouts with depression and anger remind her that, despite her deep desires to transcend her biology, she is "just like Norma."

As the book's timeline concludes in 2020, just after the onset of the COVID-19 pandemic, all three sisters are pro-choice, and all have been divorced. None ever found the stable, long-term romantic relationship they were seeking. And Shelley, having lost her job in the pandemic, is struggling to pay her bills.

Deep secrets

Prager describes himself as pro-choice and says that he believes that a fetus is only a "potential child," yet he recognizes the complexity of abortion choices. McCorvey, who never had an abortion, is tormented by the choice not to have one. Shelley, the daughter that McCorvey wanted to abort, spends a lifetime feeling unwanted and abandoned and struggles for decades with deep anger against the mother who wanted to end her existence before she was born. Both described themselves as both "pro-life" and "pro-choice" at different points in their lives, even though neither label fully fit. And if McCorvey and her daughter found it difficult to come to terms with abortion and *Roe*, so have many Americans, Prager suggests.

Throughout the book, Prager challenges readers' presuppositions and refuses to fit the book's messy stories into clear moral categories. Things (and people) are not always what they seem. Nearly all the people profiled in this book carry deep secrets that they refuse to reveal to others—but that Prager, as a master journalist, repeatedly succeeds in uncovering.

Take, for instance, Linda Coffee, the Texas attorney who represented McCorvey in *Roe*. She was both a strong abortion-rights activist and a faithful Texas Baptist who loved church and felt that she couldn't tell her fellow parishioners that she was sexually attracted to women and didn't believe in God. Or her fellow attorney Sarah Weddington. She was a Methodist minister's daughter who presented herself as a devout Christian and felt that she couldn't tell others about her own abortion in Mexico only a few years before *Roe*.

The Supreme Court justices who decided *Roe* didn't publicize the abortions and unwanted pregnancies in their own families and close circle. Henry Wade, the Dallas district attorney whose name would forever be linked with *Roe*, didn't tell people that he was actually a pro-choice liberal who only defended the Texas law out of duty, not because he believed in it. Mildred Jefferson, the president of the National Right to Life Association—for a while the nation's most visible pro-life activist—used half-truths and outright lies to keep nearly all of her life hidden from public view. She covered up her financial mismanagement, her marriage troubles, the limits of her medical experience, the reasons for her childlessness, and her deep resentment of a world that had discriminated against her on the basis of both her race and her sex, despite her being the first African American woman to earn an MD from Harvard Medical School.

But perhaps the most prolific deceiver in the book is Norma McCorvey herself, who spent a lifetime fashioning so many falsehoods that none of her associates could quite figure out what to believe. Prager, though, thinks he has uncovered the truth: McCorvey was a woman who intensely craved attention and would make up stories about herself to win people over. She also remained a deeply selfish and bitter person who nevertheless was attracted by what she thought was Christian love from the Evangelicals who sought to convert her.

She embraced the role of a pro-choice spokesperson—followed by pro-life activist—mainly to get attention and to become a hero. Inside, she was deeply conflicted about abortion. She never wanted to be a mother and she sensed that she did not have the skills. During the brief time when she cared for her oldest daughter Melissa, she locked the young girl in her car while she and her boyfriend went into her trailer to take drugs.

Yet she also longed for children. When she passed empty playgrounds, she was given to melancholy thoughts about the children who would never be born because of the case she had brought to trial. When she gave talks to pro-choice groups, she made the mistake of referring to abortion as killing. Years later, when she gave talks on the pro-life circuit, she made the mistake of saying repeatedly that abortion should be legal in the first trimester. She found interviews with both groups so unnerving that she made it a point to get drunk before each media appearance.

A useful symbol

Both pro-choice and pro-life activists exploited McCorvey. In 1970, when she came to Linda Coffee, she really wanted help in getting an abortion, which Coffee could have easily arranged by sending her to a doctor in Dallas who performed illegal abortions, or to a hospital in another state where abortion was legal. Yet Coffee did not do this, because she was more interested in winning a court case for women across the nation than in helping one woman terminate her pregnancy. McCorvey was useful to Coffee only as a symbol, not as a person.

Similarly, twenty-five years later, the pro-life activists who championed McCorvey's conversion could have taken her off the media circuit in order to offer counseling and help to the woman who still lived with her lesbian lover and who often showed up drunk and confused to the events she was supposed to headline. But her symbolic value as a convert made it too risky to insinuate that her born-again experience was anything less than complete.

Prager's story can easily be read as a near-hopeless tragedy. There's plenty of religion in the book, but most of it seems powerless to change people's lives. For most of the characters, religion is something they try for a while and then discard in frustration when members of their church reject them or when they decide they can't live by its standards. Others in the book angrily reject religion as oppressive. Dallas's leading abortion doctor grew up as a fundamentalist Baptist but then abandoned his plans for the ministry and embraced the cause of women's rights and abortion access.

Still others, like Mildred Jefferson, found that religiously based moral rectitude could not prevent loneliness and alienation. Unlike nearly every other character in the book, Jefferson, the daughter of a Methodist minister, abstained from sex until marriage and from alcohol and tobacco for life. Yet her desire to own more things than she could afford led her into credit problems that derailed her medical career almost as soon as it began and destroyed her dream of becoming a surgeon. And her workaholic tendencies and lack of affection for her husband led him to leave her for another woman—after which Jefferson never remarried and became more bitter than ever.

Welcome the messiness

What should a Christian make of this complicated and often tawdry story? Should we conclude that sex outside of marriage is inevitable, that abortion is necessary in some circumstances, that a cycle of drugs and poverty is unlikely to be broken, and that churches are usually unable to change lives?

Obviously, this is not the message of the gospel. But Prager's narrative should serve as a cautionary tale about the dangers of looking for easy solutions instead of engaging in the hard work of gospel-driven transformation. Sin is messy, and there are never any easy solutions to a sin problem.

Adoption—which Christians have often championed as the preferred solution to unwanted pregnancies—can be traumatic for both birth mothers and their children, as Prager's book reminds us. It is not a cure-all for every ill. The vitriolic condemnations of homosexuality that McCorvey encountered in evangelical Christianity and the promises that a person with same-sex desires could easily overcome them were not helpful. And religiously driven moral standards without Spirit-produced heart transformation will lead, more often than not, to frustration rather than lasting change.

Prager's book shows us the tragic results of these realities. But rather than giving an excuse for despair over the pro-life cause or evangelical Christianity in general, it should remind us not to rely too heavily on easy fixes in the campaign to save unborn lives. The lives of the people who want abortions—or who campaign against them—are more complicated than we might guess. The pro-life cause, then, should open itself to all this messiness—and the surprising people we might encounter along the way.

Daniel K. Williams is professor of history at the University of West Georgia. He is the author of Defenders of the Unborn: The Pro-Life Movement Before Roe v. Wade *and* The Politics of the Cross: A Christian Alternative to Partisanship.

Bibliography

"2020 Democratic Platform." *American Presidency Project.* https://www.presidency.ucsb.edu/documents/2020-democratic-party-platform.

Alberta, Tim. *The Kingdom, the Power, and the Glory.* New York, NY: Harper, 2023.

Alcorn, Randy. *Does the Birth Control Pill cause abortions?* Sandy, OR: Eternal Perspective Ministries, 2002.

Allit, Patrick. *Religion in America Since 1945: A History.* New York, NY: Columbia University Press, 2003.

Andersen, Ericka. "When 'Pro-Life' Isn't Enough: Abortion 'Abolitionists' Speak Up." *Christianity Today,* August 1, 2022. https://www.christianitytoday.com/news/2022/august/abortion-abolitionists-pro-life-movement-christian-roe-wade.html.

Anderson, Kate. "Dobbs Has Already Saved at Least 60,000 Babies From Abortions." *Lifenews.com,* May 24, 2023. https://www.lifenews.com/2023/05/24/dobbs-has-already-saved-at-least-60000-babies-from-abortions/.

Andros, Dan. "FBI Raids Home of Pro-life Christian With Guns Drawn as Family Watches in Horror." *CBN,* September 26, 2022. https://www2.cbn.com/news/us/fbi-raids-home-pro-life-christian-guns-drawn-family-watches-horror.

Andrusko, Dave. "Poll Shows Majority of Americans Support Overturning Roe v. Wade." *LifeNews.com,* July 5, 2023. https://www.lifenews.com/2023/07/05/poll-shows-majority-of-americans-support-overturning-roe-v-wade/.

Armstrong, Dave. "A Defense of Natural Family Planning." *National Catholic Register,* May 25, 2019. https://www.ncregister.com/blog/a-defense-of-natural-family-planning.

Armstrong, Kurt. "Serious Business: After Weinstein, Thinking of My Son." *Comment* 40.4 (2022): 84–100.

Associated Press. "As France guarantees the right to abortion, other European countries look to expand access." *Washington Post,* March 4, 2024.

BIBLIOGRAPHY

———. "Mexico decriminalizes abortion, extending Latin American trend of widening access," September 6, 2023. https://apnews.com/article/mexico-abortion-decriminalize-d87f6edbdf68c2e6c8f5700b3afd15de.

———. "Women in Idaho, Tennessee, and Oklahoma sue over abortion bans after being denied care," September 14, 2023. https://apnews.com/article/abortion-ban-lawsuits-idaho-tennessee-oklahoma-39257646d84255feff5a82f401f32b79.

Associated Press Video. "North Carolina governor discusses women's health in roundtable with medical professionals," May 10, 2023. https://apnews.com/video/womens-health.

Atwood, Margaret. "I invented Gilead, The Supreme Court is Making it Real." *The Atlantic*, May 13, 2022. https://www.theatlantic.com/ideas/archive/2022/05/supreme-court-roe-handmaids-tale-abortion-margaret-atwood/629833/.

Badger, Emily, Margo Sanger-Katz and Claire Cain Miller. "States With Abortion Bans Among Least Supportive for Mothers and Children." *New York Times*, July 28, 2022. https://www.nytimes.com/2022/07/28/upshot/abortion-bans-states-social-services.html.

Barr, Luke. "FBI offers $25,000 reward for information on attacks against reproductive health facilities." *ABC News*, January 19, 2023.

Barrett, Matthew. *Simply Trinity: The Unmanipulated Father, Son, and Spirit*. Grand Rapids: Baker, 2021.

Barth, Karl. *Church Dogmatics*, Vol 3, Part 4. *The Doctrine of Creation*. Edinburgh: T & T Clark. Authorised English Translation, 1961.

Balevik, Katie. "10 common pieces of abortion misinformation—debunked by a retired gynecologist." *Business Insider*, November 5, 2022. https://www.businessinsider.com/common-anti-abortion-misinformation-debunked-by-gynecologist-2022-5.

Bavinck, Herman. *In the Beginning: Foundations of Christian Theology*. Edited by John Bolt. Translated by John Vriend. Grand Rapids, MI: Baker, 1999.

Bayly, David and Tim. "Tim Keller addresses abortion." *BaylyBlog*, January 6, 2009. https://baylyblog.com/blog/2009/01/tim-keller-addresses-abortion.

Baxter, Richard. *A Christian Directory. The Practical Works of Richard Baxter*. vol 1. Grand Rapids, MI: Soli Deo Gloria, 2000.

Bebbington, David W. *Evangelicalism in Modern Britain: A History from the 1730s to the 1980s*. London: Routledge, 1989.

Belluck, Pam. "Abortions Increase in the U.S., Reversing a 30-Year Decline, Report Finds." *New York Times*, June 15, 2022. https://www.nytimes.com/2022/06/15/health/abortion-rate-increase.html.

———. "Abortion Pills Can Now Be Offered at Retain Pharmacies, F.D.A. Says." *New York Times*, January 3, 2023. https://www.nytimes.com/2023/01/03/health/abortion-pill-cvs-walgreens-pharmacies.html.

Berkhof, Louis. *Systematic Theology*. Grand Rapids, MI: Eerdmans, 1991, reprint.

———. *Manual of Christian Doctrine*. Grand Rapids, MI: Eerdmans, 1973, reprint.

Biesel, Nicola and Sarah Lipton-Lubet. "Appropriating Auschwitz: The Holocaust as Analogy and Provocation in the Pro-Life Movement." Unpublished paper, Northwestern University, nd.

Bilger, Micaiah. "Kamala Harris Leaves God and the Right to Life Out of the Declaration of Independence." *LifeNews.com*, Jan 23, 2023. https://www.lifenews.com/2023/01/23/kamala-harris-leaves-god-and-right-to-life-out-of-the-declaration-of-independence/.

———. "Kamala Harris Tells Pastors They Should Promote Killing Babies in Abortion." *LifeNews.com*, September 12, 2022. https://www.lifenews.com/2022/09/08/kamala-harris-tells-pastors-they-should-promote-killing-babies-in-abortions/.

———. "Merrick Garland Says DOJ Does Not Prosecute Attacks on Pro-Life Groups Because They Happen at Night." *LifeNews.com*, March 1, 2023. https://www.lifenews.com/2023/03/01/merrick-garland-says-doj-not-prosecuting-attacks-on-pro-life-groups-because-they-happen-at-night/.

———. "Texas Abortions Drop 99% After Roe Overturned, Thousands of Babies Saved From Abortion." *Lifenews.com*, January 16, 2023. https://www.lifenews.com/2023/01/16/texas-abortions-drop-99-after-roe-overturned-thousands-of-babies-saved-from-abortions/.

Bitler, Marianne and Madeline Zavodny. "Child Abuse and Abortion Availability." *The American Economic Review* 92.2 (May 2002): 363–67.

Blair, Gabrielle. *Ejaculate Responsibly: A Whole New Way to Think About Abortion*. New York, NY: Workman, 2022.

Blakeslee, Nat. "Sorting Fact from Fiction in the Story of Pro-Life Celebrity Abby Johnson." *Texas Monthly*, April 16, 2019.

Blackwell, Elizabeth. *The Law of Life, With Special Reference to the Education of Girls*. New York, NY: Putnam & Sons, 1852.

Boice, James Montgomery. *Genesis: Creation and Fall, Genesis 1-11*. Volume 1. Grand Rapids, MI: Baker, 1982.

Bonhoeffer, Dietrich. *Ethics*. New York, NY: Simon & Schuster, 1995.

Bose, Nandita. "Roe v. Wade ruling disproportionately hurts Black women, experts say." *Reuters*, June 27, 2022. https://www.reuters.com/world/us/roe-v-wade-ruling-disproportionately-hurts-black-women-experts-say-2022-06-27/.

Brooks, David. "Who is John Stott?" *New York Times*, November 30, 2004. https://www.nytimes.com/2004/11/30/opinion/who-is-john-stott.html.

Brown, Mark. "Teesside woman cleared over lockdown abortion charges after CPS offers no evidence." *The Guardian*, Tue 9 Jan 2024.

Bultan, Debbie Cox. "The hidden harms of Dobbs are coming to light." *The Hill*, June 23, 2023. https://thehill.com/opinion/judiciary/4065255-the-hidden-harms-of-dobbs-are-coming-to-light/.

Burge, Ryan. "Why 'Evangelical' is Becoming Another Word for 'Republican.'" *New York Times*, October 6, 2021. https://www.nytimes.com/2021/10/26/opinion/evangelical-republican.html.

Burke, Theresa with David C. Reardon. *Forbidden Grief: The Unspoken Pain of Abortion*. Warren, MI: Acorn, 2000.

Calkin, Sydney and Ella Berny. "Legal and non-legal barriers to abortion in Ireland and the United Kingdom." *The Journal of Medicine Access*, August 19, 2021. https://journals.sagepub.com/doi/10.1177/23992026211040023.

Calvin, John. *Commentaries On The Four Last Books of Moses Arranged In The Form of A Harmony*. Volume 3. Grand Rapids, MI: Baker, 1979.

Campisi, Tom. "Lawsuits: Pregnancy Centers Are Being Targeted, Censored by Legislation." *Care Net*, August 15, 2023. https://www.care-net.org/abundant-life-blog/lawsuits-vermont-women-and-families.

Care Net. "Guidelines for Life Advocates: 10 Things Not to Do when a Woman Tells You She wants an Abortion." https://getinvolvedforlife.com/.

Carlisle, Madeleine. "Positive Views of the Supreme Court Drop Sharply After Abortion Ruling." *Time*, September 1, 2022. https://time.com/6210293/supreme-court-pew-poll-dobbs/.

Carpenter Theological Blog. "Why Women Have Abortions," http://www.carpentertheologian.com.

Center for Disease Control and Prevention. "CDCs Abortion Surveillance System FAQs." https://www.cdc.gov/reproductivehealth/data_stats/abortion.htm.

Chao-Fong, Leonie and Lauren Gambino, "US Senate attempt to protect IVF access blocked by Mississippi Republican." *The Guardian*, 29 Feb 2024.

Chrisafis, Angelique. "France to make abortion a constitutional right after senate vote." *The Guardian*, 28 Feb 2024.

Christensen, Jen. "Journal publisher retracts studies used by Texas judge who ruled to suspend use of abortion pill." *CNN*, Feb 11, 2024.

Cline, Timothy. "Standing for the Sanctity of Life." *Westminster Magazine* 3.1 (Fall 2022) 60–62.

Clinton, Hillary. "Meet the Press." *NBC*, April 3, 2016.

Colson, Charles. "Why I Support Capital Punishment." *The Gospel Coalition*, February 21, 2017.

Concepcion, Summer. "Kate Cox, Texas woman at center of high profile-profile abortion case, will attend State of the Union address." *NBC News*, Jan 24, 2024.

Cotterill, Tom and Vivek Chaudhary. "EXCLUSIVE: Enjoying her first taste of freedom: Mother-of-three Carla Foster is pictured a day after she was released from prison after judges reduced her jail term for illegally taking abortion tablets to end pregnancy at 32 weeks." *Daily Mail*, July 19, 2023.

Council of Bishops. "Roe v. Wade Statement from Council of Bishops." *The United Methodist Church*, June 25, 2022. https://www.unitedmethodistbishops.org/files/roe+v.+wade+cob+response+062422.pdf.

Crossing Borders. "China's One Child Policy." www.crossingbordersnk.org.

Cusaac-Smith, Tiffany. "Abortion rights were on the ballot in these 5 states. Here's how voters decided." *USA Today*, November 10, 2022. https://www.usatoday.com/story/news/nation/2022/11/09/abortion-election-results-kentucky-california-michigan-montana-vermont/8302538001/.

Daniels, Kristen Whitney. "Death penalty proponents welcome Pope Francis' catechism revision." *National Catholic Reporter*, August 2, 2018. https://www.ncronline.org/news/death-penalty-opponents-welcome-pope-francis-catechism-revision.

Dastin, Jeffrey. "Amazon to reimburse US employees who travel for abortions, other treatments." *Reuters*, May 2, 2022.

Davis, John Jefferson. *Evangelical Ethics: Issues Facing the Church Today*. Fourth Edition. Phillipsburg, NJ: P&R, 2015.

de Vogue, Ariane. "DOJ and Mifepristone maker ask Supreme Court to make ultimate decision on abortion drug in 2024." *CNN Politics*, September 8, 2023. https://www.cnn.com/2023/09/08/politics/mifepristone-supreme-court-appeal/index.html.

Denes, Magda. *In Necessity and Sorrow: Life and Death in an Abortion Hospital*. New York, NY: Basic, 1977.

Desobeau, Diane with Lucie Aubourg. "After bans, American women turn to an abortion hotline." *AFP News*, June 18, 2023.

Dicaro, Vincent. "Care Net Launches First-Ever Program to Address Abortion in the Church." *Care Net*, August 30, 2016. https://www.care-net.org/churches-blog/care-net-launches-first-ever-program-to-address-abortion-in-the-church.

BIBLIOGRAPHY

Deignhan, John. "Society for Protection of Unborn Children," news@spuc.org.uk, August 1, 2023.

Donegan, Moira. "She performed an abortion on a 10-year old rape victim." *The Guardian*, July 10, 2023. https://www.theguardian.com/commentisfree/2023/jul/10/indiana-abortion-doctor-10-year-old-child-rape.

Dreher, Rod. *The Benedict Option: A Strategy for Christians in a Post-Christian Nation*. New York, NY: Sentinel, 2017.

———. "No One Gets Out of Here Unbroken." *Rod Dreher's Diary*, April 20, 2022.

Dudley, Jonathan. "My Take: when evangelicals were pro-choice." *CNN Belief Blog*, Oct 30, 2012.

Dwoskin, Elizabeth and Naomi Nix. "Sheryl Sandberg's next chapter: Pledging millions to fight abortion bans." *Washington Post*, October 4, 2022. https://www.washingtonpost.com/technology/2022/10/04/sandberg-facebook-meta-aclu-abortion/.

Edelman, Ada. "'Insidious,' 'draconian,' 'cruel': New Texas abortion law encourages vigilantism, experts say." *NBC News*, July 24, 2021. https://www.nbcnews.com/politics/politics-news/insidious-draconian-cruel-new-texas-abortion-law-empowers-vigilantism-experts-n1274642.

Edgar, William. *Schaeffer on the Christian Life: Countercultural Spirituality*. Wheaton, IL: Crossway, 2013.

Editors. "ETERNITY's analysis." *ETERNITY* (February 1971) 24.

———. "Fetal Life: what rights does an unborn baby have? Are the subject to any kind of qualifications?" *ETERNITY* (February 1971) 18–24.

Editors. "Prayers for a Post-Roe World." *Reformed Journal*, August 1, 2022. https://reformedjournal.com/prayers-for-a-post-roe-world/.

El-Bawab, Nadine. "Doctors face tough decisions to leave states with abortion bans." *ABC News*, June 23, 2023. https://abcnews.go.com/US/doctors-face-tough-decision-leave-states-abortion-bans/story?id=100167986.

Ertelt, Steven. "Charges Dropped Against Pro-life Woman Arrested for Praying Outside Abortion Clinic." *LifeNews.com*, February 2, 2023.

———. "FBI Arrests Two Pro-Life Advocates for Protesting Abortion, Ignore 160 Attacks on Pro-Lifers." *LifeNews.com*, December 16, 2022. https://www.lifenews.com/2022/12/16/fbi-arrests-two-pro-life-advocates-for-protesting-abortion-ignore-160-attacks-on-pro-lifers/.

———. "Joe Biden Celebrates Abortion, Applauds Defeat of Pro-Life Amendments in Kansas." *LifeNews.com*, August 3, 2022. https://www.lifenews.com/2022/08/03/joe-biden-celebrates-abortion-applauds-vote-defeating-pro-life-amendment-in-kansas/.

———. "Oklahoma Abortions Drop to 0 As Abortion Ban Saves Thousands of Babies." *LifeNews.com*, August 11, 2023. https://www.lifenews.com/2023/08/11/oklahoma-abortions-drop-to-0-as-abortion-ban-saves-thousands-of-babies/.

———. "Texas Has Just 17 Abortions in 2023, Abortion Ban Saves Tens of Thousands of Babies." *LifeNews.com*, September 7, 2023. https://www.lifenews.com/2023/09/07/texas-has-just-17-abortions-in-2023-abortion-ban-saves-tens-of-thousands-of-babies/.

———. "Woman Who Survived Abortion Slams Democrats for Voting for Infanticide: 'There's No Excuse.'" *LifeNews.com*, January 13, 2023. https://www.lifenews.com/2023/01/13/woman-who-survived-abortion-slams-democrats-for-voting-for-infanticide-theres-no-excuse/.

———. "Montana Defeats Ballot Measure." *LifeNews.com*, November 10, 2022. https://www.lifenews.com/2022/11/10/montana-defeats-ballot-measure-requiring-medical-care-for-babies-who-survive-abortions/.

———. "Polls Show Majority of Americans Support Dobbs." *LifeNews.com*, June 29, 2023. https://www.lifenews.com/2023/06/29/poll-shows-majority-of-americans-support-dobbs-decision-overturning-roe-v-wade/.

———. "Two Abortion Activists Arrested for Attacking Pro-Life Pregnancy Centers, They Face 12 Years in Prison." *LifeNews.com*, January 24, 2023. https://www.lifenews.com/2023/01/24/two-abortion-activists-arrested-for-attacking-pro-life-pregnancy-centers-they-face-12-years-in-prison/.

Ettachfini, Leila. "The Argument for Abortion as a Religious Right: The world's largest religions support—and sometimes require—abortion." *Vice*, February 10, 2020. https://www.vice.com/en/article/qjd3b7/the-argument-for-abortion-as-a-religious-right.

Evangelical Fellowship of Canada. "Charitable status of pro-life organizations." *Evangelical Fellowship*, December 20, 2021.

"Ex-soldier charged with praying near an abortion clinic." *Evangelical Times*, Aug 14, 2023. https://www.evangelical-times.org/ex-soldier-charged-with-silently-praying-near-abortion-clinic/.

Feminists for Life of America. "Can you really be a feminist and pro-life?" https://www.feministsforlife.org/.

Farrow, Anna. "Whistleblower claims 38-week-old unborn baby aborted in Montreal." *The Catholic Register*, February 7, 2023.

Fawcett, Eliza. "Synagogue Sues Florida, Saying Abortion Restrictions Limit Religious Freedoms." *New York Times*, June 16, 2022. https://www.nytimes.com/2022/06/16/us/florida-abortion-law-judaism.html.

Fernando, Christine. "GOP-led House passes 'born-alive' abortion bill; abortion rights advocated denounce bill." *USA Today*, January 12, 2023. https://www.usatoday.com/story/news/nation/2023/01/12/house-republicans-pass-born-alive-abortion-bill-activists-push-back/11038291002/.

———. "'It's time for us to be bold: why six religious leaders are fighting to expand abortion access." *USA Today*, February 13, 2023.

Filson, David Owen. "Living Pro-life in a Post-Roe World." *Westminster Magazine* 3.1 (2022): 16–18.

Finer, Lawrence B., et al. "Reasons U.S. Women Have Abortions." *Guttmacher Institute: Perspectives on Sexual and Reproductive Health*, September 1, 2005. https://www.guttmacher.org/journals/psrh/2005/reasons-us-women-have-abortions-quantitative-and-qualitative-perspectives.

Flavel, John. *The Mystery of Providence*. Edinburgh: Banner of Truth, 2020, reprint.

Foran, Clare and Melanie Zanona. "House passes 'born alive' abortion bill." *CNN Politics*, January 12, 2023. https://www.cnn.com/2023/01/11/politics/house-abortion-bill/index.html.

Forston, S. Donald and Kenneth J. Stewart, eds. *Reformed and Evangelical across Four Centuries: The Presbyterian Story in America*. Grand Rapids: Eerdmans, 2022.

Frame, John M. "Book Review of *Abortion: The Personal Dilemma*," by R. F. R. Gardner. *Banner of Truth* 109 (1972): 31–32.

———. *Medical Ethics: Principles, Persons, and Problems*. Phillipsburg, NJ: P&R, 1988.

———. *Systematic Theology: An Introduction to Christian Belief*. Phillipsburg, NJ: P&R, 2013.

French, David. "For Abortion Abolition, Against 'Abolitionists.'" *The Dispatch*, May 25, 2022. https://thedispatch.com/newsletter/frenchpress/for-abortion-abolition-against-abortion/.

Galli, Mark. "'When Evangelicals Were Pro-Choice'—Another Fake History," *Christianity Today*, October 31, 2012. https://www.christianitytoday.com/ct/2012/october-web-only/when-evangelicals-were-pro-choice-another-fake-history.html.

Gangitano, Alex. "Biden says as a Catholic he's 'not big on abortion,' but thinks Roe 'got it right.'" *The Hill*, June 27, 2023. https://thehill.com/homenews/administration/4070735-biden-says-as-catholic-hes-not-big-on-abortion-but-thinks-roe-got-it-right/.

Gardner, R.F. R. *Abortion: The Personal Dilemma*. Exeter: Paternoster, 1972.

Genocide Awareness Project. *abortionNO*. www.cbrinfo.org.

Gillespie, Brandon. "Wisconsin man charged with firebombing offices of pro-life group." *Fox News*, March 28, 2023. https://www.foxnews.com/politics/wisconsin-man-charged-firebombing-offices-pro-life-group.

Glueck. Katie. "Joe Biden Denounces Hyde Amendment, Reversing His Position." *The New York Times*, June 6, 2019. https://www.nytimes.com/2019/06/06/us/politics/joe-biden-hyde-amendment.html.

Godfrey, Elaine. "The Abortion Absolutist." *The Atlantic*, May 12, 2023. https://www.theatlantic.com/politics/archive/2023/05/dr-warren-hern-abortion-post-roe/674000/.

Gorman, Michael J. *Abortion & the Early Church: Christian, Jewish & Pagan Attitudes in the Greco-Roman World*. Eugene, OR: Wipf & Stock, 1998.

———. and Ann Loar Brooks *Holy Abortion? A Theological Critique of the Religious Coalition for Reproductive Choice*. Eugene, OR: Wipf & Stock, 2003.

Granberg-Michaelson, Wes. "The Real Question in the Abortion Debate." *Reformed Journal*, May 9, 2022. https://reformedjournal.com/the-real-question-in-the-abortion-debate/.

Greenfield, Beth. "Here's why people are connecting the Texas school shooting, the baby formula shortage and the fight over abortion rights." *yahoo!life*, May 26, 2022.

Gregorian, Darel *et al*. "Appeals court upholds some restrictions on abortion pill access, but drug will remain available for now." *NBC News*, August 16, 2023. https://www.nbcnews.com/politics/politics-news/appeals-court-upholds-restrictions-abortion-pill-access-rcna100255.

Griffiths, Brent D. "Biden spikes the football after Ohio voters kill an effort to stymie abortion rights." *Business Insider*, August 8, 2023. https://www.businessinsider.com/biden-celebrates-ohio-issue-1-rejected-reaction-white-house-2023-8.

Gruber, Seth. "White Rose Resistance — A Voice for the Unborn." *The White Rose*. https://thewhiterose.life/.

Guttmacher Institute. "Medication Abortion Now Accounts for More Than Half of All US Abortions." http://www.guttmacher.org/article/22/02.

Gryboski, Michael. "Nearly half of Democrats support abortion restrictions; two thirds support abortion restrictions: poll." *Christian Post*, January 19, 2023. https://www.christianpost.com/news/nearly-half-of-democrats-support-abortion-restrictions-poll.html.

Harris, Kamala. "Harris raises alarm about increased abortion restrictions but has faith in Americans." *ABC News Live Prime*, July 31, 2023. https://abcnews-nwsdynamic.aws.seabcnews.go.com/Politics/harris-raises-alarm-abortion-restrictions-faith-people-america/story?id=101768406.

Hardesty, Nancy. "When Does Life Begin? A searching inquiry into an ancient problem." *ETERNITY* (February 1971): 19–43.

Haykin, Michael A. G. and Kenneth J. Stewart. *The Emergence of Evangelicalism: Exploring Historical Continuities.* Downers Grove: InterVarsity, 2008.

Hayward, Eleanor. "Parliament poised to decriminalise abortion in historic vote." *The Times*, February 23, 2024.

Hendriksen, William. *Luke: New Testament Commentary.* Edinburgh: The Banner of Truth Trust, 1979.

Hennessey-Fiske. "Alabama lawmakers pass legislation to protect IVF treatment." *Washington Post*, February 29, 2024.

Henry, Carl F. H. "Is Life Ever Cheap? A scathing attack on abortion-on-demand." *ETERNITY* (February 1971): 20–48.

Holzwarth, Larry. "10 Weird Common Practices in Colonial America in the Early History." History Collection. https://historycollection.com/.

House, H. Wayne. "Miscarriage or Premature Birth: Additional Thoughts on Exodus 21:22–25." *Westminster Theological Journal* 41.1 (1978): 108–23.

Howard, Jacqueline. "US maternal death rate rose sharply in 2021, CDC data shows, and experts worry the problem is getting worse." *CNN health*, March 16, 2023. https://www.cnn.com/2023/03/16/health/maternal-deaths-increasing-nchs/index.html.

Hughes, Philip Edgcumbe. *The True Image: The Origin and Destiny of Man in Christ.* Grand Rapids: Eerdmans, 1989.

Hunter, James Davidson. *To Change the World: The Irony, Tragedy & Possibility of Christianity in the Late Modern World.* New York, NY: Oxford University Press, 2010.

Hunter, Joel C. *A New Kind of Conservative.* Ventura, CA: Regal, 2008.

Imes, Carmen Joy. *Being God's Image: Why Creation Still Matters.* Downers Grove: IVP Academic, 2013.

Johnson, Abby and Cindy Lambert. *Unplanned: The Dramatic True Story of a Former Planned Parenthood Leader's Eye-Opening Journey across the Life Line.* Carol Stream, IL: Tyndale, 2014.

Johnson, Alexis McGill. "I'm the Head of Planned Parenthood. We're Done Making Excuses for Our Founder." *New York Times*, April 17, 2021. https://www.nytimes.com/2021/04/17/opinion/planned-parenthood-margaret-sanger.html.

Johnson, Julia. "Anne Hathaway tells *The View*, 'abortion can be another word for mercy.'" *Washington Examiner*, November 1, 2022.

Johnson, Ben. "Christians Must Take Children to Transgender Procedures or They Can't Adopt: Oregon State Law." *The Washington Stand*, April 6, 2023.

Jones, David Albert. *The Soul of the Embryo.* New York, NY: Continuum, 2004.

Jones, Peter. "A Plea to My Evangelical Friends for Biden." *Cornwall Alliance For the Stewardship of Creation*, October 23, 2020. www.cornwallalliance.org/2020/10/.

Keller, Timothy. *Generous Justice: How God's Grace Makes Us Just.* New York: Penguin, 2010.

Kidd, Thomas S. *Who is an Evangelical? The History of a Movement in Crisis.* New Haven: Yale University Press, 2019.

Koop, C. Everett M.D. *KOOP: The Memoirs of America's Family Doctor.* New York: Random House, 1991.

———. *The Right to Life; The Right to Die.* Wheaton, IL: Tyndale, 1976.

Kubota, Samantha. "Cher recalls experiencing her first miscarriage at 18." *Today*, July 18, 2022. https://www.today.com/health/womens-health/cher-recalls-first-miscarriage-rcna38837.

Kekatos, Mary. "5 women sue Texas over abortion bans, saying their lives were put at risk." *ABC News*, March 7, 2023. https://abcnews.go.com/Health/5-women-sue-texas-abortion-bans-lives-put/story?id=97614294.

Lerer, Lisa. "When Joe Biden Voted to Let States Overturn Roe v. Wade." *New York Times*, Mar 29, 2019.

Letham, Robert and Donald Macleod. "Is Evangelicalism Christian?" *Evangelical Quarterly* 67:1 (1995): 3–33.

Lewis, Andrew R. *The Right Turn in Conservative Christian Politics: How Abortion Transformed the Culture Wars*. Cambridge: Cambridge University Press, 2017.

LifeWay Study. "Women Distrust Church on Abortion." *LifeWay Research*, November 23, 2015.

"Linsey Davis's exclusive interview with Vice President Kamala Harris on immigration." *ABC News*, July 31, 2023. https://abcnews.go.com/US/video/abc-news-live-prime-monday-july-31-2023-101886940.

Long, Colleen. "Planned Parenthood, Emily's List and NARAL Pro-Choice America endorse Joe Biden in 2024 race." *Associated Press*, June 22, 2023. https://apnews.com/article/biden-abortion-planned-parenthood-dobbs-a1afa38e1bec7c32d1dad5ba635bf99d.

Luther Martin. *Luther's Works: Lectures on Genesis: Chapters 21–25*. Volume 4. Edited by Jaroslav Pelikan and Walter A. Hansen. St. Louis, MO: Concordia, 1964.

MacCulloch, Diarmaid. *Thomas Cromwell: A Revolutionary Life*. New York, NY: Viking, 2018.

Macleod, Donald. *A Faith to Live By: Understanding Christian Doctrine*. Fearn, Ross-shire: Mentor, 1988.

———. "Embryo Research: Where Are the Fences." *The Monthly Record*, September 1984.

———. "The Highlands are now a Labour-free zone." *West Highland Free Press*, May 13, 2005.

Madani, Doha. "States with more abortion restrictions have higher maternal and infant mortality, report finds." *NBC News*, Dec 13.2022. https://www.nbcnews.com/health/health-news/abortion-restrictions-higher-maternal-infant-mortality-rcna61585.

Maher, Kit and Shawna Mizelle. "DeSantis defends record on abortion following rebuke from leading anti-abortion group." *CNN Politics*, August 1, 2023. https://www.cnn.com/2023/08/01/politics/desantis-susan-b-anthony-abortion-stance-2024-republicans/index.html.

Mandelburg, Tierin-Rose. "Christian Minister Says 'Your Faith is Too Small' If you Don't Support Killing Babies in Abortion." *LifeNews.com*, Feb 27, 2023. https://www.lifenews.com/2023/02/27/christian-minister-says-your-faith-is-too-small-if-you-dont-support-killing-babies-in-abortions/.

Mangan, Dan. "Judge suggests abortion might be protected by 13th Amendment, despite Supreme Court ruling." *CNBC*, Feb 6, 2023. https://www.cnbc.com/2023/02/06/supreme-court-abortion-ruling-questioned-by-judge.html.

March for Life. "The Women of the Pro-Life Movement: Dr. Mildred Jefferson." http://marchforlife.org/dr-mildred-jefferson.

Marsden, George M. *Fundamentalism and American Culture*. New York, NY: Oxford University Press, 2006.

Martinez, Jessica and Gregory A. Smith. "How the Faithful Voted." *Pew Research Center*, November 9, 2016. https://www.pewresearch.org/short-reads/2016/11/09/how-the-faithful-voted-a-preliminary-2016-analysis/.

Masci, David. "Where Major Religious Groups Stand on Abortion." *Pew Research Center*, June 21, 2016. https://www.pewresearch.org/short-reads/2016/06/21/where-major-religious-groups-stand-on-abortion/.

Masih, Niha. Maegan Vazquez. "Texas attorney general blocks temporary lift on abortion ban for complicated pregnancies." *Washington Post*, August 5, 2023. https://www.washingtonpost.com/politics/2023/08/05/texas-abortion-ban-pregnancy-complications/.

Matthews-Green, Frederica. *Real Choices: Listening to Women, Looking for Alternatives to Abortion*. Linthicum, MD: Felicity, 2013.

Mayo Clinic. "Stem Cells: What they are and what they do." https://www.mayoclinic.org/tests-procedures/bone-marrow-transplant/in-depth/stem-cells/art-20048117.

McCammon, Sarah. "Controversial televangelist Pat Robertson has died at age 93." *NPR*, June 8, 2023. https://www.npr.org/2023/06/08/1181131645/controversial-televangelist-pat-robertson-has-died-at-age-93.

McGill Johnson, Alexis. "I'm Head of Planned Parenthood. Were Done Making Excuses for Our Founder." *New York Times*, April 17, 2021. https://www.nytimes.com/2021/04/17/opinion/planned-parenthood-margaret-sanger.html.

Melville, Catriona. "Abortion care in Australasia: A matter of health, not politics or religion." *ANJOG* 62.2 (April 2022): 187–89.

Mercer, Joshua. "Dobbs Decision Has Saved Over 25,000 Babies From Abortion." *LifeNews.com*, June 23, 2023. https://www.lifenews.com/2023/06/23/over-25000-babies-have-been-saved-from-abortions-since-supreme-courts-dobbs-decision/.

———. "Pro-Life Advocate Mark Houck Announces Congressional Campaign." *LifeNews.com*, August 3, 2023. https://www.lifenews.com/2023/08/03/pro-life-advocate-mark-houck-announces-congressional-campaign/.

Metaxas, Eric. *Amazing Grace: William Wilberforce and the Heroic Campaign to End Slavery*. New York: Harper Collins, 2007.

"Michelle Higgins—Urbana 15." *InterVarsity Christian Fellowship USA*. YouTube video. 28:29. https://www.youtube.com/watch?v=XVGDSkxxXco.

Michels, Nancy. *Helping Women Recover from Abortion: How to deal with the guilt, the emotional pain, and the emptiness*. Minneapolis, MN: Bethany House, 1988.

Middleton, J. Richard. *The Liberating Image: The Imago Dei in Genesis 1*. Grand Rapids, MI: Baker Academic, 2005.

Miller, Matthew. "How the Evangelical Church Awoke to the Abortion Issue: The Convergent Labors of Harold O.J. Brown, Francis Schaeffer, and C. Everett Koop." *Reformation 21*, March 4, 2013. https://www.reformation21.org/featured/how-the-evangelical-church-awoke-to-the-abortion-issue-the-convergent-labors-of.php.

Miller, Paul D. *The Religion of American Greatness: What's Wrong with Christian Nationalism*. Downers Grove: IVP Academic, 2022.

Mohler, Albert. "Vaccines and the Christian Worldview: Principles for Christian Thinking in the Context of COVID." *The Briefing*. albertmohler.com/2020/12/14.

———. "Nonsense of the Quintessential Sort: MSNBC Host Argues 'Jesus Never Once Talked About Abortion'—And That the Pro-Life Position is Heresy." *The Briefing*, September 15, 2022. albertmohler.com/2022/09/15.

Moore, Russell. *Adopted for Life: The Priority of Adoption for Christian Families and Churches*. Carol Stream, IL: Crossway, 2009.

———. *Losing Our Religion: An Altar Call for Evangelical America*. New York, NY: Sentinel, 2023.
Moltmann, Jurgen. *The Way of Jesus Christ*. Translated by Margaret Kohl. London: SCM, 1990.
Morgentaler, Henry. *Abortion and Contraception*. Toronto, ON: General, 1982.
Montgomery, John Warwick. *Slaughter of the Innocents: Abortion, Birth Control, and Divorce in the Light of Science, Law and Theology*. Westchester, IL: Cornerstone, 1981.
———. "Editorial." *The Simon Greenfield Law Review* 5 (1985–86).
Montoya, Melissa, Colleen Judge-Golden, and Jonas J. Swartz. "The Problem with Crisis Pregnancy Centers: Reviewing the Literature and Identifying New Directions for Future Research." *International Journal of Women's Health*, June 8, 2022. https://www.ncbi.nlm.nih.gov/pmc/articles/PMC9189146/.
Moran, Lee. "Jen Psaki Busts 'Entirely Misleading' Republican Talking Point." *Huffpost*, August 28, 2023. https://www.huffpost.com/entry/jen-psaki-republicans-talking-point_n_64ec3ae6e4b084283f26547e.
Morris, Leon. *The Gospel According to John*. Grand Rapids, MI: Eerdmans, 1995.
Mrozek, Andrea. "Whether Feminism? Finding Hope for a New Women's Movement." *Comment* 40.2 (Spring 2022): 86–92.
Mueller, Julia. "Cooper calls North Carolina 12-week abortion bill compromise between the right-wing and the radical right-wing." *The Hill*, May 21, 2023.
Mulvihill, Geoff and Linley Sanders. "Few US adults support full abortion bans, even in states that have them, an AP-NORC poll finds." *Associated Press*, July 11, 2023. https://apnews.com/article/abortion-poll-roe-dobbs-ban-opinion-fcfdfc5a799ac3be617d99999e92eabe.
Murray, Iain H. *Evangelicalism Divided: A Record of Crucial Change in the Years 1950–2000*. Edinburgh: Banner of Truth, 2000.
Murray, Jessica. "Tory MP who backed cutting abortion time limit, named minister for women." *The Guardian*, October 30, 2022.
Murray, John. *Collected Writings of John Murray, Systematic Theology*. Vol 2. Edinburgh: Banner of Truth, 1977.
———. *Principles of Conduct: Aspects of Biblical Ethics*. Grand Rapids: Eerdmans, 1957.
Nathanson, Bernard N. *The Hand of God: A Journey From Death To Life By the Abortion Doctor Who Changed His Mind*. Washington, DC: Regnery, 1996.
——— with Richard N. Ostling. *Aborting America*. USA: Life, 1979.
National Right to Life. "Protecting Life in America Since 1968." https://www.nrlc.org.
Nawaz, Amna. "The Abortion landscape." *PBS News*, June 23, 2023.
———. "The link between a lack of reproductive rights and domestic violence." *PBS News*, July 14, 2023.
Neidig, Harper. "Thomas calls for overturning precedents on contraceptives, LGBTQ rights." *The Hill*, 06/24/22.
Ney, Philip. "The Relationship Between Abortion and Child Abuse." *Canadian Journal of Psychiatry* 24.7 (November 1979): 610–20.
Noll, Mark A., David W. Bebbington, George M. Marsden. *Evangelicals: Who They Have Been, Are Now, and Could Be*. Grand Rapids: Eerdmans, 2019.
Noor, Poppy. "Abortion pill case: where does the lawsuit against the pill currently stand?" *The Guardian*, May 17, 2023.

NRL News Today. "Former abortionist turned pro-life activist dismantles pro-abortion myths about abortion survivors," September 14, 2023. https://www.nationalrighttolifenews.org/2023/09/former-abortionist-turned-pro-life-activist-dismantles-pro-abortion-myths-about-abortion-survivors-2/.

Nsuguba, Jimmy. "Tory minister criticised after backing 'praying' woman arrested outside abortion clinic." https://www.aol.co.uk/news/tory-minister-sparks-backlash-backing-181723939.html

Ohden, Melissa. "Over 85,000 Babies Have Survived Abortions Since Roe v. Wade in 1973." *LifeNews.com*, Sep 7, 2023. https://www.lifenews.com/2023/09/07/over-85000-babies-have-survived-abortions-since-roe-v-wade-in-1973/.

Olasky, Marvin. *Abortion at the Crossroads: Three Paths Forward in the Struggle to Protect the Unborn*. New York, NY: Bombardier, 2021.

——— & Leah Savas. *The Story of Abortion in America: A Streetside View*. Wheaton, IL: Crossway, 2023.

———. "The War on Adoption." *National Review*, June 7, 1993.

Olohan, Mary Margaret. "Biden Official Admits FBI Targeting Pro-Life Americans to Protest Overturning Roe." *LifeNews.com*, Dec 13, 2022. https://www.lifenews.com/2022/12/13/biden-official-admits-fbi-targeting-pro-life-americans-in-a-response-to-overturning-roe/.

Olson, Roger and Christian T. Collins Winn. *Reclaiming Pietism: Retrieving an Evangelical Tradition*. Grand Rapids: Eerdmans, 2015.

Owen, John. *Indwelling Sin in Believers*. Edinburgh: Banner of Truth Trust, 2022.

Packer, James. "The Uniqueness of Jesus Christ: Some Evangelical Reflections." *Churchman* 92 (1978).

———. *Knowing God*. Downers Grove, IL: IVP, 1973.

Patterson, Calli. "Pelosi Received Communion at Vatican, despite abortion stance." *New York Post*, June 29, 2022.

Pew Research Center. "Pro-Choice Does not Mean Pro-Abortion: An Argument for Abortion Rights Featuring the Rev. Carlton Veazey." September 20, 2008.

Piper, John. "Jesus Died to End Abortion and Racism," *Desiring God*, October 20, 2021. https://www.desiringgod.org/articles/jesus-died-to-end-abortion-and-racism.

Pitts, Leonard Jr. "Are you anti-abortion?" *Baltimore Sun*, Feb 12, 2016.

Plotkin, Stanley. "The Future of Immunization." *Vaccine Makers Project*. YouTube video. 03:26. September 20, 2022.

Pope Francis. "Address of His Holiness Pope Francis to Participants in the Meeting Promoted by the Pontifical Council for Promoting the New Evangelization." 11 October, 2017. https://www.vatican.va/content/francesco/en/speeches/2017/october/documents/papa-francesco_20171011_convegno-nuova-evangelizzazione.html.

Posner, Sarah. "That Christianity Today Editorial Won't Change Anything." *New York Times*, December 22, 2019. https://www.nytimes.com/2019/12/22/opinion/christianity-today-trump.html

Pro-life Evangelicals for Biden. "Open Letter on The American Recovery Act," March 7, 2021.

"A Protestant Affirmation on the Control of Human Reproduction." *Christianity Today* 18.33 (November 8, 1968) 18.

Quinones, Julian and Arijeta Lajka. "'What kind of society do you want to live in?' Inside the country where Down syndrome is disappearing." *CBS News*, August 15, 2017. https://www.cbsnews.com/news/down-syndrome-iceland/.

Rachel's Vineyard. "Welcome to Rachel's Vineyard." http://www.rachelsvineyard.org.

Rafferty, Philip. *Roe v. Wade: Unraveling the Fabric of America*. Mustang, OK: Tate, 2012.
Rainey, Jane G. "Church of the Holy Trinity v. United States (1892)." *The First Amendment Encyclopedia*. www.mtsu.edu/first-amendment/article.
Ramsay, Paul. *Who Speaks for the Church*? Nashville, TN: Abington, 1967.
Randall, Rebecca. "3 Bioethical Questions About COVID-19 Vaccines." *Christianity Today*, January 2021. https://www.christianitytoday.com/ct/2021/january-web-only/covid-19-vaccine-christian-ethical-questions-fetal-cells.html.
Rahman. Khaleda. "Anti-Abortion Movement Faces Devastating Setbacks in Multiple States." *Newsweek*, August 9, 2023. https://www.newsweek.com/anti-abortion-movement-setbacks-multiple-states-1818519.
Rasmussen Reports. "Abortion: Half of Voters Approve Supreme Court Ruling." June 28, 2022. https://www.rasmussenreports.com/public_content/politics/general_politics/june_2022/abortion_half_of_voters_approve_supreme_court_ruling.
Reagan, Ronald. *Abortion and the Conscience of the Nation*. Nashville, TN: Nelson, 1984.
Reardon, David C. *Aborted Women: Silent No More*. Wheaton, IL: Crossway, 1987.
Reynolds, Nick. "A Powerful Minority, Christian Nationalism is Democracy's 'Greatest Threat.'" *Newsweek*, February 2, 2023. https://www.newsweek.com/christian-nationalism-democracy-greatest-threat-brookings-public-religion-research-institute-survey-1780236.
Red Rose Rescue. "Mission Statement." redrose rescue.com/about.
———. "Code of Conduct." redrose rescue.com/about.
Richards, Dr. Chris. "When Does Life Begin?" *Banner of Truth* 681 (June 2020) 13–14.
Richardson, Katelynn. "Pro-Life Democrat Launches Presidential Campaign to Challenge Joe Biden: 'I'm a Voice for the Voiceless.'" *LifeNews.com*, Sep 14, 2023.
Robertson, David. "What does the case of baby killing nurse Lucy Letby tell us about our society?" *Christian Today*, August 28, 2023. https://www.christiantoday.com/article/what.does.the.case.of.baby.killing.nurse.lucy.letby.tell.us.about.our.society/140673.htm.
Rogers, Katie and Jason Horowitz. "Biden: Pope said he should receive communion, despite US bishops' rift on abortion rights." *New York Times*, October 29, 2021. https://www.nytimes.com/2021/10/29/world/europe/biden-pope-communion-abortion.html.
Rogin, Ali. "Why a growing number of Latin American countries are legalizing abortion." *PBS*, May 14, 2022. https://pbswisconsin.org/watch/newshour/abortion-latin-america-1652551881/.
Roelofs, Katie and Emily Helder. "Adoption: Two Voices." *Reformed Journal*, October 31, 2022. https://reformedjournal.com/adoption-two-voices/.
Runia, Klaas. "Abortion Perspective." *ETERNITY* (February 1971) 16–17.
Sargeant, Leah Libresco. "Red Rose Rescue." *Comment* 42.2, (Summer 2023) 74–84.
Saur, Prudence B. *Maternity: A Book for Every Wife and Mother*. Chicago: L.P. Miller, 1889.
Schaeffer, Francis. A. *A Christian Manifesto*, Wheaton, IL: Crossway,1981.
———. *He is There and He is Not Silent*. Downers Grove, IL: IVP, 1968.
———. *The Complete Works of Francis A. Schaeffer*, Vol 5. Wheaton, IL: Crossway, 1982.
———. *Whatever Happened to the Evangelical Church*? Wheaton, IL: Crossway 1984.
——— with C. Everett Koop, MD. *Whatever Happened to the Human Race? Exposing our rapid yet subtle loss of human rights*. Old Tappan, NJ: Fleming H. Revell, 1979.

Sellers, Frances Stead and Fenit Nirappil. "Confusion post-Roe spurs delays, denials for some lifesaving pregnancy care." *Washington Post*, July 16, 2022. https://www.washingtonpost.com/health/2022/07/16/abortion-miscarriage-ectopic-pregnancy-care/.

Serwer, Adam. "The Myth That America's Abortion Laws are More Permissive Than Europe's." *The Atlantic*, July 22, 2022. https://www.theatlantic.com/ideas/archive/2022/07/roe-overturned-europe-abortion-laws/670539/.

Sharp, Rachel. "Her baby was dying. She needed an abortion to survive. But Texas was ready to let her die too." *Independent*, July 26, 2022. https://www.independent.co.uk/news/world/americas/abortion-law-texas-medical-emergency-b2130937.html.

Shiffer, Emily. "There's No Such Thing as 'Late-Term Abortion'—Here are the Facts." *Parents*, December 15, 2022. https://www.parents.com/pregnancy/my-body/pregnancy-health/theres-no-such-thing-as-late-term-abortion-here-are-the-facts/.

Shimron, Yonat. "3 Jewish women file suit against Kentucky abortion bans on religious grounds." *Religious News Service*, October 7, 2022.

Sider, Ronald J. "Biden Won. Now What?" *Ron Sider Blog*, November 7, 2020. https://ronsiderblog.substack.com/.

———. *Completely Pro-Life: Building a Consistent Stance on Abortion, the Family, Nuclear Weapons, the Poor*. Downers Grove, IL: InterVarsity, 1987.

———. "Pro-Life Evangelicals for Biden." *Ron Sider Blog*. https://ronsiderblog.substack.com/p/pro-life-evangelicals-for-biden.

———. *Rich Christians in an Age of Hunger*. Downers Grove, IL: IVP, 1978.

———. ed., *The Spiritual Danger of Donald Trump: 30 Evangelical Christians on Justice, Truth, and Moral Integrity*. Eugene, OR: Cascade, 2020.

Singer, Peter. "Sanctity of Life or Quality of Life?" *Pediatrics*, 72.1 (1983) 128–29.

Smietana, Bob. "COVID vaccines are moral to use, say ethicist, Catholic bishops." RNS, religionnews.com/2020/11/25.

Smedes, Lewis B. *Mere Morality: What God Expects from Ordinary People*. Grand Rapids: Eerdmans, 1972.

Smith, Gregory A. "Like Americans overall, Catholics vary in their abortion views, with regular Mass attenders most opposed." *Pew Research Center*, May 23, 2022.

Smith, Peter. "US Catholic bishops worry about abortion views in the pews." *Associated Press*, November 17, 2022. https://ny1.com/nyc/queens/ap-top-news/2022/11/17/us-catholic-bishops-worry-about-abortion-views-in-the-pews.

Sproul, R. C. *Abortion: A Rational Look at an Emotional Issue*. Colorado Springs, CO: NavPress, 1990.

SPUC. "Stem Cell Research." https://www.spuc.org.uk/News/ID/383567/Stem-Cell-Research.

Spiers, Elizabeth. "I Was Adopted. I Know the Trauma It Can Inflict." *New York Times*, Dec 3, 2021. https://www.nytimes.com/2021/12/03/opinion/adoption-supreme-court-amy-coney-barrett.html.

Stacey, Dawn. "How Griswold v. Connecticut Led to Legal Contraception." *Verywell Health*, July 17, 2022. https://www.verywellhealth.com/griswold-v-connecticut-1965-906887.

Stackhouse, John G., Jr. *Evangelicalism: A Very Short Introduction*. Oxford: Oxford University Press, 2022.

Stewart, Kenneth J. "Did evangelicalism predate the eighteenth century? An examination of David Bebbington's thesis." *Evangelical Quarterly* 77.2 (2005) 135–53.

Stoker, Amanda. "'Babies Born Alive' bill will introduce 'birth equality' on a federal level." *SkyNews*, 11 June, 2023. YouTube video. 02:50. https://www.youtube.com/watch?v=fLqd39rJLHo.

Stott, John, R. W. "Abortion, Deformity and 'Vegetables.'" *Church of England Newspaper*, November 5, 1971.

———. *Decisive Issues Facing Christians Today*. 2nd ed. Grand Rapids, MI: Revell, 1993.

———. "Does Life Begin Before Birth?" *Christianity Today* 24.15 (September 5, 1980) 50–51.

———. *Evangelical Essentials*. Downers Grove, IL: InterVarsity, 2000.

———. "A Plea for Evangelical Christianity." *Christ the Controversialist*. Downers Grove, IL: IVP, 1972.

Sullivan, Kate. "Biden campaign spotlights abortion as it looks to find its 2024 footing." *CNN Politics*, September 8, 2023. https://www.cnn.com/2023/09/08/politics/new-ad-biden-campaign-abortion/index.html.

Suri, Sameer. "Paris Hilton, 42, reveals she had an abortion in her early 20s." *DailyMail*, 24 February 2023. https://www.dailymail.co.uk/tvshowbiz/article-11789425/Paris-Hilton-reveals-abortion-early-20s-kid-not-ready.html.

Susan B. Anthony Pro-Life America. "About." https://sbaprolife.org/about.

Talbot, Christopher. "The Pro-Life Legacy of Francis Schaeffer." *First Things*, September 5, 2022. https://www.firstthings.com/web-exclusives/2022/09/the-pro-life-legacy-of-francis-schaeffer.

Taylor, Justin. "The Case Against Pro-Life Voting for Joe Biden." *The Gospel Coalition*, October 7, 2020. https://www.thegospelcoalition.org/blogs/justin-taylor/the-case-against-pro-lifers-voting-for-joe-biden/.

Tucker, Emma. "An abortion clinic on wheels: Planned Parenthood in Illinois to reduce travel times for patients in red states by bringing abortion to them." *CNN*, November 5, 2022. https://www.cnn.com/2022/11/05/us/planned-parenthood-illinois-mobile-abortion-clinic/index.html.

Threedy, Debora. "Slavery Rhetoric and the Abortion Debate." *Michigan Journal of Gender & Law* 2.1 (1994) 7–14.

Tisby, Jemar. *The Color of Compromise: The Truth About the American Church's Complicity in Racism*. Grand Rapids. MI: Zondervan, 2020.

Thomas, Cal and Ed Dobson. *Blinded by Might: Why the Religious Right Can't Save America*. Grand Rapids, MI: Zondervan, 1999.

Torrance. Thomas, F. *The Being and Nature of the Unborn Child*. Lenoir, NC: Glen Lorien for Presbyterians Pro-Life, 2000.

———. *The Soul and Person of the Unborn Child*. Haddington: Handsel, 1999.

———. *Test Tube Babies: Morals, Science and the Law*. Edinburgh: Scottish Academic, 1984.

Tozer, A.W. *Keys to Deeper Life*. Louisville, KY: GLH, 2019.

Turley, Jonathan. "Federal Judge Suggests Abortion May Be Protected Under 13th Amendment's Ban on Involuntary Servitude." *Jonathan Turley*. https://jonathanturley.org/2023/02/07/federal-judge-suggests-abortion-may-be-protected-under-13th-amendments-ban-on-involuntary-servitude/comment-page-3/.

Umholtz, Kaytelyn. "More out-of-state patients are traveling to Mass. for abortions, study says." *Boston.Com*, September 7, 2023. https://www.boston.com/news/health/2023/09/07/more-out-of-state-patients-getting-abortions-massachusetts/.

United Methodist Church. "What is the UM position on abortion?" https://www.ucm.org/en/content/.

United States Conference of Catholic Bishops. *Catechism of the Catholic Church*. 2nd Edition. Washington, DC: First Printing, November 2019.

———. "Moral Considerations Regarding the New Covid Vaccines." nd.

URGE. "Bro-Choice Links." https://urge.org/category/bro-choice.

U.S. Food and Drug Administration. "Plan B One-Step (1.5 mg levonorgestrel) Information."

Vastag, Brian. "Nobel Prize for medicine awarded for stem cell discoveries." *Washington Post*, October 8, 2012. https://www.washingtonpost.com/national/health-science/nobel-prize-for-medicine-awarded-for-stem-cell-discoveries/2012/10/08/ebd55128-1139-11e2-ba83-a7a396e6b2a7_story.html.

Vander Broek, Allison. "The Texas Abortion Law, the Anti-Abortion Movement, and the Politics of Cruelty." *Reformed Journal*, November 15, 2021. https://reformedjournal.com/the-texas-abortion-law-the-antiabortion-movement-and-the-politics-of-cruelty/.

VanDrunen, David. *Bioethics and the Christian Life: A Guide to Making Difficult Decisions*. Wheaton, IL: Crossway, 2009.

Vlamis, Kelsey. "A Texas minister helps fly dozens of women to New Mexico every month to get abortions. He's one of many religious leaders coordinating abortion care with Roe v. Wade overturned." *Business Insider*, June 30, 2022. https://www.businessinsider.com/network-religious-leaders-abortions-roe-v-wade-clergy-consultation-service-2022-5.

———. "Catholic bishops' effort to deny Biden communion risks alienating church members, a majority of whom support abortion rights." *Business Insider*, July 18, 2021. https://www.businessinsider.com/catholic-bishops-clash-with-biden-on-abortion-potentially-alienating-parishioners-2021-7.

Waltke, Bruce K. "Reflections from the Old Testament on Abortion." *Journal of the Evangelical Theological Society* 19.1 (1976) 3–13.

———. "The Old Testament and Birth Control." *Christianity Today* 18.33, November 8, 1968.

Wang, Amy B and Caroline Kitchener. "Graham introduces bill to ban abortion nationwide after 15 weeks." *Washington Post*, Sept 13, 2022. https://www.washingtonpost.com/politics/2022/09/13/abortion-graham-republicans-nationwide-ban/.

Warren, Roland C. "Why the Pro-Life Movement Must Be Pro-Abundant Life." Care Net, Dec 1, 2022. https://www.care-net.org/abundant-life-blog/why-the-pro-life-movement-must-be-pro-abundant-life.

Watson, Kathryn. "Pelosi responds to archbishop denying her communion over abortion stance." *CBS News*, May 25, 2022. https://www.cbsnews.com/news/pelosi-communion-archbishop-san-francisco-abortion/.

———. "They're Not Religious, But They Oppose Abortion." *Christianity Today*, November 21, 2022. https://www.christianitytoday.com/ct/2022/december/pro-life-none-non-religious-secular-atheist-feminist-ally.html.

Weixel, Nathaniel. "Poll: most don't trust Supreme Court to decide reproductive health cases." *The Hill*, May 26, 2023. https://thehill.com/policy/healthcare/4021997-poll-most-dont-trust-supreme-court-to-decide-reproductive-health-cases/.

Weszley, Angie. "A New Christian Response to Abortion," *Pro Grace.org*. https://s3.amazonaws.com/kajabi-storefronts-production/sites/2147506037/themes/2149437002/downloads/cGvEUYYtSTCYEHHciMvp_ProGrace_E-Book.pdf.

———. "Does the Roe decision impact the ProGrace strategy?" *Pro Grace.org*, July 27, 2022. https://www.prograce.org/blog/does-the-roe-decision-impact-the-prograce-strategy.

White, Rebecca. "I Had a Carefree Sex Life." *Daily Beast*, July 24, 2022. https://www.thedailybeast.com/i-had-a-carefree-sex-life-the-next-generation-will-have-fear.

Whitford, Chris. "Deep Wells of Mercy." *Comment* 40.4 (Fall 2022) 81–82.

Wikipedia. "Abortion in the United Kingdom." *Wikipedia*. https://en.wikipedia.org/wiki/Abortion_in_the_United_Kingdom.

Wicks, Amanda. "The Loudest Political Voice on SNL." *The Atlantic*, November 6, 2022. https://www.theatlantic.com/culture/archive/2022/11/snl-takes-stance-abortion-ahead-midterms/672019/.

Williams, Alithea. "Update on the Carla Foster case & what YOU can do to help." *SPUC*, July 20, 2023.

Williams, Daniel K. *Defenders of the Unborn: The Pro-Life Movement Before Roe v. Wade*. Oxford: Oxford University Press, 2016.

———. *The Politics of the Cross: A Christian Alternative to Partisanship*. Grand Rapids: Eerdmans, 2021.

———. "The Prolific Deceivers at the Heart of 'Roe v. Wade.'" *Christianity Today*, December 6, 2021. https://www.christianitytoday.com/ct/2021/december-web-only/family-roe-wade-joshua-prager-norma-mccorvey-deceiver.html.

Wilson, Douglas and N.D. Wilson. *Black and Tan: A Collection of Essays and Excursions on Slavery, Culture War, and Scripture in America*. Moscow, Idaho: Canon, 2018.

Wolf, Elizabeth. "These are the states where abortion rights are still protected after the Supreme Court overturned Roe v. Wade." *CNN*, June 24, 2022. https://www.cnn.com/2022/05/13/us/abortion-rights-access-states-roe-v-wade/index.html.

Wolfe, Stephen. *The Case for Christian Nationalism*. Moscow, Idaho: Canon, 2022.

World Health Organization. "Abortion." https:/www.int/news-room/fact-sheets/detail/abortion.

Wright, Jasmine. "Kamala Harris found her voice on abortion rights the year after Dobbs. Now she's making it central to her 2024 message." *CNN Politics*, June 24, 2023. https://www.cnn.com/2023/06/24/politics/kamala-harris-abortion-rights/index.html.

Yilek, Caitlin. "Harris dismissed GOP claims on Democrats' abortion stance." *CBS News*, September 8, 2023. https://www.cbsnews.com/news/abortion-kamala-harris-roe-v-wade-face-the-nation/.

Young, Curt. *The Least of These: What Everyone Should Know About Abortion*. Chicago, IL: Moody, 1984.

Zielgler, Mary. *Abortion and the Law in America*. Cambridge: Cambridge University Press, 2020.

———."Opinion: A crushing loss for Republicans on abortion rights." *CNN*, August 9, 2023.

———."Opinion: The twisted irony in Alabama's court decision on embryos." *CNN*, February 21, 2024.

———."Opinion: Walgreens' abortion pill decision sends a chilling message." *CNN*, March 8, 2023. https://www.cnn.com/2023/03/08/opinions/walgreens-abortion-medication-ziegler/index.html.

Index

ABC (American Broadcasting Company), 149
ABC News, 137n79, 138, 139n91
Abernathy, Gary, 22
Abortion Act (Britain, 1967), 9, 141
ACLU (American Civil Liberties Union), 126
Adam, 81, 85, 86, 90n24
Affordable Care Act of 2010, 98
Aid Access (European website), 12, 163
Alabama Supreme Court, 80
Alan Guttmacher Institute. *See* Guttmacher Institute
Alberta, Tim, 26, 26n19
Alcorn, Randy, 98, 98n14
Alliance Defending Freedom (ADF), 161, 162
Allit, Patrick, 28n23
Ambrose of Milan, 49
American Birth Control League. *See* Planned Parenthood
American Civil Liberties Union (ACLU), 126
American College of Obstetricians and Gynecologists (A.C.O.G.), 63
American Medical Association, 52, 53
Amnesty International UK, 142
And Then There Were None, 16

Andersen, Ericka, 139n92, 140, 141n95
Anderson, Kate, 14n25, 136n77
Andros, Dan, 135n70
Andrusko, Dave, 138n86
Anthony, Susan B., 10
Apocalypse of Peter, 48
Aquinas, Thomas, 50, 61, 87
Archer, Gleason, 76
Aristotle, 46, 46n2, 47, 50, 61, 66, 84
Armstrong, Dave, 97n10
Armstrong, Kurt, 157n150
Associated Press, 128n40, 144n111
Attorney General, US, 134
Atwood, Margaret, 127, 127n33
Augustine, 49, 50, 86, 107
Augustus Caesar, 113
Aultman, Kathi, 124, 125n20
Austin American-Statesman, 150
Avail NYC, 152–53, 155

Badger, Emily, 153n142
Balevik, Katie, 121n6
Balmer, Randall, 22, 22n4
Baptist National Convention, 20
Barnabus, Epistles of, 48
Barnes, Peter, 145, 145n115
Barr, James, 96

INDEX

Barr, Luke, 134n67
Barrett, Amy Coney, 117, 126
Barrett, Matthew, 87n16
Barrows, Jeffrey, 103n22
Barth, Karl, 53, 53n33, 82, 82n7, 92
Basil of Caesarea, 49
Bavinck, Herman, 78, 78n19, 85, 85n11
Baxter, Richard, 51
Bayly, David, 85n10
Bayly, Tim, 85n10
Bebbington, David W., 23, 23n7, 25, 45
Bellarmine, Robert, 81
Belluck, 161n5
Benedict XVI, Pope, 106
Benham, Flip, 171
Berkhof, Louis, 81n3, 88, 88n19, 88n22
Bernard, Caitlin, 127n34
Berny, Ella, 142n100
Berry, R. J., 95
Bethlehem Baptist Church, Minneapolis, 157
Bible Institute of Los Angeles, 26
Biden, Jill, 128
Biden, Joe, 32, 35, 36, 37, 37n50, 38, 39n60, 122, 123, 126, 137, 138, 161
Biesel, Nicola, 93n35, 165n22
Bilger, Micaiah, 37n53, 37nn55–56, 38n59, 129n47, 130n53, 135n69, 163n12
Biola Univesity, 26
Birthright, 57, 58
Bitler, Marianne, 13n20
Blackmun, Harry, 51, 52
Blackwell, Elizabeth, 10, 10n3
Blair, Gabrielle, 115, 116n9, 155, 155nn146–148, 156
Blakeslee, Nat, 16n38
Boice, James Montgomery, 88, 88n23
Bonhoeffer, Dietrich, 54, 54n34, 165
Born-Alive Abortion Survivors Protection Act, 122, 124
Bose, Nandita, 127n35
Boucher, 11n9
Brennan, Margaret, 123
Brewer, David J., 30, 31
Brigham and Women's Hospital, Boston, 163

Britton, John, 165
Brooks, Ann Loar, 12n10
Brooks, David, 24, 24n12
Brown, Harold O. J., 42, 43, 44, 68
Brown, Mark, 143n104
Brown, Michael, 157
Buckley, William F., 42
Bukovinac, Terrisa, 137
Bultan, Debbie Cox, 137n81
Burge, Ryan, 28n21
Burke, Teresa, 12, 12n17
Burnaby CPC. *See* Crisis Pregnancy Centre (CPC)
Burnaby Safe House, 2
Bush, George W., 29

Calkin, Sydney, 142n100
Calvin, John, 51, 51n22, 76, 92
Campisi, Tom, 149n129, 163n10
Capraro, Chiara, 142
CAPS (Center for American Political Studies), 121n10
Care Net, 2, 14, 43, 147–49, 148nn126–127, 150–52, 155, 165, 166, 168
Carlisle, Madeleine, 121n4
Carpenter Theologian Blog, 151n136
Carter, Jimmy, 27
Catholic Church, 11n9, 15, 19, 21, 31, 32, 39n60, 50, 107
Catholics for Choice, 19
Catholics for Free Choice. *See* Catholics for Choice
Center for American Political Studies (CAPS), 121n10
Center for Bioethics and Human Dignity (CBHD), 105
Center for Reproductive Rights, 128
Centers for Disease Control and Prevention (CDC), 17n42, 122, 123, 124, 125n20, 163
Centre for Women's Justice, 143
Charlotte Lozier Institute, 14
Chaudhary, Vivek, 142n101
Cher, 127n36
Christan Coalition, 36
Christensen, Jen, 162n6

INDEX

Christian Action Council (CAC), 2, 42–43, 76, 147, 152, 168
Christian Advocacy Society of Greater Vancouver, 2
Christian Broadcasting Network, 28
Christian Coalition, 28
Christian Medical and Dental Association, 103n22, 105
Christian Medical Fellowship, 66
Christian Medical Society, 61
Christian Reformed Church, 131
Christian Today (British publication), 143
Christianity Today (US magazine), 140, 171
Christians for Life (CFL), 2
Christians for Social Action, 27
Chrysostom, 49, 50
Church of England, 33
Church of England Newspaper, 66
Church of Scotland, 67n32
Cicero, 47, 48
Civil Rights Division, of DOJ, 133
Clapham Sect (or Saints), 33
Clement of Alexandria, 48
Clergy Consultation Referral Service, 15
Cline, Timothy, 98n12
Clinton, Bill, 11, 164
Clinton, Hillary, 18n47, 122
Coffee, Linda, 175, 176
Colson, Charles, 27, 108, 109n36
Common Council, New York City, 52
Common Ground Network fof Life and Choice, 13
CompassCare, 134
Comstock Act, 161
Concepcion, Summer, 128n41
Condon, Guy, 147n124
Constatine, 48
Constitution, US, 132
    First Amendment, 136
    Second Amendment, 136
    Thirteenth amendment, 34n42, 121
    Fourteenth amendment, 97, 121
Cooper, Karl, 166
Cooper, Roy, 125
Cotterill, Tom, 142n101
Cottrell, J. W., 65, 76

Council of Ancyra, 49
Council of Canadian Christian Charities, 149
Council of Elvira, 49
Cox, Kate, 128
Crisis Pregnancy Centre (CPC), 2, 3
Criswell, W. A., 1
Cromartie, Michael, 24
Cromwell, Thomas, 24
Cussac-Smith, Tiffany, 37n52

Dabney, R. L., 34n42
Daily Mail, 142
Dallas Theological Sminary, 64
Daniels, Kristen Whitney, 107n32
Dastin, Jeffrey, 126n27
David, 78
Davis, John Jefferson, 77, 77n16
de Vogue, Ariane, 162n9
Deignhan, John, 141n99
Delitzsch, Franz, 76
DeLuca, 130n54
Democratic Party, 32, 36, 160
Democrats for Life, 137
Denes, Magda, 11n8
Department of Justice (DOJ), US, 133, 135, 161, 162
DeSantis, Ron, 125
Descartes, René, 89
Dicaro, Vincent, 150n134
Dickson, John, 26
Didache, 48
Dobbs decision (*Dobbs v. Jackson Women's Health Organization*), 1, 121, 126, 136, 137, 144, 146, 163
Dobson, Ed, 28n24
Dobson, James, 43
Doctrine of the Faith, 104
Donald, Ian, 16
Donegan, Moira, 127n34
Dorsett, Walter, 53
Dreher, Rod, 120-21, 120nn1-2, 146, 147, 147nn121-122
Dudley, Jonathan, 42, 65, 65n23, 67, 68
Dwoskin, Elizabeth, 126n29

Ebenezer Baptist Church, 129
Edelman, Ada, 121n8
Edgar, William, 44n74
Einstein, Albert, 90, 91
Epistles of Barnabus, 48
Ertelt, Steven, 17n41, 37n51, 37n53, 123n14, 130n49, 133n64, 134n68, 135n71, 137n77, 144n108, 163n15
ETERNITY (magazine), 56, 56n3, 58, 59–60, 59n10, 60n11
Ethics and Public Policy Center, 24
Ettachfini, Leila, 65, 65n24
Evangelical Fellowship of Canada, 149n128
Evangelical Theological Society, 65
Evangelicals for Social Action, 27, 35. *See also* Christians for Social Action
Eve, 81

FACE. *See* Freedom of Access to Clinic Entrances Act (FACE)
Facebook, 126
Falwell, Jerry Jr., 28
Falwell, Jerry Sr., 28, 42, 43
Farrow, Anna, 145n113
Fawcett, Eliza, 129n46
FBI (Federal Bureau of Investigation), 134, 135
Feminists for Life of America, 10
Fernando, Christine, 129n44, 134n66
Fessler, Ann, 116
Filson, David Owen, 132, 133n62
Finer, Lawrence B., 17n43
Fitzsimmons, Ron, 149
Flavel, John, 51, 51n23
Foley, 136n72
Food and Drug Administration, US (FDA), 12, 98, 98nn13–14, 161, 162
Foran, Clare, 123n13
Forston, S. Donald III, 34n42
Foster, Carla, 142, 143
Fox News, 126

Frame, John M., 56, 56n4, 57nn5–6, 69, 73, 73n1, 77, 83, 83n9, 85, 89–90, 89n24, 90n24, 93, 94
Francis, Pope, 106
Fraser, J. Cameron, 16, 16n35
Fraser, Margaret, 2, 16, 83
Free Church of Scotland, 95
Free Presbyterian Church Synod of the United States, 34n42
Freedom of Access to Clinic Entrances Act (FACE), 133, 134, 135, 165
French, David, 22, 140n93, 141, 141n96
Friedan, Betty, 15n30
Fuller Theological Seminary in California, 27, 35, 60, 108

Gabriel, 131
Galli, Mark, 21, 67, 68, 68n35, 69, 69n36
Gallup, 17n39
Gardner, R. F. R., 1, 55–58, 55n2, 58n7, 60, 69, 87, 87n17, 90n24, 96, 96nn3–4, 116, 116nn10–11, 131
Garland, Merrick, 134, 135
Genocide Awareness Project, 33n40, 34n41
Gerson, Michael, 22
Gillespie, Brandon, 133n64
Giroux, 11n9
Godfrey, Elaine, 124, 124n19
Gore, Al, 164
Gorman, Michael J., 12n10, 46nn1–2, 47, 47nn3–6, 48, 48nn7–11, 49nn12–16, 50nn17–19, 67n32
Gosnell, Kermit, 148
Graham, Billy, 27, 28, 42
Graham, Franklin, 28, 159
Granberg-Michaelson, Wes, 77, 77n18, 131, 131n58, 132
Greenfield, 136n75
Gregorian, Darel, 162n8
Gregory of Nyssa, 92
Gregory XIV, Pope, 50
Griffin, Michael, 165
Griffiths, Brent D., 126n26
Griswold v. Connecticut, 97
Guardian, The, 143
Gunn, David, 165

Gupta, Vanita, 134
Gurdon, John, 100
Guttmacher Institute, 13, 13n21, 14n26, 17, 125n20

Haley, Nikki, 121–22
Harden, Jim, 134
Hardesty, Nancy, 60, 60n12, 60nn14–15, 61, 61nn16–17, 62, 62n18, 69, 88, 88n21
Harris, Kamala, 37, 122, 123, 138–39, 161
Harvard Medical School, 175
Harvard University, 43
Hathaway, Anne, 127
Havel, Vaclav, 147
Hawkins, Tim, 151
Haykin, Michael A. G., 23, 23n8
Hayward, Eleanor, 143n103
"heartbeat law" (Texas), 132, 163
Helder, Emily, 132n59
Helms, Jesse, 39
Hendriksen, William, 91n26
Hennessy-Fiske, Molly, 80n2
Henry, Carl F. H., 27, 60
Hern, Warren, 124, 125
Higgins, Michelle, 114, 114n6
Hill, Anita, 126
Hill, Paul, 165
Hill Country Bible Church, Austin, Texas, 151
Hilleman, Maurice, 103
Hilton, Paris, 126–27
Hippocrates, 46, 46n2
Hippolytus, 47n3
Hitler, Adolf, 165
Hodge, Charles, 34n42
Horowitz, Jason, 39n60
Houk, Mark, 135, 136
House, H. Wayne, 76, 76n11
House of Commons of Canada, 144
House of Representatives, US, 122, 134, 149
Howard, Jacqueline, 130n50
Huffington Post, 42
Hughes, Philip Edgcumbe, 82n5

Human Fertilization and Embryo Act of 1990, 88
Hunter, James Davidson, 120–21, 120n3
Hunter, Joel C., 36, 36n47
Hyde amendment, 36, 36n45, 38, 38n58

Imes, Carmen Joy, 85n12, 86n15
Income Tax Act, Canada, 148
Institute of Advanced Catholic Studies, at the University of Southern California, 39n60

Jackson, Jesse, 164
"Jane Roe," of *Roe v. Wade*, 171
Jefferson, Mildred, 11, 175, 176–77
Jehovah's Witnesses, 173
Jennifer (Norma McCorvey's daughter), 173
Jeremiah, 58
Jerome, 49
Jesus Christ, 23, 28n21, 29, 49, 67, 78, 81, 82, 83n9, 85, 86, 87, 90, 90n26, 92, 93, 113, 131, 148, 150, 153
Jewett, Paul K., 60, 62, 68
John Paul II, Pope, 106
John the Baptist, 78, 90, 90n26
Johnson, Abby, 16, 16n37
Johnson, Alexis McGill, 133, 133n63
Johnson, Ben, 115n8
Johnson, Boris, 141n97
Johnson, Julia, 127n32
Johnson and Johnson, 104
Joint Commision on Accreditation of Hospitals, 63
Jones, David Albert, 46n2
Jones, Peter, 36n48
Judson Memorial Church, Manhattan's Greenwich Village, 15

Kacsmaryk, Matthew, 161, 162
Kantzer, Kenneth, 61–62
Keele University, 67
Keil, Carl Friedrich, 76
Kekatos, Mary, 128n39
Keller, Timothy, 25, 32n37, 33n37, 83–85

Kennedy, John F., 31
Kennedy, Ted, 39, 164
Kerby, Laura R., 136, 136n76
Kidd, Thomas S., 22, 22n6, 23, 25
King, Larry, 106
King, Martin Luther, Jr., 32, 32n37, 129
Kitchener, Caroline, 121n9
Kline, Meredith, 76
Knox Seminary, 64
Koop, C. Everett, 1, 16n35, 20, 39–42, 40nn61–63, 41nn64–65, 42n66, 43, 44, 45, 69, 78, 78n21, 156
Kubota, Samantha, 127n36

Lader, Larry, 15, 15n30
LaHaye, Beverly, 43
LaHaye, Tim, 43
Laika, Arijeta, 144n112
Lee, Bandy X., 22
Letham, Robert, 24n9
Lewis, Andrew R., 32, 32n36
Liberty Foundation, 28
Life Chain, 156
LifeWay, 14n27, 151, 152nn137–140, 156
Lipton-Lubet, Sarah, 93n35, 165n22
Little Sisters of the Poor, 98
London Institute for Centemporary Christianity, 66
Long, Colleen, 137n78
Luther, Martin, 51, 51n21
Lutherans for Life, 12

MacCulloch, Diarmaid, 24, 24n13
Machen, J. Gresham, 26
MacKay, Donald, 67
Macleod, Donald, 24n9, 87n16, 95–96, 96n2
Macron, Emmanuel, 141n97
Madani, Doha, 130n51
Maher, Kit, 125n23
Making Life Disciples, 150
Mandelburg, Tierin-Rose, 129n45
Mangan, Dan, 121n4
March for Life, 11n7
Maria Caulfield, 143–44
Marsden, George M., 25, 26n20

Marshner, Connie, 165
Martinez, Jessica, 21n1
Mary, 78, 90n26, 92–93, 131
Masci, David, 20n50
Mathewes-Green, Frederica, 13, 13n23, 14, 14n24, 14n26, 115, 115n7, 117, 117n12, 118, 118nn14–15
Mayo Clinic, 102, 102n21
McCammon, Sarah, 29n25
McCorvey, Norma, 171–77
McFadden, James, 42
McWhinnie, Alexina, 116
Means, Cyril Jr., 51
Melissa (Norma McCorvey's daughter), 173, 175
Melville, Catriona, 145n114
Mercer, Joshua, 136n73, 136n77
Meta, 126
Metaxas, Eric, 33nn38–39
#MeToo movement, 156, 156n150
Mexican Supreme Court, 146
Michels, Nancy, 12n16
Middleton, J. Richard, 82n6, 86, 86n14
Miller, Claire Cain, 153n142
Miller, Matthew, 42, 42n66, 43n70, 43n72, 44, 44nn73–74
Miller, Paul D., 29–30, 29nn28–29, 30n30, 42
Mizelle, Shawna, 125n23
Moderna, 104
Mohler, Albert, 105, 105nn27–28, 131, 131n57
Moltmann, Jurgen, 54, 54n35
Montgomery, John Warwick, 77, 77nn13–14
Montoya, Melissa, 147n125
Moody, Howard, 15
Moore, Russell, 21, 22n3, 30, 30n31, 114, 114nn4–5, 118, 118n16, 157n152
Moral Majority, 27, 28, 44n74. *See also* Liberty Foundation
Moran, Lee, 122n11
More, Thomas, 23
Morgentaler, Henry, 9, 11, 11n9, 13, 13n19, 14, 14n28
Morris, 154n143
Moses, 107

Mouw, Richard, 35
Mrozek, Andrea, 157n150
MSNBC, 131
Mueller, Julia, 125n22
Muggeridge, Malcolm, 16n35, 42
Mulvihill, Geoff, 138n88
Murray, Iain H., 24, 25n14
Murray, Jessica, 143n106
Murray, John, 81, 81n4, 89n24, 90n24, 108, 108n35

Nathanson, Bernard N., 9, 12, 12n14, 15, 15n29, 15nn31–34, 16, 16n36, 17
Nation Women's Coalition for Life, 13
National Abortion and Reproductive Rights Action League, 15
National Abortion Rights Action League (NARAL), 15, 15n30
National Association for the Repeal of Abortion Laws, 15, 51
National Association of Evangelicals, 27
National Baptist Convention, 37
National Coalition of Abortion Providers, 149
National Domestic Violence Hotline, 137
National Right to Life, 10, 139
National Right to Life Association, 175
National Right to Life Committee, 11
Neidig, 156n149
Nelson, 37n50
Neuhaus, Richard John, 1
New York Daily News, 149
New York Times, 22, 117, 133, 149
Newsmax, 126
Newton, John, 33
Ney, Philip, 13n20
Nirappil, Fenit, 127n37
Nix, Naomi, 126n29
Nixon, Richard, 27
Noah, 108
Nobel committee, 101
Noll, Mark A., 25
Nsubuga, Jimmy, 144n107

Obama, Barak, 29, 36, 98

Ocasio-Cortez, Alexandria, 129, 130n49
O'Donovan, Oliver, 66–67
Ohden, Melissa, 123n15
Olasky, Marvin, 10, 10n3, 11, 11n6, 12nn11–13, 13nn21–22, 15n30, 46n2, 50, 51, 52, 52nn24–28, 53, 53nn29–32, 61, 97, 97nn7–9, 115, 115n7, 118, 118n14, 140, 140n94, 149, 149nn130–131, 150, 150n132, 163n13, 164–65, 164nn16–19, 165nn20–21, 165n23, 166, 166n27, 167, 167nn28–30, 168, 168n31
Olasky, Susan, 150
Olohan, Mary Margaret, 134n65
Olson, Roger, 25, 25n17
OnlineCare Canada, 2
Operation Rescue, 164–65, 166, 171
Origen, 47n3
Orthodox Presbyterian Church (OPC), 73, 76, 77
Ostling, Richard, 15, 15n29
Ovid, 47n3, 48
Owen, John, 51

Packer, James I., 24, 24n10, 46, 113–14, 113n1, 114n2
Patterson, Calli, 39n60
Paul, 58, 89n24, 108
Paul VI, Pope, 97
PBS (Public Broadcasting Service), 137n82, 138n89
PCUSA. *See* Presbyterian Church, USA (PCUSA)
Pelosi, Nancy, 32, 39n60, 122
Pence, Mike, 121
Peters, Rebecca Todd, 130
Pew Research Center, 17n39, 18n44, 20, 38n60
Pfizer, 104
Piper, John, 157, 157n151
Pius IX, Pope, 50
Planned Parenthood, 13n21, 14, 15n30, 16, 18, 18n45, 114, 126, 133, 134, 135, 149, 151, 163
Plato, 46, 47, 89
Plotkin, Stanley, 103

Polanyi, Michael, 90, 92
Pontifical Academy for Life, 104
Posner, Sarah, 21n2
Post Abortion Community Services, 2
Prager, Joshua, 172, 174–77
Pregnancy Care Centre, 148
Pregnancy Decision Line, 147
Presbyterian Church, USA (PCUSA), 53, 92, 130
Presbyterians Pro-Life, 92
Prime Time Live, 149
Princeton Seminary, 34n42
Prison Fellowship, 27, 108
ProGrace, 153–55
Progressive Anti-Abortion Uprising, 137
Pro-Life Evangelicals for Biden, 35, 36, 36n46, 38, 38n57, 44–45
Psaki, Jen, 122

Quebec College of Physicians, 144n113
Quinones, Julian, 144n112

Rachel's Vineyard, 12–13
Rafferty, Philip, 52, 52n26
Rahman, Khaleda, 126n25
Rainey, Jane G., 31n33
Ramsay, Paul, 30, 30n32
Randall, Rebecca, 105n26
Rape Victims Support Network, 2
Rasmussen Reports, 138n87
Reagan, Ronald, 16, 16n35, 27, 39, 42, 44
Real Choices, 13
Reardon, David C., 12, 12n15, 12n17
Red Rose Rescue, 165–66, 166nn25–26
Redeemer Presbyterian Church, New York, 83
Reed, Ralph, 28
Reformed Church in America, 77, 131
Reformed Presbyterian Church (Covenanters), 34n42
Reformed Seminary, 64
Regent College, 64
Regent University, 28
Religion News Service, 130

Religious Coalition for Abortion Choice, 11
Religious Coalition for Abortion Rights, 15, 19, 130
Republican Party, 27, 28n21, 29, 32
Reynolds, Nick, 29n27
Richards, Chris, 88n18, 97–99, 98n11, 98n15, 99n16
Richardson, 137n84
Rinfret, 11n9
Robertson, David, 143, 143n105
Robertson, Pat, 28, 29
Roe v. Wade, 1, 3, 4, 32, 37, 38, 42, 51, 52, 55, 59, 68, 97, 113, 117, 120, 121, 123, 126, 127, 129, 130, 131, 132, 134, 136, 137, 138, 140, 141, 146, 147, 149, 156, 156n150, 158, 160, 164, 166, 171, 172, 174, 175
Roelofs, Katie, 132n59
Rogers, Katie, 39n60
Rogin, Ali, 146n119
Roman Catholic Church. *See* Catholic Church
Rosen, Dr., 116
Royal Society for the Prevention of Cruelty to Animals, 33
Runia, Klaas, 50, 50n20, 59

Sandberg, Sheryl, 126
Sanders, Linley, 138n88
Sanger, Margaret, 15n30, 133
Sanger-Katz, Margo, 153n142
Sargeant, Leah Liberesco, 166n25
Saur, Prudence B., 10, 11n6
Savas, Leah, 10, 10n3, 11n6, 12, 12nn11–13, 52nn24–28, 53nn29–32, 97nn7–9, 140n94, 163, 163n13, 164, 164nn16–19, 165nn20–21, 165n23, 166, 166n27, 167, 167nn28–30, 168n31
Scarborough, Joe, 131
Schaeffer, Francis, 1, 2, 32, 42, 43, 43n71, 44, 44n74, 69
Schaeffer, Frank (son of Francis), 43
Schaeffer, Priscilla, 43

Secular Pro-Life, 19
Sellers, Frances Stead, 127n37
Serwer, Adam, 144n110
Shannon, Shelley, 165
Sharp, Rachel, 128n38
Shelley (Norma McCorvey's daughter), 174
Shiffer, Emily, 122n12
Shimron, Yonat, 129n48, 130n52
Sider, Ronald J., 22, 22nn4–5, 35, 35n43, 36, 36n49, 55, 55n1
Singer, Peter, 82, 83, 83n8
Sixtus V, Pope, 50
Slave Trade Act of 1807, UK, 33
Slavery Abolition Act of 1833, UK, 33
Smeaton, John, 101, 102n19
Smedes, Lewis B., 58–59, 58n8, 59n9, 107n33
Smietana, Bob, 103n22
Smith, Gregory A., 21n1
Smith, Peter, 38n60
Snyder, Monica, 19
Society for the Protection of Unborn Children, UK (SPUC), 101–2, 102n20, 141
Sojourners Community in Washington, DC, 27
Southern Baptist church, 173
Southern Baptist Convention, 68, 139
Southern Baptist Ethics & Religious Liberty Commission, 105
Southern Baptist Theological Seminary, 105, 131
Spiers, Elizabeth, 117, 117n13
Sprinkle, Joe M., 77, 77n17
Sproul, R. C., 77, 77n15, 106n29, 107, 107n34
SPUC. *See* Society for the Protection of Unborn Children, UK (SPUC)
Stacey, Dawn, 97n6
Stackhouse, John G., Jr., 25, 25nn15–16
Steel, David, Lord Steel of Aikwood, 9
Stewart, Kenneth J., 23–24, 23n8, 24nn9–11, 34n42
Stewart, Lyman, 26
Stiller, Brian C., 26, 26n18
Stoker, Amanda, 145n116

Stott, John R. W., 24, 24n11, 46, 66–67, 66nn28–30, 67nn31–32, 68nn33–34, 160, 160n1, 168
Studnicki, Jim, 162
Sullivan, Kate, 1
Supreme Court, Canada, 144
Supreme Court, US, 28, 30, 37, 37n50, 42, 43, 97, 98, 121, 126, 132, 136, 137, 139, 144, 146, 162, 163, 175
Surgeon General, 39, 40, 44
Suri, Sameer, 127n31
Susan B. Anthony Pro-Life America, 10, 125
Sutnick, Amy, 149

Talbot, Christopher, 2n1
Taylor, Justin, 36n48
Terry, Randall, 164, 165
Tertullian, 47n3, 48, 48n11, 49, 67, 67n32
Testimony Publishing Company, Chicago, 26
Thomas, Cal, 28n24
Thomas, Clarence, 126, 156
Thornwell, J. H., 34n42
Threedy, Debora, 34n42
Thurman, Chris, 22
Tiller, George, 165
Tisby, Jemar, 28n22, 34n42, 114n6
Torrance, Thomas F., 67, 67n32, 90, 90n25, 91nn27–28, 92n29, 93, 93nn33–34, 94
Tozer, A. W., 157n152, 158n152
Trinity College, Deerfield, IL, 60
Trinity Evangelical Divinity School, 61
Trinity International University, 105
Trudeau, Justin, 32, 141n97
Trump, Donald, 21, 28, 28n21, 29, 36, 38, 120, 137
Tucker, Emma, 126n28, 136n74
Turley, Jonathan, 34n42
Twelve Tables, The, 47
Tyndale, William, 24

Umholtz, Kaytelyn, 163n14

United Church of Christ (UCC), 129, 130
United Free Church of Scotland, 56
United Methodist Church, 130
United States Conference of Catholic Bishops (USCCB), 104, 104n24, 105n25
University College, London, 95
University of Oxford, 104
URGE (Unite For Reproductive and Gender Equality), 9
US Constitution. *See* Constitution, US
US Food and Drug Administration (FDA). *See* Food and Drug Administration, US (FDA)
US House of Representatives. *See* House of Representatives, US
US Supreme Court. *See* Supreme Court, US
USA Today, 149

Vancouver CPC. *See* Crisis Pregnancy Centre (CPC)
Vander Brock, Allison, 132n61
VanDrunen, David, 100, 100n17
Vastag, Brian, 101n18
Vlamis, Kelsey, 39n60, 129n43

Wade, Henry, 171, 175
Wagner, Mary, 165
Walgreens, 163
Waltke, Bruce K., 64–65, 64n22, 65nn25–27, 67, 68, 74, 88, 88n20
Wang, Amy B., 121n9
Warfield, B. B., 26
Warnock, Raphael, 129–30, 130n49
Warren, Roland C., 150, 151n135
Washington Post, 22, 136
Washington Times, 36n46
Waters, Matt, 165
Watson, Kathryn, 19nn48–49, 39n60
Weddington, Sarah, 175
Weinstein, Harvey, 156
Weixel, Nathaniel, 162n7

Wesley, Charles, 157
Wesley, John, 33, 157
Westminster Seminary, California, 26, 64, 75–76
Westminster Theological Seminary, Philadelphia, 73
Weszley, Angie, 154, 154n144, 155n145
Wheaton College, Illinois, 26
Whelan, Patrick, 39n60
White, Rebecca, 128n42
Whitefield, George, 157
Whitford, Chris, 153, 153n141
Wichita Eagle, 164
Wicks, Amanda, 121n7
Wilberforce, William, 33, 139, 157
Wilkinson, Julie, 125
Williams, Alithea, 142n102
Williams, Daniel K., 18n46, 31, 31n34, 32, 32n35, 96n5, 160–61, 160n2, 161n3, 163, 169, 171, 177
Wilson, Douglas, 34n42
Winn, Christian T. Collins, 25, 25n17
Wistrich, Harriet, 143
Wolf, Elizabeth, 37n54
Wolf, Naomi, 14n23
Wolfe, Stephen, 29, 29n26
Woolley, Paul, 75–76, 78
World Health Organization (WHO), 17, 145–46, 146nn117–118
Wright, Jasmine, 138n90
Wyden, Ron, 149

Yamanaka, Shinya, 100, 102
Yancey, 22n5
Yilek, Caitlin, 123nn16–17, 124n18
YMCA (Young Men's Christian Association), 167
Young, Curt, 76, 76n12, 85, 86n13

Zagorski, Sarah, 123
Zanona, Melanie, 123n13
Zavodny, Madeline, 13n20
Zielgler, Mary, 80n1, 126n24, 147n124, 163n11

www.ingramcontent.com/pod-product-compliance
Lightning Source LLC
Chambersburg PA
CBHW050145170426
43197CB00011B/1971